Last House on the Road

Other volumes in The Concord Library

Series Editor: JOHN ELDER

Eighty Acres: Elegy for a Family Farm
RONALD JAGER

Tarka the Otter
HENRY WILLIAMSON

The Insect World of J. Henri Fabre
EDWIN WAY TEALE, editor

A Land
JACQUETTA HAWKES

In Limestone Country
SCOTT RUSSELL SANDERS

Nature and *Walking*
RALPH WALDO EMERSON and HENRY DAVID THOREAU

Following the Bloom
DOUGLAS WHYNOTT

Finding Home: Writing on Nature and Culture from Orion *Magazine*
PETER SAUER, editor

The Very Rich Hours: Travels in Orkney, Belize, the Everglades, and Greece
EMILY HIESTAND

Thoreau on Birds
FRANCIS H. ALLEN, editor

Staying Put: Making a Home in a Restless World
SCOTT RUSSELL SANDERS

The Geography of Childhood: Why Children Need Wild Places
GARY PAUL NABHAN and STEPHEN TRIMBLE

Family of Earth and Sky: Indigenous Tales of Nature from around the World
JOHN ELDER and HERTHA WONG, editors

Writing the Western Landscape, by Mary Austin and John Muir
ANN H. ZWINGER, editor

A Beginner's Faith in Things Unseen
JOHN HAY

Last House on the Road

Excursions into a Rural Past

Ronald Jager

Beacon Press
Boston

Beacon Press
25 Beacon Street
Boston, Massachusetts 02108-2892

Beacon Press books
are published under the auspices of
the Unitarian Universalist Association of Congregations.

Printed in the United States of America

99 98 97 96 95 94 8 7 6 5 4 3 2 1

Library of Congress Cataloging-in-Publication Data

Jager, Ronald.
Last house on the road: excursions into a rural past / Ronald Jager.
p. cm. — (The Concord library)
ISBN 0-8070-7062-9
1. Country life—New Hampshire—Washington. 2. Washington (N.H.)—Social life and customs. 3. Jager, Ronald—Homes and haunts—New Hampshire—Washington. I. Title. II. Series.
F44.W25J33 1994
974.2'75—dc20 94-14640
CIP

This book is dedicated
in love and gratitude
to my wife,
Grace Otten Jager,
and to our son,
Colin Lovell
Jager

Contents

Preface

This book had its remote beginnings some years ago as my wife and I negotiated a lapsed road in New Hampshire's scenic backcountry. We were following up the worn ruts to track down a fresh rumor: back here somewhere there was said to be an old house that might be for sale. Turned out there was.

We know now—countless couples before us have learned it well—that the adventure of transforming an old house into a new home is exceedingly rich and complex. Many-layered. As with peeling back old wallpaper, you never know what local color you may uncover. In any old house, or around it, there is often a story or two if you care to heed it, but there may be a whole saga there if you cultivate the habit of looking. In New England the saga is likely to reach out into a wider, older culture—although that depends on what you are looking for, how many layers down you want to peel. You may slice deeper than you first intended, making it hard to know where to make a cutoff and stop scraping. We tended to keep going.

As it turned out, we not only had to appropriate the old house—which is different from just buying it—and make it do, but we also took on, one after another, the writing of several books on New Hampshire history. Early on, we got into the habit of scraping down to origins. It was the old house that got the juices going, but quickly the demands and seductions of New England itself took over, and together they eventually secreted this book.

This book begins with our home and hearth—as we found it, made it, and enriched it with what we extracted from the ghosts of previous owners who built and lived and farmed here. It explores the surrounding fields and forests—literally, mentally—and takes excursions into the rural past of New England and beyond. It includes sketches of actual people and small-town routines which make up our community. It looks in on town meetings and reviews New Hampshire's political culture from the angle of the presidential primary. But most of my story is of the earth, earthy: salvaging an old house, a well, a meadow, a stone wall; going hunting and giving it up, swinging a double-bitted axe, building a pond, walking the woods, listening to the voices of the landscape.

I might not be looking at country affairs in this particular light if I hadn't recently tried to take the measure of another landscape in another state. A few years ago, in *Eighty Acres: Elegy for a Family Farm*, I sketched my version of what it was like to be young and rural in the 1940s. My family worked a typical farm of the time, powered by horses and by our own hands, in a typical Michigan farming community. Although some of the near fields are hilly there, the long landscapes are flat as flapjacks and the soil at best is only fair. Of course the farm work was long and hard, and profits slim, but all in all the harvest of that old style of rural life was rich and lasting. In the 1950s I went off to college, and it was just at that time too that changes in Midwest farming cranked up the pace dramatically, so that most eighty-acre farms like ours either died out or were eaten alive by their neighbors.

In *Eighty Acres* I was writing about yesterday's Michigan from a particular angle, namely, today's rural New England, peering back across a span of nearly forty years. Readers from many states wrote to me: thank you for telling *my* rural story, they said—How did you know? Some readers urged me to say something next time about the mental move from rural

Michigan to rural New England, about "getting your head out of that piece of landscape and into this one," as a friend put it. This book responds to that.

Like that earlier book, this one alternates the broad view with a narrow focus, since I'm deciphering the fine print from a small script, to wit, the little patch of New England where we have now put down roots. I'll admit this: my wife and I see ourselves not simply as living in the Northeast, the national attic, but rather as adopted New Englanders, locating ourselves comfortably within an assumed past. Yet this book frequently still leans on the Midwest—everyone's formative perspective is unique, and that happens to be mine—so *Last House* is a natural sequel to *Eighty Acres*.

On one level, rural New England is, of course, a straightforward piece of history and real estate. It is also a rhetorical achievement, a piece of mental artifice, with the village on the green as the centerpiece and the town meeting as the soundtrack. Granted. But if New England and its state of mind are partly mythic fabrication, then literature, art, history, politics, and journalism are all in on the conspiracy; and there is no way to call it off now. In this stern environment I try hard to stick to the literal truth, even if I sometimes find that truth so whimsical or ironic that I cannot forever keep a straight face myself. As I see it, all three parts of this book start out sedately enough, but there are weak places where I warm to the subject and cheerfulness is pretty rampant. I can't really do much about that—except to say that it looks like sobriety invariably breaks out again.

I'd like especially to thank my wife, Grace, and also our son, Colin, for patiently and lovingly sharing this adventure with me—the swift years living it and the long hours writing it. Without them, no hearth and home, and no book. And I'd like to thank Chapter Two, which appeared in a different version in the *New York Times*, for generously lending its title to the whole book.

Ronald Jager
Lovellwood
Half Moon Pond Road
Washington, New Hampshire

Last House on the Road

Part I

Hearth and Home

Who knows but if men constructed their dwellings with their own hands, . . . the poetic faculty would be universally developed, as birds universally sing when they are so engaged? But alas! we do like cowbirds and cuckoos, which lay their eggs in nests which other birds have built, and cheer no traveler with their chattering and unmusical notes.

—HENRY DAVID THOREAU, *Walden*

That's Thoreau stretching his "poetic faculty" as he constructs his own dwelling at Walden Pond. We who dwell in nests which other birds have built, do we ask: What if the cowbird and the cuckoo really sang? What would be the burden of their song? I know: Praise for the bluebird and the swallow, who built the nests they borrowed!

Our house, which we now call Lovellwood, is a nest built by others, but it is not borrowed. Buying a house and coming to own it is a comparatively simple matter; it may be done in a moment, but it is only a first step. Coming to possess it is another matter entirely, and takes much longer. Of that I sing—of the slow process of taking possession, renewing an old nest.

As we worked our way into the old house we had bought, we also worked our way into the lives of the Powers families, two generations, who had struggled and sweated, lived and died here over the course of nearly ninety years. Working farther into the house, back toward its origins, we got into the lives of the Wood families, two generations, who had cleared the trees and built the house two hundred years ago, and lived here sixty years. Slowly we uncovered and absorbed both their stories, developing our own poetic faculty in the process; and to them we added our own story—as birds universally sing when they are so engaged. Three stories now merge in the house into one story. That, briefly, is how we took possession and made the house our own. The ensuing chapters tell the story the long way.

1

Abandoned Houses

Hearts go out to strays. People adopt things. Something deep inside us responds to what is woebegone, forlorn, abandoned. Is it not a widespread if not quite universal human story, transcending cultures, time, and place: a couple spots an old house, be it ever so bereft and unlovely, and feels a yearning to take it into their very own custody? It happens. Deep within us lurks a caregiver—wherefore they call us human beings. And, yes, sometimes the impulse leads down a steep path to a stern wisdom.

I have now to introduce two acquaintances. Both of them are abandoned houses, one living in New Hampshire, the other dying in Michigan. The one in Michigan I knew but briefly, and she is just a fading memory now, tinged with melancholy, like an old courtship that never had a chance to flourish. The New Hampshire house forms the very roof over my head as I write.

A decade after leaving the Michigan farm that I now call "Eighty Acres" but then called home, after college and marriage and travel and some graduate school, I was doing a brief teaching stint in Evanston, Illinois. Occasionally, my wife Grace and I went back to Missaukee County to visit parents, visit the family farm, drive through the old familiar neighborhoods.

On one occasion we took the road from my parents' farm north and then west a few miles past the swamp where Stick Crick seeps into Clam River, then on the dirt road north across the bridge and up the slope, where we saw upon the open landscape a large abandoned farmhouse, faintly gray and lonely as a ghost. You could look into its hollow eyes and see right out the other side. In Michigan, then as now, many a country house like that, whether dead or alive, and standing on flat and fallow land, sticks out bluntly on the landscape, making a firm statement, as it was probably meant to do, though the manner is often brusque and short on style.

We parked and walked the near meadows to the woods and then turned to stare at the house, so stark against the western skyline. It seemed to call aloud for an artist or photographer to capture its mood, winsome and melancholy. We ventured nearer, walking obliquely toward it, attracted, curious, hesitant to intrude. With its odd angles and arbitrary roof lines, the house was a sharp and barren silhouette, devoid of trees, solitary in the tall timothy and broom grass that swayed in beige and pale green waves in the gusts of summer wind. Fallen fragments of an old fence, of sagging posts and rusty wire, seemed to mark a former garden. The house itself was solid and upright, the walls unbent and the roof still true. It might not have been sixty years old, but left untended it might not see another twenty. This was about four miles from my native Eighty Acres.

Grace and I heard voices whispering in our mind's ear. We responded with furtive glances down the road and then quickly pulled ourselves through a backwall window frame and dropped down inside. We were trespassing in what had been a kitchen. Perhaps we should walk on tiptoe. Instead, we lowered our voices—listening to an inner voice—inspecting empty rooms, and hesitantly climbing the stairs, hearing only the crunch of bits of broken plaster as they crumbled to chalk beneath our shoes. From unglazed upper windows we looked out over unplowed fields, overgrown . . . but in a glance we swept away the brush, cleared the fields, put up pasture fences, plowed the garden, cleaned the yard, installed the glass and paint and shutters and. . . .

This is what we were hearing: *maybe this place is salvageable; maybe we should do it*. Pastoral visions rolled in upon unresisting brains: we would buy and restore this old farmhouse; we would live and work in Illinois, and periodically—summers, weekends—retreat to this native soil, to Missaukee County, Michigan. Reclaim roots.

There were some wispy clouds in this blue-sky dream, of course: we had no money; I had no secure job, nor even a final academic degree, for that matter. Had not countless other couples heard similar voices, some to their sorrow? Voices of the tempter? For us, yanking a dying house back from the brink should be at the bottom of any reasonable list of priorities. Still, the voice spoke its *idea* to us, its urgings so plain we would never unhear it. Just because I had chosen an academic life, we needn't capitulate totally to the city; it wasn't inevitable that I relinquish the countryside and my native place: we could get hold of a piece of something out there, or back there, and just hang on. We could hold hands with two worlds.

It took some months before we traced down the owner of that old house, who lived in Detroit; by that time we were living in New England again, and I was writing a dissertation in Cambridge. But we imagined that our New England stay might be temporary, for we fancied ourselves Midwesterners and expected to return there. I wanted a windward anchor. So we wrote a scrupulous letter to the owner of the great gray house, gave our candid assessment of his property, declared our interest and our intentions, and made him a definite proposal. This flirtation unnerved us considerably: what if he accepted?

I was thirty years old at that time. And that time was thirty years ago. He hasn't answered our letter yet. Good thing, maybe.

Waiting for a reply didn't silence the voice within or extinguish the idea at all. Instead, it prospered and got transplanted intact, native soil still clinging to the bare roots, into another environment. This time it was New England.

Instead of returning to the Midwest when I completed my studies, we succumbed to an invitation to housesit for friends for a year in the New Hampshire countryside. What seemed a detour became a turning point, and going back to the Midwest became the road not taken.

We had already acquired a stock of images of rural New Hampshire, partly fabricated from myths and books and partly observed by driving through it: the wildlife and the accents and stone walls; the decorum of its villages and its colonial architecture; the rocky landscapes and their layered history; the people, swamp Yankee and flatlander, and the natives, real and adopted, with their crusty integrity and their cranky politics. We had sensed the poetry and the history and the richness of these regions; but we had not *lived* among these things. And we had not yet learned to enjoy and deplore the state's exasperating and attractive political culture. When we first lived in New Hampshire as housesitters, unpaying guests, our situation was quite unrepresentative: nearly penniless, we nonetheless lived in a well-restored old house with a huge library, sequestered upon a hillside where we could watch the morning mist drift up from the Contoocook River across the face of the minor mountains on the other side. We were bitten, smitten, and became permanently infected.

As it turned out it was in the middle of this first heady and intimate encounter with New Hampshire countryside that I was also granted a choice for the future, whether to teach in Illinois again or in Connecticut—for us, not only a choice of universities but also of wider cultural contexts. And in our hearts we were transferring loyalties, were becoming New England converts. So when we went to Connecticut instead of again to Illinois, we had also voted for the New England countryside, so to speak, as our cultural backup. At least for now, we said. It was then the mid-sixties.

Inevitably, we began to scout New Hampshire backroads looking for rural property, for we had the implausible idea that we might again find a creaky old farmhouse, perhaps lost in the woods and pleading for rescue before it collapsed. Most of the backroads in central New Hampshire are flanked by woodlands that were meadows and farmyards a century and a half ago; and the land under those trees is pitted and pocked with cellar holes, scars from thousands of farmsteads now reverted to forest. Some of these residual stone structures are seven-foot walls and chimney foundations masterfully constructed without mortar of quarter-ton granite boulders up to two hundred years ago. They remain rigidly intact to this day, as if buildings had never stood upon them, though they surely did.

We spent little time with real-estate agents, rightly believing we couldn't afford most of what they would offer. We needed a bargain: more than a cellar hole but less than a colonial, something in between that wasn't leaning too far the wrong way. This was in fact at the very end of the long era of rural New England bargains. We worked out an unusually scientific search formula, consisting of correct proportions of these activities: just poking around on scenic backroads; casually following leads, hearsay, and rumor; pursuing impulse and whim; and waiting. We noted that this formula was a considerable advance on the one that had led us to the gray house in Michigan, and it surprised my wife Grace not at all that it yielded results—though I had been sure it wouldn't, even as I agreed it was fun anyway.

Did it get results! A tendril on the local grapevine led us to a nearly abandoned road in a somewhat abandoned town where we found a very abandoned little old center-chimney Cape Cod–style farmhouse, parked in the middle of a hundred acres, more or less, of retired farmland. Here was both seclusion and picturesque decline, and here was even a shaggy mountain in the background, less than a mile away and rising nearly a thousand feet. In the foreground, the predatory forest had already nibbled away most of the pastures, swallowed some stone walls, and supplanted most of the fields.

The little story-and-a-half farmhouse, vaguely white and the only building on the site fully upright, had a resigned sag on the far side; it hadn't seen paint in two decades, or tenants in five years; it was nearly two hundred years old and looked it (but that's a compliment). Comfortably unobtrusive on its benignly neglected landscape, mellow and enduring like the gray and moss-grown stone walls that splayed off in all directions from the yard, it seemed, on second and third glance, not so much abandoned as . . . just waiting. To us, New England converts without resources save for energy and idealism, plus a dash of bookish nostalgia for old New England, quiet dereliction on such a modest scale registered as authenticity and charm. Rusty farm machinery poking up through the long grass here and there added character to the scene.

The owner of these precincts, who had never lived there, was as candid as a hunk of granite: he just didn't think the house was worth saving, and he frankly said so. The place had lots of possibilities, we all agreed, but not much else. And we were right about that.

However, we not only thought the house worth saving, we even thought something in the air—or was it something from that earlier unrealistic and failed courtship in Michigan?—invited us to do it. We took the project under active advisement. We admitted we didn't really need it and we couldn't really afford it, cheap as it was. We merely loved it. It was a stray. Several times we drove up from Connecticut to inspect the place in its different lights, and we surreptitiously planted daffodils near the little old house late that fall, even though we didn't arrange the purchase until the next spring. But when the flowers bloomed we went to the bank and got a small mortgage and signed the papers. Thus we bought the little house on Half Moon Pond Road, at that time the last house on the road, not counting the old schoolhouse, bought it cheaply, and over a hundred acres of land with it, but without any idea when we might ever really live there. That first summer, which was 1966, might best be classified as camping at home.

The next year a leave of absence from teaching gave me opportunity to go off somewhere to write a book. We quickly decided that the cheapest way to do that would be to make this old house secure enough so that we could survive a winter, and then just settle down and scribble. So we did that.

Ensconced in the last house on the road, more than a mile and half beyond the other winter-occupied houses on the road, we hunkered down and went to work. The fact that we handled that first winter—the woodcutting, the snow, the road, the lack of a telephone—validated us in the eyes of the townsfolks, who had been skeptical. For wasn't I, despite having a nice wife, merely a professor, hence just a softie, probably even a liberal, used to an easy life? Anyway, we were from somewhere else, and we probably couldn't hack it up here. ("He's back in there . . . *writing*?") A few asked us blithely in October when we were leaving. They didn't know about our secret weapons, about the inextinquishable disciplines of life picked up on an eighty-acre farm in another state, didn't know the hardihood of Grace, city girl now turned country wife. We passed the test. At the end of that year and that summer we headed back to the university as usual, loaded with blisters and memories and manuscript and ripe tomatoes and not a few regrets that we had to go.

That is a couple of decades ago now, and that is when *Last House on the Road* really began its slow gestation. But at the time I did not know it.

The next January, when we returned to see how the house had fared in our absence, it appeared that we had inherited a huge rusty truck. We wondered if this was usual in New England.

The big blue beast stood, unasked and unlicensed, smack dab in the front yard where the lawn was to be. It was clearly a stray, something else abandoned; so we went to work at mentally adopting it. As winter wore on to spring and we returned weekends as we could, we found that our truck was gathering a little local notoriety. Even today ours is a small community here, but it was smaller then, and for a time during the doldrums of winter it seems that our big blue truck was the only show in town. Folks looking for diversion would drift up Half Moon Pond Road just to see it, to verify the rumors ("Ayah, it's a big blue truck, awright") and scratch their heads about it ("Jus settin' right there front t'house!"). It was certainly an odd piece of sculpture to have so near our restoration project, but it put us firmly on the social map in town. As newcomers we were still new, but we were clearly comers.

An old-timer stopped by to say that the road agent had reported in town that the truck's wheels were "froze up" and that the thing was nearly immovable. But, he said, what the heck, he'd just as soon look out the window and see an old truck as see a big stupid rock any day. What'd I think? Well, nothing in my philosophy had prepared me for this particular value judgment; but the fact that he'd said it and meant it kept me cheerful for about three days.

For a time we affected a perverse kind of affection for the monster; after all, it *was* part of the landscape. In June I mowed the grass around it and somebody suggested that we plant geraniums in it. We thought about that and talked about it as much as we could. ("Ayah, might's well plant some geraniums in it—use it for a greenhouse! Ha Ha.") We were getting the conversational hang of rural life. The thing obstructed the view of the lilac bushes, but we tried to imagine that the old blue flivver had a kind of goofy charm. Nobody else had one like it. Perhaps I should put it up on blocks to make it look a little more natural in these parts.

However, when we noticed an undertow of sympathy for our plight down in the village we decided it had to go, and I arranged with the local police chief to have it dragged away. Before the yellow spot on the lawn had healed, a confessed owner showed up demanding to know about a big blue truck with no brakes and a busted axle. Had I seen it? Under the circumstances his accusative tone did not please me a whole lot. I admitted I had seen it but explained that it had disappeared recently, it might have been stolen; and I gave him directions to the police. His tone then changed completely.

He looked me over carefully, looked at the overgrown fields and the unpainted house, looked at the tiny beachhead of lawn and garden that we had created, and asked me what business I might be in way back here. I explained that I was a philosopher, and when this merely puzzled him I switched my profession to writer, adding by way of illustration that sometimes I even recycled old trucks into literature. He did not appear to be reassured by this. But we parted in a friendly spirit, and I was glad to learn later that he had retrieved his truck—though I kept its story.

For a number of years we came weekends whenever we could and came each summer without fail—came to plant the garden and hack at the underbrush and pick blueberries, but mostly to pull this old house carefully back from the brink. "Restoration" may be a word too fancy for it, for we had no impulse to create a museum in the woods, and in fact some modernization back in 1909 had sacrificed several original features, including the center fireplaces. But the farmhouse had much of its original character, worth preserving and enhancing, and gradually it became livable again. We started calling our place Lovellwood, for reasons I'll come to later.

In the mid-1970s we again took leave for a year from the academic life to tackle a different kind of book, a joint venture this time, which turned out to be a co-authored five-hundred-page history of Washington, New Hampshire, our adopted town. The house had engaged us originally, but writing the book on the town got us married to this world. In the late seventies we were back again, this time for a longer stay. Now we would try to make it on a freelance basis: teach, speak, write, consult, recycle trucks, whatever. That meant a larger garden and a leaner lifestyle, but we've carried on for fifteen years now. If we add that time to the preceding decade of intermittent residence, we can claim credit for a quarter of a century here at Lovellwood on Half Moon Pond Road. The place doesn't look abandoned anymore.

I mention the numbers because outsiders like us who were careless enough to be born elsewhere need all the credit we can get.

Last House on the Road

On the eighty-acre farm where I was born in Michigan, the farmhouse stood far back from the road, nearly two hundred yards, and as a youngster I disliked that. Nobody else was stuck off in the fields—why were we? But I early came to appreciate the advantages: it cut down on road dust, noise, commotion, and accidental visitors. When Grace and I hunted for a house in New Hampshire we automatically wanted it to be off on a side road, even out of sight if possible. It was possible. When we found it, not only was ours the last house on Half Moon Pond Road, but the road itself didn't last much farther either. And, indeed, there was a fallen sign at the road edge near the house: "End of town road."

During our first summer here we frequently saw grass growing down the center of the road, and that gave us a comfortable sense of seclusion. Grass doesn't grow there anymore; and there are a few houses up the road too, a kind of development on the mountainside. We're not the only ones around anymore, though the other folks are even less visible than we are. It's the road in that earlier lapsed condition that is the hero of this chapter, and through the years three things about it have not changed: it's still richly scenic and seductive; it's still a dead-end road; and I'm still reconciling the citizenry to these facts.

"Where does this road go?" "Does this road go through?" "What is up this road?"

Wayfarers who stop at our door to get their bearings have so often asked these questions that I am forever tempted to draw upon stock New Hampshire wit for answer: "Go? It's been here for nigh two hundred year and ain't gone nowhere yet." Or maybe: "Go? Well, mister, I'll tell you this: each March it goes to mud and it stays there for about six weeks." But I haven't the courage for that, for these are cautious folk trying to be reasonable, and they are concerned about the road. They should be.

Hill country in southwestern New Hampshire is where they are, and I certainly cannot blame them for sampling these byways. Even the short trip from Washington village is worth the trouble. Of course you pass Half Moon Pond, about as idyllic as ponds come, and for years there was an old house with a lilac bush growing not into but out of the window; there used to be a neat hunters' cabin with a plastic squirrel in the yard; there has always been a good stand of hobblebush and wild azalea; there are two brooks, a couple of dams and old millsites, and a double row of sugar maples ageing ungracefully; and from our yard, though no place else, you can even see the mountain. Half Moon Pond Road ranges through continuous woods, and it wends and winds and bumps along at a casual pace, sloppily escorted all the way by venerable stone walls put in place two hundred years ago, some of them now thrown apart by lumbermen and road crews, but some also rising majestically from splendid natural beds of hayscented fern. And, yes, it's true: there are discarded beer cans beneath the waving fronds of ferns, just as there are thorns among roses. Used and much abused, such tracks as Half Moon Pond Road are yet seductions for any traveler with leisure or curiosity.

But if you have drifted onto this road by mistake, supposing it was or would soon become another road, you may think you are deep in the boondocks when you come to our opening and see the sunlight again. The sun falls here on about five acres of brushy fields, and our recycled farmhouse, as old as the eighteenth-century road, is the last relic in a valley that once supported a dozen farmsteads—all of them long since faded away, closed down, fallen in, or burned out. It is a town-maintained road to our place and a bit farther, but beyond that it declines into a timber road, alternating rocks and ruts, enveloped in thousands of acres of wilderness.

It's a deep question: How completely must a rocky, rutted road peter out before it comes officially to a dead end? We have unbelievably high standards for dead-endedness in these parts, and some of our locals, with four-wheel-drive pickups and egos perpetually in overdrive, simply don't acknowledge the concept. Yet somewhere in there this road is dead to ordinary autos—they'll never get through alive—although hikers or headstrong bikers with time and a yen for adventure can get through to Bradford. That's beyond the rock slide, where the surface is pure granite and the trajectory is, to say the least, unusual for a road.

But I don't go into this philosophical stuff with the wayfarers at our door. I can be blunt about the road if bluntness is what my guests need. "The farther it goes, the worse it gets," I may say. But I know that truths as humble and melancholy as that do not rest comfortably in their all-American souls.

Our national religion is against it. Things will get better—were we not reared on this idea? In a way it is surprising that anybody stops to inquire at all. By now, I've got those who do pretty well classified.

Some inquire out of idle interest; but there is a second group of visitors whose wanderlust has heated up to alarm before they arrive at our door. Although they ask, pro forma, where the road goes, they suspect that I have guessed their guilty secret, and they face it bravely. "We're lost," they say. I make a quick assessment: will they try to get me interested in where they thought they were (pretty hard), or do they want to know where the heck they are? In the latter case I go straight for the unvarnished facts. "You're on Half Moon Pond Road, which as recently as a hundred years ago went through to Bradford, but lately it just peters out in the woods. There is nothing much but timberland beyond here, so you will have to go back to the village center." Why is this always received as bad news?

I quickly throw in the good news. "You're not very lost: it's only two-and-a-half miles." Their looks tell me they think it's about ten. Clearly, I'm not to be trusted and, moreover, my cheerfulness is threatening. Feeling truly lost, they would like me to share a little of their alarm. Travelers are lured in this far by the certainty, born of whimsy and hope, that this scenic road is a shortcut to somewhere. I have damaged but not dislodged this conviction. I offer the following proposition to whatever science it is that keeps track of these things: The human race has an innate belief, hard to stifle on a random drive, that every rotten road is joined at both ends of its ruts by smooth pavement.

A third group of callers is neither seeking information nor spreading their alarm. They are intrigued with what they think they have found in our clearing, and after asking with genuine interest where the road goes, they will pose one of two questions, never both: "Do you mean you really live way back here?" or "Your place isn't for sale by any chance, is it?" What appalls or captivates them about this place is probably just that there is a dwelling back here at all. For that matter, we were surprised ourselves, twenty-five years ago, when we found it, getting here just in time to rescue the old farmhouse. Today, however, the house is a home and comfortably into its third century; we do live here, yes; it's not for sale, no; and it provides a splendid sanctuary for earwigs, ghosts, wide boards, writer's blocks, and other domestic gear.

Although our road and location have brought us into touch with the special classes of nomads mentioned—the cautious who inquire, the lost who despair, and the intrigued who express pity or envy—there is a fourth group whose makeup is somewhat more complex, and our acquaintance with them is rather more extensive. Their trademark is that they are on a pleasant trip to nowhere, so they do *not* stop on the way in, but *afterward* wish they had. Restive and true believers in the American Way, they are certain that easy street is just around the bend. But it's not. What's around the bend is potholes. So we make their acquaintance when they come out—on foot—for they have had some mishap up the road and need help. They are the hardcore innocents. I'll introduce some of my favorites.

Shortly before sundown one summer evening we saw a car go zipping past the house, much too fast for this road. An hour later a young teenage girl hurried into the yard, slight sandals on her feet, fright on her face, despair in her heart. Part of her story she volunteered and part of it we deduced. Desperate to find a familiar road, she had apparently plunged on, faster and faster, as the sun sank lower and the road got worse. Panic was driving her into thoughtlessness and she was driving her car into wilderness. It was the season of road ruts, and eventually the car's rear axle got hung up in the middle of the so-called road, the wheels spinning freely in a black wallow of pure New Hampshire mud. As darkness fell she collected her wits enough to scamper back down the road to our house. She said she had been hunting for a shortcut to Greenfield, Massachusetts, and we were obliged to point out that she was in western New Hampshire going straight north.

It was now dark. Grace proposed that she stay for the night, and since at that time we had no telephone, I offered to drive her to the village to line up help for the morning and to call her parents. Very reluctant at first to report the facts to her home, she eventually agreed that not reporting them might be worse. When I saw in her words and face as she talked by phone with her mother that Mom was not warming to her story, I took the phone, identified myself and tried to be reassuring.

That's when I realized precisely what sort of selling job I had on my hands. So I was the nice man proposing that her young daughter stay the night! (Incidentally, how *do* you persuade an unmet mother that her wandering child is safe with you?) Would she call the F.B.I.? Would state police set out to track us down to our lair deep in the woods where we imprisoned juveniles in a gingerbread house and. . . . But probably not. As I closed off the conversation as best I could, it occurred to me that it might have been wiser to let Grace make this call. We fed the daughter, gave her bed and breakfast, got the tow truck, and finally saw her off. She forgot to say thanks. Was she a runaway, as we suspected, blaming us for thwarting her? Maybe just a lost and scared kid.

Not all of the innocents who arrive at our yard have driven

in; some have wandered into the valley on foot, found the road by accident and walked in our direction because it seemed downhill. To those we are not so much the last house on the road as the first. One summer day a young girl lost her way on the mountain and suddenly found herself in our clearing. We knew of her coming because we had heard a plaintive voice in the woods calling "Alexandre!" Then she was there, and so distraught that we could not fathom her words when we offered help; it sounded like Greek to us. Finally we deciphered where she was staying, and took her there, a nearby lake cottage, discovering that she had indeed been speaking Greek, for she was a native of Crete visiting New Hampshire relatives for the summer, and had wandered away from a blueberry-picking party.

Although daylight visitors continued at a regular pace, it was a few years before we had any more involuntary overnight guests. We made up for lost time one early September when a whole squadron arrived in our yard. It was windy, raining, cold and near midnight when the knock came. A bedraggled spokesman stepped from a huddle of shapes in the dooryard mist and said, "Sir, you are not going to believe this, but. . . ." Two hours earlier his party, camping on the mountain, had fallen heir to a lost party of three hikers. The three, not camping, lost and ill-clothed, drenched and chilled, one of them already appearing to be desperately ill, had thought they were in a park. The camping party had broken camp and the whole group then slithered down the mountain in the cold rain to seek help. Did we have a garage or barn where they could be dry until morning, and perhaps a warmer place for the invalid? "I'm awfully sorry to bother you like this, Sir," he said, and then presented the sick one in the door light as a specimen for my inspection—and mercy. The story was too implausible to be disbelieved.

I suggested our kitchen floor as the only bunkhouse available and invited them in, the sick and the lame first. Grace had dressed and joined me at the door in time to learn that there would be a few guests. She had the wit to ask, "How many?" "About thirteen, I'm afraid," came the reply out of the shadows and rain as the parade started in. Then there ensued an hour of cheerful chaos as we lit fires, brewed cocoa, stacked gear, moved furniture, and found spaces for sleeping: thirteen extra people trying in various ways to deploy their bodies inconspicuously in a small house. In fact, kitchen and dining-living room offered still too little space for all the sleepers and baggage, so Grace and I eventually retreated to the rafters and turned the entire first floor over to the invasion.

We had diagnosed the ailment of the sick one as panic aggravated by chill, not likely to be fatal—except to innocence. When we overheard her say that she would call a taxi in the morning we added an acute case of Urbanitis to the diagnosis, a malady that can provoke temporary mind damage as a side effect when the victim is exposed to raw countryside. A taxi indeed! Passing cocoa, we picked up bits of introductions, the most memorable being this: "She goes to Harvard and her and me go to M.I.T." (Scout's honor, that's exactly what she said!) Well, it was the day before registration for freshmen down in Cambridge, and these three had found a state forest—called a park here—on the road map, driven to it and started walking, heedless of directions, weather, maps, terrain, time. They were game spirits. They were many miles from their car, going up a mountain in the dark and rain and in the wrong direction when they stumbled on the ten-person camping party, which undertook to deliver them. The campers came en masse, not knowing their destination and not wishing to disperse their group on a black night. Over the cocoa the campers' leader eyed the "her and me" set benignly and quietly asked us what we knew about college admissions standards down on the Charles River. "Won't touch it," I said.

By morning everyone was alive and well. Some clothes were almost dry and the keen autumn sun was pouring down, putting sparkles on every leaf. The ten seasoned campers took breakfast on the lawn from their own mess kits and then returned to the trail. We transported the three future scholars back to their car, seven miles, and pointed the direction out of the forests of New Hampshire toward the groves of academe. Their long innocent summertime of adolescence was over, we hoped, and we had been privileged to witness the rites of passage. I'm an optimist: somewhere today I know they are teaching Environmental Studies.

One evening four stylish women dressed for shopping tripped briskly into the yard. They had been out antiquing and were, they had supposed, taking an interesting route home. Going beyond our place as far as possible on the antique road, they had finally stopped in despair, tried vainly to turn around and stopped again in mud. With the car mired up to where the runningboards used to be, they had blithely high-heeled and tiptoed themselves back a couple of muddy miles to the last house on the road, arriving just as Grace was about to serve up the season's first rhubarb pie. So they joined us for dessert, and after that we delivered them to the brusque mercies of the town road agent, who told them plainly to just stay clean out of the way. At Christmas we got a thank you note signed "The Four Sillies" from somewhere in Kentucky, commemorating their all-time-favorite New England adventure.

One man, who said he had traveled our road dozens of times, took his brand new Jeep out for a trial spin one warm day in June and stalled it three miles up the road. When he got back to our place his face was shining with chagrin and blackfly bites. While I took him home to get his old Jeep to retrieve the new one, we talked about the blackflies and the merits of various insect repellents. He had always carried a can of his favorite brand in his old vehicle but had not yet put one in the new one, and he chided himself for this foolish oversight. Later, I found that he had left at our door a thank-you note and a half-full can of his favorite repellent, a brand unavailable in stores. It's terrific stuff, I find, very potent. A neighbor of ours thinks the man used the first half to spray in the carburetor to start his new Jeep. I can believe that.

It was below zero and storming violently one night when we were awakened by pounding on our door at 2:30 A.M. Our visitors were two lost hikers who said that they had tried to ski to Mt. Sunapee—which is impossible even in daylight unless there are fifteen feet of snow, in which case it would be exciting but stupid. Discovering the inevitable much too late in the day, they had turned back at about dusk, taken a wrong turn, got lost, but didn't dare stop for fear of freezing. Eight hours later and barely upright, they had stumbled upon Half Moon Pond Road, luckily followed it in the right direction, and arrived at our door, where they had used their last strength to awaken us. I drove them—only partially thawed out, since they wanted to reassure their hosts as soon as possible—to the designated house in the village. There we found a convivial party still going on, and nobody seemed worried about the skiers—for them the final ignominy. . . . I've never been able to fully believe this story, but I tell it anyway, simply because it is true.

Our encounters with innocents abroad are frequent enough (eight adventures is the record for a summer) to be interesting but not really troublesome. They give us a certain knowing perspective on human impulse and sometimes the pleasure of seeing misfortune dissolve in gratitude. In every case there is some unlikely but possibly true story to relate on our doorstep, and we are seasoned enough to credit anything they can tell us. We've probably heard it before—whether from Kentucky or Crete or Harvard. Some have just run out of gas before they ran out of courage. Or did they hit a moose up the road? Not yet, but that will come too. People haven't been able to take No for an answer from this road. *Why* ramblers who have no particular destination in mind, or who are seeking a quick way out, just keep going on a road as it gets steadily more bleak and the scenery runs to swamp is not something I shall ever fully fathom. But I shall continue to sympathize with their rashness, for I know that retracing steps is not an innate human impulse. When they do retrace, they are not bursting with pride or self-esteem.

The most charming vagrant at our door was a yellow tomcat. Perhaps he was a summer resident who was forgotten in the autumn, or maybe he just found life dull in the village or at the town dump and so moved on up the most scenic road in town. But before he got stuck or lost he shrewedly retraced his steps by an innate impulse to the last house on the road and put himself at our mercy like all the rest. "I'm lost" is what he clearly said as we opened the door to his call, but "You mean you really *live* way back here?" is what he was probably thinking. And he was not one of the innocents; he was the smartest wayfarer of them all. We put him up for the night like a lost camper. Having been introduced to our hearth, he seemed to forget his former plans and he lived out his life right here.

Three years ago a major lumber operation moved in up the road beyond our place. Uncharacteristically, these lumbermen repaired the road before they used it; then last year they came back for more lumber and made the road even better. Now they are back again, still harvesting trees, still fixing up the road too. Fewer and fewer people are getting stuck and lost back there—the downside of progress, as I see it. The trees the lumbermen cut go into pulp, which makes paper for books, including books about living on old forgotten roads. If ordinary citizens can't depend on our abandoned road to have their troubles on anymore, or me to report on them, these lumbermen will have shut down a whole genre of literature, and I won't be able to complete the circle by creating prose to help them dispose of their pulp. Somewhere up the road I see things coming to a dead end.

The Old Powers Place

Let us return to origins. When we first came up Half Moon Pond Road in the mid-1960s what we found was leftovers from a traditional eighteenth-century New England farmstead: a reclining one-hundred-eighty-something-year-old house, plus accumulations. Among the latter was a grim little ramshackle shack of a barn that left us unsaddened when it sank to the ground within a few years, and also a sugar house that had seen far better days which hadn't ever been very good, and a hundred-something acres of trees and rocks and brushy meadows haphazardly but scenically stone-walled and cheerfully called "abandoned farmland."

"The Old Powers Place" the locals called it; they didn't think of it as a farmstead anymore, though a few of them remembered old man Powers and his wife and his oxen.

Eventually, we learned quite a bit about the Powers families, two generations, who had taken over the farmstead a hundred years before we got here, and today it's as if we have been living with them for quite a while—walking in their footprints, alert to their lingering ghosts. We're on a first-name basis especially with Anson and Auren Powers, father and son. *We* are; they respond only through fragmentary evidence left for us to discover and decipher.

Anson Powers married a neighbor girl, Amy Spaulding, when they were both just seventeen, and they probably lived here a few years before he bought this farm in 1857, the day after he turned twenty-one. What they got was a Cape Cod–style house, already old, two barns and, in the standard deed language of the time, "a hundred acres, more or less." He was a preacher's son and evidently a courageous farmer to stick it out here for over forty years. Lots of his neighbors pulled up stakes and went west for better farms, but Anson Powers farmed here to the end of his days at the end of the nineteenth century, when the farm passed to his son, Auren, born here in 1872. Auren Powers lived all his life in this house, about seventy-five years in all; in later years he became Old Man Powers, and when he died during the 1940s, perhaps in the same room where he had been born, this farm, as farm, sort of died too; it was already then the last holdout in the valley. Thereafter, the shrinking meadows were pastured occasionally, sometimes by goats, but usually by young cattle visiting from Massachusetts, and eventually the farmstead was sold for taxes and bought for speculation. The house, which only then entered the local discourse as The Old Powers Place, was home to renters briefly, but mostly it just waited another decade for us, nonfarmers, to wander up Half Moon Pond Road and, against all evidence, affirm that it still had a future.

What it boils down to is essentially this: two long Powers generations carried the house and spanned the century from the Civil War to our day. It wasn't a great century for New England farming. In fact, a hundred years of slow rural decline and sometimes bleak New England history is miniaturized and personalized in those two Powers generations.

When the young Powerses moved here before the Civil War, the town of Washington was prosperous. There were two hundred farms and about a thousand people in town (an area the size of a Midwest township, roughly six miles by six), all working on farms or in the dozen small water-powered mills and shops that served the farms. A hundred years later in 1960 the population was down to less than two hundred, and there was only a handful of farms. Today, we have just two working dairy farms that support their families, plus a couple of smaller part-time farms. And there is almost as much woodland as there was when the Abenaki Indians lived here. Something similar goes for nearly all surrounding New Hampshire communities, except the riverbank mill towns. The decline and fall of farming here between the Civil War and World War II was stretched out over so many decades that it was sometimes possible to believe that it wasn't happening at all; indeed, during the 1870s and eighties and nineties the wise men in the New Hampshire state agriculture department repeatedly insisted that the revival of New England farming was just around the corner. What was really around the corner was the further erosion of New Hampshire farming and the rising breadbasket in the Midwest.

The Civil War was the first sign of stress in the Washington community. More than fifty sons of the town served in the Union army. So too did another thirty-four whom the town hired from elsewhere as quota-filling substitutes, seventeen of whom deserted—all quite typical. The "war of the southern rebellion"—so called in this town—touched everything, even in remote New England communities. Three of Anson Powers's brothers enlisted shortly after he moved to this place: two were discharged after service and reenlisted, and a younger brother, Lewis, was killed in South Carolina. Of Washington's fifty enlistees, twelve were killed or died in service. That's a lot of pain to be absorbed in a town only six miles square. To honor their fallen neighbors the returned veterans erected a handsome granite obelisk on the Washington town common in 1867, the first Civil War monument in New Hampshire. It is still faithfully cared for by the town.

To the time of the Civil War, Washington, though nearly a hundred years old then, had remained an insular place. The steady shift of New England rural folk to the cities and to the Midwest—which began with the Erie Canal and the building of railroads and was hastened by the Civil War and the Homestead Act—might not have seemed ominous, or very noticeable even, to Anson Powers in his first years in this house. The record shows that he mortgaged the farm during the Civil War, but he stayed with it. Meanwhile, more and more of his neighbors left to seek a better life elsewhere, and by the 1880s many who clung tenaciously to the granite were part of a culture of survival.

A thick *History of Washington* was published in 1886, and it is heavy with community pride; but you can also flutter the pages and hear the whispers of stress and melancholy, hear too a sigh for the old days, the prosperous times of self-sufficient family farming, the 1830s and 1840s, already idealized, and even for the heroic era when the town made costly sacrifices to save the Union and suppress the southern rebellion. Rural wistfulness punctuates family genealogies: "he lived on the mountain road, but the farm is now abandoned" . . . "their place has not been farmed for many years" . . . "these building are now neglected." In their lament for lands left untended, the local authors are knowingly touching an eternal note of human sadness, which poets and elegists have sounded since the days of ancient Rome. They could not know it then but that song of the 1880s would linger in the town's air for decades to come, as the forests recaptured another and yet another of the neighbors' farms.

New Hampshire soil was rocky, the climate marginal for farming, and the terrain bluntly inhospitable to the new machinery, plows, mowers, and binders being manufactured in city shops. Railroads brought barley to Boston from rich Ohio farmlands more cheaply than it could be raised and sent to Boston by wagon and train from New Hampshire. Worse yet, New England city factories gobbled up cottage industries in far-flung rural districts; they undersold and closed the little mills on a thousand village brooks and siphoned droves of young people from the countryside. Hundreds of farmsteads, once bravely carved piece by piece from the wilderness, returned to wilderness before a century was up. "Go West, young man," said New Hampshire–born Horace Greeley, and whole families simply left New England, and the town of Washington too, to seek a better life on better farmland.

But Anson and Amy Powers, like a fair number of their neighbors, were pretty stout survivors. Son Auren must certainly have known what he was in for when he became sole owner of the Powers place in 1898. Sometimes the Powerses supplemented their income by boarding the teacher of the local school, a privilege they acquired—it was an old rural custom—by being the low bidder when the teacher's board was auctioned off at the district school meeting. What the teacher thought of this practice is not in the record. I've checked the state agriculture records, and they confirm that Washington farmers' main cash crops then were eggs, cheese, butter, meat, potatoes—and awesome amounts of maple sugar. Well into the twentieth century Auren Powers—like his father before him, I presume—harnessed up his horse each April and took a wagonload of his maple sugar and syrup to a distant city, Manchester or farther, and returned with staples. It was a trip that sometimes took several weeks.

Maple trees outlive man and beast, and even in old age they still bear tales of their vigorous youth: now and then I will salvage for firewood a great old gnarled maple that has been dying for fifty years and has finally expired, and deep, deep inside the trunk, maybe even a hundred years inward toward the core, I'll still find the stained heartwood where last century's tap hole drew sweet sap from the young tree. It puts me in touch with Anson and Auren and the world they knew.

The first decade of the twentieth century brought a major change to young Powers's place. It started with a fire. A local newspaper reported in August of 1905:

> A fire destroyed both barns of Auren Powers last night. It appears that the fire started in the well shed, where there was no combustible material. It is supposed a tramp must have gone in there to lodge and either dropped a match or set it from his pipe.

Auren's barns burned, and also the well shed, but the well itself remained and still does. It's the traditional New England sort, hand-dug, round, about six feet in diameter, only a dozen feet deep and carefully laid up with a cylinder of stone, originally fed by the eaves of the barn. Once during a dry spell I was poking around in the soup and the sludge in the bottom of the old well and I fished up a smooth piece of wood, hollow, about five inches by five, and four feet long. It was the main part of a wooden pump, made of tamarack I presume, and sound and solid as green wood. Unwittingly, I had excavated beyond the iron age down to the wood age and found Auren's pump, probably discarded for an iron one when he built his new barn. Anyway, now that I have published my archaeological results, I intend to fill up the old barn well, ninety years after the fire, lest someone tumble in. Many, many years ago Auren apparently dragged an old trailer over the well and left it there to cover the opening, and the trailer rotted, leaving only its springs and axle. I think I'll drop them into the well before I fill it; that should puzzle the archaeologists of the future.

But back to the barn fire. The tramp started it, the paper said. I wasn't there, but I doubt it. Poor tramps! How often have they served the purpose that "defective wiring" does for a later generation of fires: a handy and irrefutable explanation of the inexplicable. But farmers have long known that many a barn burns in August, a month after the haying season, and they also know that poorly cured hay stacked in a tight barn mow will heat severely and may spontaneously combust. Auren knew that too, and I would guess that he had bad luck with his haying that summer. However, why blame a farmer like Auren Powers whom we all know, if we can blame a stranger we don't know? Sure, a tramp did it.

But now Auren was without barns, and would have to build a new one. Judging by the well and foundations remaining today, the burned barns had stood apart, fifty yards from the house. For his new barn Auren was to follow the more modern idea that had sprung up all over New England during the late nineteenth century: attaching the barn to the house through a short sequence of intervening service sheds and outbuildings. This connected "big house, little house, back house, barn" sequence is sometimes taken as a New England trademark, which it is, but a late nineteenth-century one. After that it became quite common for farmers to do just what Auren did: he attached a twentieth-century barn to his eighteenth-century freestanding house. Between his big new barn and the little old house were just two structures: the wing or ell of the house, used as summer kitchen and general service area, and a smaller structure, which I presume was the outhouse.

Here and elsewhere, I have to fill in some details of the Powerses' family story, using fragments from all the usual suspects: newspaper accounts, hints in deeds, relatives' reports, archaeological data, diaries, printed genealogies, common sense, old maps, structural evidence, county records, background reading, state reports, town records, and an old photo which an elderly neighbor, Ernest Cram, took down from his wall to give us. The photo shows the Powers place when the attached barn was new and the house had been modernized. Another picture comes from a distant Powers relative who showed up here with photos garnered from his grandfather's attic: it shows Auren in front of his barn with his yoke of oxen, looking as stolid as either of them. Auren and I never met, of course, but I think I get the picture of his tenure here. I never got to see his new barn, which went up before 1909, stood for fifty years, and came down just before we got here.

There are real advantages to the New England attached

farm buildings system. Everything is near at hand, and in bad weather you needn't go outside to use the outhouse or to do the milking and chores. Many northern European farms of an earlier era, and some few American ones, took the idea a step farther, combining house and barn into one large brick or stone structure under a single tile roof, with space so deployed that the living or sleeping quarters could benefit from the animal heat and the hay insulation. But when the structure is a New England wooden connected house-sheds-barn sequence there is a massive disadvantage too, namely the danger of fire. Most connected buildings in New England were built before modern firefighting equipment, but even today if one building lights up, the whole string may sail to heaven in flames. With the house attached to the barn you may be about twice as likely to have a fire and it may destroy twice as much.

In 1905 Auren Powers lost two barns by fire but saved his house because it stood by itself. So why did he attach his new barn to his old house? That's something I'll have to ask him if I see him.

Within a few years of the fire the Powerses not only built a new barn but modernized the house as well. This suggests unusual prosperity for a period of rural decline, but it is probably easily explained: in the county registry of deeds I find record that they made a major timber sale in 1909, and from this, I think, came the cash for the house improvements and the lumber for the barn. Fortunately for Auren, he had some land too rocky and rough for anything but growing timber. All during his youth that western hillside had been quietly preparing to rescue him from disaster when his barns burned; and when they did he had timber for a new barn and plenty left over to sell. It was a once-in-a-lifetime opportunity and he made the most of it.

Perhaps the Powerses also thought of modernizing the house as something that would pay for itself, for Mrs. Powers went briefly into the "summer boarder" business. In the early years of this century it became fashionable for city people, women and children especially, to vacation on a farm for a month or two during the summer. So farm women would "take in boarders," as the phrase had it. The state government vigorously promoted the practice and issued pamphlets for farmers' wives, explaining how to satisfy their customers: urban gentlewomen would not be impressed with old-fashioned or delapidated farmhomes, they said. Whatever the motive, the Powerses did often have summer boarders—it was more profitable than bidding for the teacher's board—and they did make some major changes in the house. They took out the old-fashioned window sashes with their small eighteenth-century six-by-nine panes and replaced them with modern two-pane sashes. And they made a massive change in the interior.

The house the original Powers family had acquired in the 1850s, though small, had the standard large center chimney, accommodating three fireplaces—for kitchen, parlor, and bedroom. By the beginning of the twentieth century, installing stoves in farmhouses was common, even in the poorer rural regions. The fireplace had long since come to be fervently despised as drafty, dirty, and monstrously inefficient. Many simply boarded and papered over their fireplaces and cut new holes in the chimney flue to accomodate a stovepipe—the cheap way to do it. The Powerses, going modern all at once, took the more drastic approach. They got rid of the hated fireplaces altogether; and they took out the massive center chimney, from the topmost brick to the basement, and built a new and much smaller stove chimney in its place. Auren apparently recycled the surplus bricks in his sugarhouse chimney.

They would have had their reasons, whether they were going into the summer boarder business or not: removing the fireplaces and supporting brickwork in the three major rooms yielded lots of new space, which they turned into stairs to the basement, stairs to the second floor, a walk-in pantry, and a closet. Such modern conveniences, plus the immense practical advantages of the new stoves, surely warmed the cockles of Mrs. Powers's heart. Modern at last! For good measure she papered the walls of the parlor, not failing to cover the ancient cracks with underlying layers of newspaper. Thanks to that little touch, we could date her work exactly when we peeled back the old wallpaper.

At least two and perhaps all three fireplaces had been serviced by a large slab of rock, each carefully chiseled to perfect rectangular shape and to surface smoothness. Granite hearthstones. Whatever central place, or whatever honor and dignity they had had for over a hundred years since somebody else had built this house and smoothed those stones, there was no place for them now in the Powerses' new and modern arrangement. So they took out the old hearthstones too. Probably Auren himself dragged two of them out into the yard and dumped them (temporarily, did he suppose?) out of the way and into a ditch between the stone wall and the narrow roadway, not thirty feet from the house.

Time went by. World War I came and went, then the Depression, then World War II. Auren Powers aged, became Old Man Powers, and finally died. Farms in the valley were abandoned, one by one; derelict houses progressed to scenic cellar holes, till only the Powers farmstead was left, the last one on the road—and it wasn't very much. Year after year grass grew up and died down upon Auren's ditched hearthstones, and they sank a little lower as the mud and gravel washed in. Eventually, they just disappeared from sight, and from memory. For more than sixty-five years they rested there undisturbed.

4

Lieutenant Ebenezer Wood: "Original Settler"

Some of the modernizing that the Powerses did long ago was such that our first thought was how we should undo it—undo it for ourselves, and for the sake of the house and what it had originally been.

What had it been? In our minds today the origins of the house itself are recollected jointly with the beginnings of our own stay within it. At first we had no very clear idea where we were or whose handiwork was on this place: no knowledge of the Powers family who had discarded the hearthstones, of Auren Powers who had farmed here all his years. And no inkling of the Wood family who had spent sixty years here before that. Indeed, what we had acquired appeared at first to be just a forgotten little old house in an obscure little old town, a town with a long history perhaps, but of that we were entirely innocent too.

The first summer, between bouts of clearing out a house that had not been a home for some years, except to wildlife, we did what we could to tune in on our chosen environment. New England communities are notably self-conscious about their past, a pleasantly infectious malady, we found, and since about the time of the Civil War, hundreds and hundreds of these towns have produced a big book, or maybe two, on their town history. No recent book on Washington then existed, but the local library promptly served up a brittle copy of *History of Washington New Hampshire 1768–1886*, eighty years old, nearly seven hundred pages long, and crammed with myriad minor details of another century. Evidently, this community trailed a long past.

New owners of a house may become obsessed with it, even if it is worn and unkempt. New parents do not think *their* baby is homely, and even if it is they don't care. In the flush of new romance we swept and hammered away at our old place: it was newly ours, after all, not homely to *us*, and every sad sag of floor, every hewn beam or scrap of ancient wallpaper, every hand-planed board or rusty wrought-iron nail drew us on and in. The possessor becomes possessed. In the wing of the house, where we launched the first assault, we discovered that the floorboards, when we had excavated down to them, would need some repair—which, when done, would at least yield a level place to place our sleeping bags. First things first.

I was cheerfully banging away in that wing beachhead one day, when Grace rushed in, holding the big town history book spread open in both hands: "Hold it!" she said. "I've found our house." Evidently, this obsession of ours was about to shift to another mode. Hammer poised, I attended while she solemnly read aloud from page 670 of the brittle book:

> Ebenezer Wood . . . was born in Littleton, Mass., Jan. 20, 1754. He married Phebe Brooks, . . . and settled in Washington, in 1780 or 1781. He resided in the mountain district, on the farm now owned by Anson S. Powers, and was the original settler on that place. Previous to his settlement in Washington he was a soldier in the Revolution, with the rank of lieutenant. He was a cooper by trade, and worked at that business after coming to Washington. He died Dec. 28, 1840.

". . . the original settler." For us, that passage was also the original datum.

Evidently, Grace had opened for us another beachhead, another diversion: the first was in the house itself, the second in its history. Such a short passage, such a minor string of simple facts! But they beckoned us to look for more, and that led to farther fields than we had ever imagined. We had literally to write books before we started to recover from the diversion.

Anyway, this big book clearly implied that we were not just on Half Moon Pond Road but back in "the mountain district." Not much doubt about that: to the east, starting right there from the swamp behind the house, the land slopes upward, then rises sharply, knoll over hillock, very steeply at last, to the top of Lovell Mountain, a mile away as the bluejay flies and nine hundred feet above us. It's no place to get lost in a storm, but from the back yard it's a benign and neighborly mountain, big enough to snag and hold its own cloud sometimes; and in fall or spring its crown of spruces is frequently spangled with snow when we have none down here. Altogether it's a serene mountain, such as raises your spirits as it lifts your eyes. We had landed in "the mountain district."

In the big book Ebenezer and Phebe Wood stood at the head of a long line: four pages listed the eleven Wood children and slews of further descendants, about a century's worth. Tough folks, the original Woods. He cleared this land of trees, moved rocks, framed the house, built stone walls, farmed and coopered until the youngest son took over the farm; he lived here till age eighty-seven, she till ninety-two. If Anson Powers could lead us back to the Civil War, Ebenezer Wood could take us back to the Revolutionary War, back to beginnings: of the nation, the town, the road, the farm, the house. We had met Mr. and Mrs. Original Settler.

It is true that the house of the original settler—our house—was at that precise moment a scene of unlivable clutter and disarray, but then and there everything felt comfortably perplexing and challenging and oddly exhilarating. We were standing, after all, on nearly two hundred years of yet unsifted historical compost. Roots might grow in such soil.

We sought out the Revolutionary War muster rolls to follow the tracks of Massachusetts Minuteman Ebenezer Wood. Like hundreds of other young men he had grabbed his musket and hurried to Boston immediately upon hearing of the battles of Lexington and Concord. He stayed that summer of 1775, fought in Captain Wilder's Company at the battle of Bunker Hill, and was probably with General Washington on Dorchester Heights in the successful breaking of the siege of Boston. When the British left Boston he went back to the farm. Like many New England farm lads, Ebenezer was an intermittent soldier: he enlisted, returned home, married, farmed, reenlisted, got promoted, left to harvest the crops, returned, and was again discharged well before the end of the war. He put in about two years. Washington town records first use for him the title "Lieutenant" five years after the war ended, a title he carried thereafter to the end of his life. (His neighbors wore titles too: town records show that there was many a "Col.," "Capt.," "Lt.," and "Maj." in town, along with the usual suspects, "Esq." and "Deacon." In land-sale deeds Wood also moved up from "Yeoman" to "Gent." during the same period.)

When peace came, Ebenezer Wood was twenty-seven, had a wife and three children, and was clearing land and building a house in the mountain district of Washington, New Hampshire. Whether his coming to a remote town already then so named had anything to do with his service under General Washington I do not know.

But why come at all? For one thing, land was dirt cheap—if you could find it between the rocks. Better yet, this was the frontier, testosterone country, and agents in Portsmouth, New Hampshire, were hawking bargains in towns far off in the wilderness. A lot of undeveloped land was being snatched up by sharp speculators, then retailed in 100-acre lots to potential settlers who had not seen it; if they had seen it they might have thought twice about coming here to plant potatoes. In fact, the earliest government report on the rectangle that is now the town of Washington, dated 1738, stated flatly that the area was just too rocky to farm. Period. However, a town was chartered here in the 1750s, and then abandoned after a futile decade: too many rocks, too many Indians, not enough buyers, no permanent settlers.

After all that, a settlement did finally get going in 1768, and by the stern process of self-selection and endurance, it came about that only the hardiest of the hardy, pioneers from Massachusetts all, made a go of it in Washington, New

Hampshire. An early survey map of Washington, dated 1773, is neatly drawn, but it doesn't show the topography, the open ledges and precipices or, for that matter, the dozen ponds and the looming, impossible-to-farm granite bulk of Lovell Mountain—a map drawn somewhere else, and made strictly for marketing. Yet by the outbreak of the Revolutionary War there were several dozen families who had cleared land, built mills, put up log houses, moved rocks, and settled in for the long haul; so the town was cheerfully on its way and ready to be incorporated and named. To this young town Ebenezer Wood brought his family before war's end, and here he bought one hundred acres in the mountain district and built the house where he lived for the next sixty years.

What kind of house? *Cape Cod*, the style is called now, but not then. Then it wasn't a style; it was just a farmhouse. It's my guess that Wood was replicating the sort of farmhouse he had grown up in, following a design already well entrenched in country vernacular. From early colonial days to the end of the eighteenth century, the Cape Cod style was repeated thousands and thousands of times all over New England. Smaller than the two-story "Colonial," the Cape Cod is just a story and a half, rectangular, with a steep roof, a center chimney, and two or three fireplaces. Usually it's symmetrical: a front door centered on one side; opposite it the kitchen and large fireplace, bedroom and borning room on one end, dining and parlor on the other. The basement too is symmetrical, U-shaped, with an unexcavated area in the middle upon which the large center chimney stands, and basement walls are of large fieldstone, laid up without mortar. Like everybody else in town at the time, Ebenezer framed the entire house with hand-hewn posts and beams, and he also made it of average size, thirty-six by twenty-four, with an attached wing.

Countless Cape Cod houses, conceptually identical with

individual variations, dotted the colonial landscape. For in rural and village New England there had evolved a style almost perfectly suited to its time and needs: simple, convenient, built from nearby trees, and requiring no special expertise to do it. Dozens of them, maybe a hundred, sprang up in this town too during the fifty years after its founding, and some still stand today. Very often, as in this case, when the farmer built the house he also put on an ell or wing, a smaller, lower rectangle attached to one end, providing entry and utility space. In time, another farmer might come along and attach other sheds to the wing and then, maybe a generation or two later, still another might add a large barn to the wing and sheds—which is what Auren Powers did.

So in the early 1780s Ebenezer Wood did what nearly everybody else was to do in the mountain district in the next few decades: he built a simple Cape with a strong wing. You can tell what his neighbors did by the identical U-shaped cellar holes up and down the road. However, here in the mountain district on Half Moon Pond Road this one is the last surviving house of its kind.

"Post and beam"—that's today's phrase for the colonial method of framing a house like this. The colonials got the method from medieval Europeans, who got it from the ancients. Two hundred years ago, they usually bypassed the *term* and spoke simply of a "framed" house in distinction from a "log" house, for almost all framing was post and beam. All the timbers for the Woods' house—spruce, pine, and hemlock—were chopped down, dragged to the site with oxen, and then neatly squared up, four sides, with an axe and a broadaxe. Some places I detect also the finishing marks of an adze. In this house twenty-two rafters support the roof, each six inches square and twenty feet long. Lower beams—stringers, plates, corner posts, and joists—are sturdier and heavier.

Supporting the second floor are eleven massive twenty-six foot stringers notched into three beams, each running the thirty-six foot length of the house, all upheld by a dozen upright posts and all expertly hand-hewn on four sides. Put all the hand-hewn timbers from the main house, omitting the wing, together end-to-end and they will stretch over a quarter of a mile. And it's a small house.

When Ebenezer put the frame together he secured all joints by mortise, tenon, and cross-brace, everything pegged with oak treenails, which they pronounced and wrote, "trunnels." He used no iron nails. (There was copious iron in the water of the well but none in the frame of the house.) Nails were expensive in the 1780s, used for boarding, not framing; anyway, wooden framing trunnels expand and contract with the beams, stay tight, and will long outlast nails, which gather moisture and rust, or rot the wood and loosen. So cash outlay was reserved for nails, glass, brick, and lime for plaster; the rest came from the farm and the sawmill.

I'm thinking now about just the skeleton of the house that Wood built. Auren Powers, living here later for over seventy years, had no opportunity to *see* most of that powerful skeleton at all, for of course Ebenezer had plastered the walls and ceilings. We too, unaware at first of the house's vintage or its builder, didn't know what sort of framing stood behind the plaster that crumbled behind the brittle wallpaper; didn't really realize at first that it was a typical old New England farmhouse: simply, elegantly, powerfully done, merely built to last forever.

Thomas Jefferson was a slightly older contemporary of Ebenezer Wood, more learned, certainly, undoubtedly wiser in most respects. They never met, I'm sure, though I like to think Wood might have voted for President Jefferson, agreeing with him in matters of state. On some things they differed: Jefferson had no respect for wooden buildings. On this point Lt. Wood—yeoman, carpenter, cooper—may have understood something that Jefferson—gentleman, architect, statesman—did not. In *Notes on the State of Virginia* Jefferson directs a nice diatribe at the American prejudice against buildings of brick and stone. His sharpest attack is aimed at the lowly idea that homes of brick and stone are damp and unhealthy. Nonsense, says Jefferson. "The inhabitants of Europe, who dwell chiefly in houses of stone or brick, are surely as healthy as those of Virginia." Besides, brick and stone houses are "warmer in winter and cooler in summer . . . and cheaper in their first constuction, where lime is convenient, and infinitely more durable."

So far Ebenezer might have agreed, but he didn't build his house of brick or stone. No bricks were made in this town at the time and lime for mortar was distant and expensive; as so often, transportation problems were decisive. Actually, the town has good brick clay and later saw good brick houses; but there has never been a stone house here. What was everywhere, and free for the taking, was good virgin timber; so all the men learned wood chopping and carpentry as they learned milking and mowing. No wonder that American builders became biased toward wooden construction. Ebenezer Wood did what everyone did and built himself a modest farmhouse of wood. And Thomas Jefferson said:

> A country whose buildings are of wood, can never increase in its improvements to any considerable degree. Their duration is highly estimated at fifty years. Every half century then

> our country becomes a *tabula rasa*, whereon we have to set out anew. . . . Whereas when buildings are of durable materials, every new edifice is an actual and permanent acquisition to the State, adding to its value as well as to its ornament. [Query XV]

That's the leading sage of the age: a wooden building is not a permanent addition to the nation, since it will hardly last fifty years. Ebenezer Wood never thought of that, probably never read Jefferson's book. Good thing maybe. He might have snickered.

Jefferson's words were penned in the early 1780s—at precisely the time when Ebenezer Wood was finishing his house. Over two hundred years later I sit in this same wooden house, and as I type these words the computer screen is nestled against one of the beams Ebenezer hewed with his axe. Two technologies, axestroke and keystroke, cheek by jowl. That spruce beam is almost as hard as a brick, every finishing stroke of the broadaxe still preserved, and the beam is just as sound and strong as the day it was installed. Would that the strokes of my keys last as long! The house has stood not fifty, but two hundred years, and everything suggests that, if fire and tornado spare it, it will last another two centuries.

Of course, Jefferson's broad aesthetic vision of an enduring American architecture was entirely valid and justly famous. He was our most eloquent and farseeing architectual critic and our best practitioner to boot. Ultimately, he wanted to shift architecture from the domain of engineering to that of the fine arts. But he got some details of his vision flatly wrong, overlooking a humble democratic possibility right under his eyes, namely, an indigenous rural wooden architecture that did in fact add an enduring note of serenity and decorum to the pastoral landscapes he so much admired. I think Wood would have understood.

Every house secretes its private symbolic meanings for those who call it home. For the Wood tribe, this house, where eleven children once trooped over the threshold, was first of all a haven pitched against the blast of the still-unconquered wilderness. When Jefferson was elected president in 1800, the Wood household here held parents and ten children, ages two to twenty-three. Town inventories and the terrain itself prove that the Woods never had significant cash crops. Mainly, the farm supplied the cooper shop and fed the livestock and the family. Where did they all sleep? we sometimes ask the silent walls. Wasn't it cold upstairs in winter, with only the dying embers on the hearth below? Did the big hearthstones absorb heat during the day and radiate it at night?

There were grandchildren and great-grandchildren in the Wood tribe by the time the old folks passed away in the 1840s. The spare records that remain, lists and references, dates and gravestones, hint at poignant dramas of life and death: the grandson, also named Ebenezer Wood, who married at age forty-two and then fathered seven children; another grandson, Daniel Wood, who lost five of his eight young children in the space of eight years while their great-grandparents still lived. Two sons build homes on Half Moon Pond Road, one toward the village, the other pitched toward the wilderness. The first of these still stands. The other lasted a Jeffersonian fifty years, was abandoned, then quietly died down to a cellar hole.

Like every farmer in these regions, original settler or not, Ebenezer Wood struggled all his life with New Hampshire's endless storehouse of granite. He lugged rocks from the fields, built miles of stone walls, built foundations for buildings, dug wells and stoned them up. And he made hearthstones.

Today, nobody makes hearthstones by hand anymore—the stones and the task are both too hard. But it is not hard to figure out how Ebenezer did it. Granite splits fairly easily—frost has been doing it for thousands of years—often leaving flat faces. You start with something roughly smooth and six to ten inches thick, and then it's just a long and dull story of hammer and chisel. It doesn't take a Michelangelo. It takes patience. Eventually, the granite gives up and releases its hearthstone.

The stones Lt. Ebenezer Wood painstakingly dressed for his fireplaces in the 1780s, hearthstones the Powerses long used and then discarded a hundred and thirty years later, were not lost forever. After more than sixty years we found them, well-preserved and ripened for recycling.

Sticks and Stones

So far as I know, the Woods never met any of the Powers family, and certainly neither of them ever met the Jagers. Yet I fancy that we are often engaged in a continuing three-way conversation. It falls to me to name our respective roles: pioneers, survivors, stewards.

The Woods were pioneers: coming during the Revolutionary War they built the house, cleared the land, and lived to see the Washington community prosper. All around them in this rocky town, and in hundreds of very similar New England communities, there evolved and briefly flourished a nearly finished way of life, a self-sufficient agriculture: milling and coopering and local manufacturing and a dozen cottage industries all intimately tied to cultivating the resistant land and harvesting its forest. Theirs was an American success story. They were New England pioneers.

The Powerses who followed them, coming from another part of town and settling in this homestead about the time of the Civil War, were survivors. By then the best American farming was shifting to the Midwest. But the Powerses dug in and hung on in the old Wood place in the mountain district—kept their few cows and made their cheese and butter and sold their timber and built a barn and modernized their house and tapped their maple trees and made the best of it. Perhaps the life of the survivors was easier in some ways than that of the pioneers, but I doubt that it was as satisfying.

The evidence is that Ebenezer Wood once cleared his west slope along Bog Brook and pastured it, after which Anson Powers let it grow back to forest, and his son Auren sold another timber crop off it, using the money to build his new barn. Then that slope went back to forest, and eventually I came along and cut the timber and sawed out boards to build a barn to replace the fallen one that Auren built, which had replaced the ones that Ebenezer built, which burned. . . . The conversation goes on among us.

Sometimes I interrogate both old families about the things we share—and don't share—wondering what they would make of us, the next generation on this spot. Not pioneers, not survivors, we are inheritors; at best, stewards. True, we bought the place with hard money and valid mortgage, but in a deeper sense we fell heir to the choicest part, which no money buys, gleaned and winnowed it from others who worked the land for generations and left their prints in the homely eloquence of roadway and fieldscape and architecture.

"So what do you cultivate here?" they may ask me.

"Whatever of the past is in the present," say I, possibly adding to their mystification. "I do a lot of listening. Sermons in sticks and stones, you know."

As a writer I draw from the capital stored up here, listening and ruminating in the lands they fertilized, the house they built and repaired, but not by living directly off the land itself, as they did. Where they farmed and toiled and often failed, I cheerfully garden. And I could not, for the life of me, figure out a way for this rough hundred acres of forest land and former farm to support my family, as it did theirs. I plow and forage in the same fields they did, though differently; theirs was the land itself, mine the landscape too, and all its captured history.

By the time Auren Powers took out the center chimney, about 1909, and with it the fireplaces, the hearthstones, and even the small-paned windows, the Powers families, one generation or another, had lived here in Ebenezer Wood's house for about fifty years. So it's not for me to say they didn't know what they were doing. Let's say they did—say they were yanking the old house out of the eighteenth century and into the twentieth. In our conversations I don't chide them for that.

Turning up a couple of generations later we, however, were bound to regret that particular stroke of progress; for we had become owners of a traditional New England Cape, yet one without a fireplace. It was comparatively easy to restore the eighteenth-century-style small-paned windows, but it seemed to us that at the heart of the house a vital organ was missing. It hadn't seemed so to the Powers family, we were very sure of that. The fact is that many farm families who didn't modernize their homes neglected them, couldn't afford to keep them up, abandoned them, or let them fall to ruin. With many a Cape like ours, the price of survival was that it be valued enough as a home to get itself readied for the twentieth century. By modernizing it, in their fashion, the Powers family helped it survive to become an antique. Still, we early resolved to efface the face of progress if we could, although restoring the center fireplaces seemed out of the question, as that would eliminate our stairways, closets, and pantry. And our solvency. We would await an inspiration.

The storied New England Cape and Colonial all have a tender Achilles heel. It is called the sill. Those beams, near the ground, underlying the walls of the house and resting upon granite foundation stones, are notoriously prone to rot. Inside moisture from a damp cellar, a shifting of the unmortared foundation stones, outside moisture sucked from the soil or from rainwater splashing on the lower clapboards, fungus, carpenter ants—these take a toll. Typically, a sill goes soft and the house settles a bit, the floors heave, doors bind and are recut, the house sags just a little more. To be sure, a house, like a person, acquires character from the strain of remaining upright in a shifting world. Decline is often slow, like a glacier, measured in decades or generations. Posted and beamed with massive timbers, mortised and tenoned and braced and pegged, the entire house forms a wonderfully strong box, incomparably more resilient than its successor style, the balloon-framed, timber-saving, studded houses that gained ascendency in the nineteenth century. Sometimes a Cape will stand straight and stiff as a brick, but upon almost wholly rotten feet. For local carpentry in old New England, replacing sills is, so to speak, a serious cottage industry.

(Early in our stay here we hit upon an apt analogy that dramatizes the ability of a New England Cape to hold itself together despite bad feet. In the late 1960s we purchased a French automobile, a Citroen, bought for its unique hydraulic suspension system which enabled us, with the flick of a lever, to raise the body of the car to a road clearance of about fourteen inches—this to accommodate the ruts, potholes, and general uncouthness of Half Moon Pond Road. A related extraordinary feature of the Citroen is this: it was so designed that in an emergency you could remove an entire rear wheel, put it into the trunk and drive away on three wheels—inevitably to eye-popping stares of disbelief from onlookers. The internal bracing and balance of this Citroen (no, they don't make them anymore) is like a Cape Cod farmhouse. If a tire, or a sill, goes flat, the rest of the structure absorbs the strain, but doesn't collapse.)

Our sills? Most are Wood's originals. But the far side of the house has a magnificent sag, one that accrued slowly over the course of about a hundred years, I would judge. The very beams are bent from the strain of holding the house erect, decade after decade, while one sill, in the darkness under the clapboards, was quietly turning to mush, like a tire going soft from a slow leak. I think it happened on Auren's watch. Maybe the slow sag didn't matter much: farming was pretty well finished here in the mountain district, all but two neighboring homes had retired to cellar holes, and Auren was getting old. After Auren Powers died and before we arrived, a brief owner replaced a piece of that sill, but he did not take out the sag in the wall and the roof line: no doubt the job was easier to do that way. We assessed the situation carefully, tapping into local advice, always copious and free in these parts, and then elected to do nothing about it: consequently, by installing new window frames and a kitchen cupboard against that wall we accommodated the sag—since then known affectionately as The Sag—and consolidated it in place, so that it cannot now be removed without doing serious damage. It's an historic Sag, after all.

One of the present glories of this little Cape is something which the Powerses never saw, which the Woods could not appreciate: it is the bare axe-hewn ceiling beams (stringers, in architecturalese) now exposed to full view, beams eloquent with rhythms of the pioneering past, beams that hold the whole house together and perfectly combine strength with comeliness.

In the 1780s, after Lt. Wood (maybe he wasn't Lt. yet but only Ebenezer) had framed and boarded and roofed his house, he finished the interior. To do this he took short hemlock boards, green and springy and half an inch thick, and split them gently with an axe at the ends and in many places in the center, being careful to leave the board in one piece. He nailed an edge of each board perpendicularly to the ceiling beams, then forceably stretched the split board out as far as possible, opening up all its cracks, and nailed it there in place. He did the same to the walls. "Split hemlock lath" it was called, a standard device of the time, and really quite simple to do. Then Ebenezer took horsehair and cow hair that he had curried from his animals and saved for the purpose, mixed it with lime to form a stringy, bonded plaster, very strong when dried, and plastered the ceilings and walls, forcing the plaster into the cracks of the split hemlock. The wood cured and the plaster dried together and the walls and ceilings became tough and rigid, stronger by far than any sheetrock.

So the downstairs was now nearly airtight. Its smooth white interiors would well reflect the candlelight, though they would eventually turn gray from soot and in some distant, wealthier day require the freshening grace of wallpaper. But the Woods were now rid, once and for all, of the unsightly beams, unsawed and axe-marked, including also the upright corner posts which had been carefully boxed in with lumber planed by hand for the purpose.

We didn't see Ebenezer and Phebe do any of this work: we just read the evidence. Almost all of that wall plaster is in place today. The ceilings are another story.

Right from the beginning of our stay here, in the 1960s, our attention was drawn to the bedraggled ceilings. Up there, entirely hidden from our eyes, we suspected, lay the secret of the inner strength of the house: something, surely, had kept the walls plumb and the roofline true despite The Sag on the far side. In one room, some plaster from the ceiling was fallen and falling, a few connected bits dangling in the air as if on a string. Apparently, layers of wallpaper on the outside and networks of animal hair inside had kept the plaster in place. We didn't yet know enough about our new mansion to realize that the horsehair was Woodwork and the wallpaper was Powerswork, and that together they had contrived, over the years, to keep all the walls and most of the ceilings intact until we came along. However, the ceiling in the southwest room appeared almost beyond saving and, furthermore, it was under suspicion of concealing something interesting. That ceiling would be our next beachhead.

Maybe everyone has a touch of the vandal in his soul. At any rate, once the decision was made, it was not a time for gentleness. I went to work on the ceiling with contrived vengeance and with maul and hammer: and that was just for openings. Then with a wrecking bar for prying and twisting, I blasted away at the openings in the ceiling, pounding and yanking and tearing away at the lath and the ancient plaster. A prodigiously dirty and dusty business it was, but I scarcely stopped or looked until the entire ceiling was hacked to pieces and dragged to the floor: an appalling mess of splintered hemlock and plaster, wallpaper, snake skins, squirrel nests, nut shells, bat residue, old sawdust, rusty nails, a mousetrap, ages and ages worth of dried rat droppings and bushels of mouse turds. Down it all came, cascades of grime and litter, trailing clouds of noxious dust. The wreckage was so extravagant that I retreated into another room and shut the door and read a book.

When I called for Grace to join me to return to the scene of the grime to assess the damage, it was really to peer back in time, though unwittingly then, by peering directly into the inner life of the old house. For there they were, freshly surprised in their dark and ancient hiding place but now plain as day: five solid beams, hand-wrought and smoothed on four sides, each eight to ten inches square, each locked into a plate and summer beam of similar dimensions. Although we had hoped, we had not known they would be there. We surveyed what we had found and what we had wrought, running our eyes over the heaped-up litter that was now everywhere layered with a coating of grey plaster dust, like dirty snow, and we looked about at the walls and sagging doors, and up at the venerable beams, caught in the act of quietly holding up the house by holding it together, and we looked at each other and we said, "Beautiful!"

What we thought was this: Long ago, someone with axe and broadaxe and nearly faultless workmanship carefully hewed those beams to dimension, framed the house with them, and then, since their job was wholly utilitarian, properly sealed them away behind the split lath and plaster.

And we, having thus established our credentials for benign ruthlessness, were now committed to wrecking ceilings. The ghost of Ebenezer Wood, if it walked abroad, must have dreaded our coming; but we were just getting to know the Woods, and this was one way to do it. We were liking them better with every beam exposed. The next summer, having selected another target, we banged away in the kitchen and dragged its ceiling in pieces to the floor and shoveled it out the window; the following year we assaulted the last two rooms and did the same. Each time we forced more handsome beams out of hiding and into daylight, for that was the purpose of it, and each time we praised the craftsmanship of the old-timers. Wood was a cooper, after all, we said, and should be good with wood. It was a more meticulous job to cut and fit sheetrock up between the beams, fastening it to the underside of the double layered floor of the upstairs, but we did that too; and Grace painted the sheetrock white and wiped the beams with linseed oil. Then we got cricks in our necks looking up in admiration.

All this took more time and effort than it takes to tell it, but we have never doubted the worth of it. We weren't pioneering in any of this, and it's not to be confused with restoration. Restoration? That wouldn't be Wood's word. We think of it as stewardship. It's what you do in these precincts if you suspect buried treasure above the farmhouse ceiling and find it. Today, when people newly enter the house their sightline inevitably sweeps upwards, and the truth of what they see there is evident even to the inexperienced. The beams were put away as rough and raw, unsuitable for domestic eyes, but after they had incubated for a few centuries we had only to peel away the brittle shell and release them, fully formed, to be appraised for what they are.

It was not the long years of dim light in the company of rat manure that beautified them. Time itself had changed them only a little, deepening, enriching their ageless reddish hue. It is the world around them that really changed: generations of farmers have come and gone; children were born here, lived, died; rural economies were upset, righted, upset again; flatlanders have invaded. The bare functional objects of one day take on rare aesthetic value for another, and today the beams compel both eye and mind. For them the whole process is a splendid kind of reverse rot: instead of decaying to something lesser they rise to something higher.

And they still retain some secrets. The summer beam, for instance, which runs through the center of the house lengthwise, binding everything, doesn't run perfectly parallel with the two plates, but somewhat diagonally by nearly a foot, and I cannot figure out why. Though harmless, it seems a gross mistake—if mistake it was. Again, on most beams the axemanship is expert, but a few are markedly inferior and show the marks of a true wood butcher. Was there more than one axeman? To create for me a study in contrasting techniques? Who? Ebenezer Junior was a mere boy, not a likely candidate. Mrs. Wood? Pro tem, I'm crediting a neighbor. I see the beams nearly every day, and have for nearly twenty years, and I don't expect ever to exhaust them.

Vincent Scully, the architectural historian, writes that buildings, like works of art, "never embody one truth . . . but multiple truths, always exceeding the intentions of their makers in depth, ambiguity and variety, and changing over time as those who perceive them change." I think he was meditating on the ancient Greeks and their temples; but he spoke also for the yeoman of yore and their New England farmsteads. ". . . always exceeding the intentions of their makers." That's the idea. Ebenezer Wood exceeded his intentions, all right, and he scarcely knew what kind of raw material he was putting down for later generations to chew over. Did he put more "depth, ambiguity and variety" than he imagined into his house? You bet he did. It is ours to view in larger, cultural terms the things which he had to view within the narrow constraints of necessity—landscapes, woodscapes, stone walls and posts and beams, sticks and stones and whatnot.

Posts and beams are merely pieces of dead trees, sticks of wood; and stones are merely pieces of rock. Of course they are. Of course they are not. Not merely.

Comes the summer of 1976 and I am idly rubbing the toe of my shoe on a flat stone embedded in the edge of the yard and recently exposed by the lawn mower. The visible surface is smaller than this page. Absentmindedly I toe the sod, and now it rolls back easily to double the exposed surface. Still remarkably flat, smooth. Idly, I bend to tear out a piece of turf and then expose a sharp right angle in the stone. Intrigued, I push back more sod and—surprise!—there appears another sharp corner like the first. Might be a nice stone, I think, though the rest of it is deeply buried, so I let it go for now.

Mowing again a week later, I come upon that puzzling stone, note again its smooth face and perfect right angles, and decide to do something about it. That requires a shovel and some work but eventually I uncover the entire stone, laying bare a striking rectangle, about three feet by four, and clearly too perfect to be entirely natural. I think of a gravestone, but it is much too thick, too massy for that, the corners too sharp; I have no idea what it is, except that it is granite and shapely. The next day my son Colin, who is four, "helps" me dig it out and lever the stone to the surface. It is implausibly heavy, and even with Colin's help, I cannot lift an end.

Grace and I had been thinking of putting a fireplace and chimney on the north end of the house, but were still uncertain about the design. It would be a brick fireplace, recycled bricks of course, and we had thought vaguely of creating a firebase and hearth of flat stones plucked from an old wall. Almost imperceptibly, the idea seeped in that we could use a stone like this for that purpose, maybe make it into a kind of, well, a hearthstone. *Make* it into a hearthstone? Suddenly it hits us like a rock that perhaps this already *is* a hearthstone. "Perhaps" turned to "certainly" when more digging in the vicinity yielded a second, nearly identical stone, slightly smaller and with a corner broken off. Verily, we were excavating the discarded remnants of Ebenezer's Wood's original fireplace!

We let these solemn thoughts settle into our souls for some months. They would not go away. So we hired a mason. On the north end of the house we cut open the wall, discarding more split hemlock lath and hair plaster, took out a chunk of solid sill, and poured a cement footing. We rolled the old hearthstone on poles back toward the house, realizing full well why Auren didn't take it very far away. Then we tenderly levered the stone into its new bed, flush with the floor and even accommodating its sag, and secured it firmly there with a mixture of mortar and ardor. The mason built a brick fireplace upon it, using Count Rumford's principles, and he also used the bricks I had salvaged from Auren Powers's collapsed sugarhouse, something Auren had built, I reckoned, early in this century with recycled bricks from Ebenezer Wood's original center chimney. So the old bricks were now reworked again into new networks of history and of memory, returned at last to the old home's hearth.

We needed but one hearthstone, so I reshaped the other one with hammer and chisel and assigned it a place of honor as a fireback. While I mixed mortar and hauled in old bricks, the mason put in the flues and built the exterior chimney, and then I finished the fireplace mantle with paneling found in the attic. The new fireplace was born old.

There came finally a cool evening of Indian summer when we kindled a small fire on the hearth, feeding it with sticks of dried hemlock lath, which snapped and popped with old, very old, hemlock pitch, and flicked bright sparks upon the hearthstone. The three of us, Grace and I and four-year-old Colin, spread our fingers toward the flames, and we sensed that something was right, some circle complete. We imagined all the Woods and the Powerses smiling down upon us, and we felt at home.

Of Wells and Water

Before he built his house, Ebenezer Wood dug a well. The well was shallow, hand-dug with pick and shovel down into the brick-hard white clay subsoil. When he was deep enough he stoned it up into a perfect cylinder about six feet in diameter. Whereupon he built his house—that is, right on top of the well he built it, letting the outside of the well serve as part of the foundation of the house. The well itself is inside, in the basement and under the kitchen, and being near the edge of the house it is copiously fed by water from the eaves. It's a great and simple idea: the well is accessible from the cellar; because of the eaves it seldom goes dry; its pipes do not freeze; and Ebenezer could build a shaft from the well top up through the kitchen floor and to the tabletop. With that, Phebe Wood had direct access to water right in her kitchen. She would merely raise the wooden cover beside her cupboard and crank up a bucket of fresh well water.

It's a charmingly practical and integrated conception, which is what you'd expect from an eighteenth-century farmhouse, built in the era when ecology was still a subdivision of common sense. The Woods' water system, put into place in the 1780s, compares most favorably with the system my mother and many of her neighbors in Michigan coped with as late as the 1940s, when we still carried water into the house from a pump in the yard.

Long before we got here, however, the Woods' system, so ingenious for its own day, had been modernized several times. The first improvement, I suspect, linked the well to the kitchen with a pump, probably a wooden pump like the one I found in the barn well. Later, the Powerses installed an electric pump and pressure tank in the basement. They sent two iron pipes upstairs, one of which was directed through the fire box of the cookstove and then to the sink, yielding hot water on tap all winter. I don't suppose Mrs. Powers regretted the loss of the old oaken bucket in the well.

On our first exploratory visit to this house we saw the rusty water pipes and followed them down to see whence they came. There in the musty dimness of the basement we found the well, against the far wall, exquisitely fenced in with years of cobwebs. We broke through the veil and levered up the heavy well cover; then we poked the bright beam of a flashlight into the black hole, hesitantly peering over the edge behind it. A long round chamber of smooth damp rocks came into view, ending in a shining disk that shimmered and quivered as it caught bits of sand dropping from the well opening. When the disk came to rest we could dimly see through it to reddish rocks at the well's bottom—a well even older than the house itself. We were contemplating the beginning of things.

From the day we first peered into it, we took pride in that well, its origin and rationale, the way it respected interdependencies. Living in the city, we found it easy to fall prey to certain illusions—that water comes from a tap, for example. Not here. First the Wood families, then the Powers families, then the Jager family drew and drank gratefully from that basement well. Our turn was fifteen years; altogether, it watered the households here for over two hundred years. Occasionally, when academic friends dropped by to get the flavor of our efforts to salvage Lt. Wood's house, we would make a point of explaining the well and its rationale. Sometimes they would arch their eyebrows, say something clever like "How interesting," and then immediately edge over for more gin to dilute the homemade ice cubes we'd manufactured from the produce of that well. They wanted to know where the ice cubes really came from about as much as they wanted to know what really goes into a frankfurter. For some years, however, we could validly assert that periodic tests of the water showed that it was as wholesome as it was delicious.

But one summer our beloved well mysteriously went foul. First the smell, then the taste. I managed to clear up the mystery, and eventually, the foulness, more or less, by dragging up from the well bottom a wad of something that looked for all the world like a long-discarded fishnet. It turned out to be just a huge clump of fine roots that had crept into the well from the nearby butternut tree. That explained the sudden prodigious growth of the tree and proved that our systems were even more closely integrated than we had realized. For most of the summer there was an identifiable butternut-root flavor to the water. "How interesting," we said. Apprehensively.

For butternut roots were but a foretaste of things to come. That tree was still dormant the next spring when we sensed a new flavor in the water. Again, I levered open the well-cover and peered in to discover that a heavy rainstorm had somehow washed an entire convoy of nightcrawlers into the well! It was a decidedly awkward business to fish them out since the top of the well is less than four feet from the ceiling of the cellar, making it difficult to manipulate a twelve-foot pole to reach to the bottom of the well. The next spring, nightcrawlers washed into the well again, but this time—due to jaded palates?—we didn't notice them immediately. In fact, we didn't know about their visit before a good many of them had, well—let's face it—had, so to speak, as it were, died. Consequently, I can accurately report (although I've found that not many people are interested in this) that deceased nightcrawlers have a different color on the well-bottom when carefully studied by flashlight. They are rather grayish, instead of the familiar healthy pink. Also, they don't wiggle—that's another good way to tell. And, finally, they tend to break up rather easily if you scratch around for them with a long-handled apple picker. I actually learned all this by direct experience, and it amounts to more than I really thought I needed to know.

At this point a helpful neighbor suggested that I put in a trout to fish out the worms—an old New England trick, he said. I could even keep the trout on a leash, he suggested, recall him after he had done his chores in the well, and dispatch him again whenever necessary. Well, perhaps a trout well-trained, so to speak, in this particular line of work exists somewhere, but casual inquiry didn't turn one up in our vicinity. I had to go back to scratching for the gray mincemeat with the apple picker. Even today I won't concede that this experience was driving us to drink, but I will admit to putting ever fewer and smaller ice cubes in my gin.

Our carefully cultivated rural equanimity was suffering a little wear and tear. For the most part we try to appreciate all God's little creatures, but we actually began, about this time, to be suspicious of the entire cellar floor crowd: all the wimpy little denizens of those dark and damp basement corners. After a lifetime of skulking about down there, eating each other, eluding the flashlight, where did these little crawlers creep to when they neared the end? Maybe to take a final plunge into our well? Too often, as I tried to contemplate higher things upstairs in my study, I felt my thoughts inexorably sink to what we cheerfully called "the ecological situation" in the basement. Certainly we owned a lovely old well, but it seemed rather too intimate with its surroundings.

And we had still more to learn. It was the next summer that the pipe from our sink drain sprang a small leak, completely unnoticed at the time. Investigating one more novel odor in the water, we eventually found (I'm not making this up) that we were actually recycling our sink water, which was leaking into the well, right up into our drinking water. Although we subsequently adjusted to importing ice cube water from the neighbors, it was hard to adjust to the prospect of bathing in secondhand dishwater, even if it was occasionally free of butternut-flavored nightcrawlers.

Boldly looking the situation in the face at last, we admitted that we liked the *idea* of living with a two-hundred-year-old basement well more than we liked living with the well itself. This well, anyway. We called a family council and considered the melancholy fact that our historic well had a chronic problem—excessive rapport with its immediate surroundings—and we then voted, three to zero, to fight back by giving up. One thing we must do: dig a new well. And a second thing we must do: control its illicit relations with its environment.

In fact, however, we had been dreaming other dreams entirely—big and exciting dreams about timber harvesting and pond building. Now the well was forcing us to recognize how interconnected everything really is.

East of our house and west of our woods lay a grassy area, low-lying and swampy, perfect for a pond. Beyond lay the brook and the forest. The mixed hardwood and softwood forest climbs a long rocky slope toward the mountain, and includes specimens of every local species. So far as I can see, these trees feed on granite. With a diet so austere, one does not expect much timber growth. Nevertheless, we had early formed the thought: shouldn't we sell the timber that has matured on the hillside and use the proceeds to build a pond in the swamp? However, pond building had always seemed complicated and expensive (a correct estimate, it turns out), and timber harvesting had always seemed economically marginal and aesthetically brutal (another correct estimate, incidentally). And there were other complications. It always proved easier to postpone these projects, since there was plenty of other work, lesser tasks, to chose from. But the well was forcing our hands.

Wherever we looked, new webs of interconnectedness sprang into view. First, the placement of a new well would be determined by the placement of the pond; they had to be planned and done together: no well without a pond. Second, constructing a pond at all was contingent upon thinning the forest and harvesting the trees to pay for it. However, third, timber cutting was not feasible until we resolved a boundary dispute down toward Bog Brook. To do that, we had, fourth, to get a surveyor, restudy deeds as old as the house, and convince the neighboring landowners of our results. The question was whether we were really *that* thirsty.

The boundary dispute was with a large landholding trust, which owned the adjoining forestland. For more than a century all deeds hereabouts had defined one named farm as bounded by the other named farms without saying where any farm was. Everybody was supposed to know that. But by the time the trust got into the act a generation ago all the local old-timers were dead or dying, and nobody knew where the boundaries actually were. Instead of tracing the references back to their origins the land trust hired a surveyor who simply drew a couple of straight lines through the puckerbrush—land was dirt cheap anyway—and made a map. Good-looking map, too. As it happens, it's also bogus. After we had concluded from several days' research in the county Registry of Deeds that the real line ran along the old cart road and not along the stone wall indicated on the map, that the map rested upon convenience but not upon documents, and—most importantly—that it deleted some fine timberland from our assets, we began to make overtures to the land trust. It was hard to get their attention, hard to keep it, and harder yet to get them to consider seriously our suggestion that their map of our common boundary was mistaken, and that we were, shall we say, thirsting to get it corrected. That is how time passes in the countryside.

Meanwhile, back at the house the venerable well went right on serving up exotic drinks, occasionally in three flavors—butternut, worm, and sink. Sometimes we drank a toast to the bogus map. Our friendly adversaries at the land trust could not discern what our urgency about an old boundary had to do with our graphic tales about an old well. But we were beginning to see it ever more clearly. Drinking from the old well caused us to see visions.

This was the vision. Part of the forest we would thin down to a sugar orchard; the logger's skidder roads we would recycle as cross-country ski trails; the timber would go to the mill, the waste wood to firewood, and the swamp topsoil to garden loam. With the pond we would have additional fire protection, and we could also swim, skate, and irrigate. The vision was of walkable, skiable forest roads and a sugar orchard sloping past the garden toward the edge of a swimmable, fishable, skateable pond. The new well, dug deep into the raw clay and sealed in cement tiles, would perch on the hither side of the pond.

It was such an entrancing five-year plan that we undertook to complete it in five months. We never did resolve the boundary dispute; we just steered clear of that line. And one day we let the invasion begin. Surveyors and neighbors, plumbers and well-diggers, two species of forester, an engineer, a biologist, loggers, conservation officers, lumbermen, dozermen, and choppers—a long line of participants, observers, supervisors, spectators, friends, and advisers came and went. Some worked. Wanting to keep things simple, we did not call in a water dowser.

Even so, there was quite a bit of slack in the network, and my family and I had to take that up, which we did by becoming experts on title research, forestry, selective timber harvesting, landscaping, gardening, maple sugaring, pond design, and several other ancillary and connecting disciplines, ecology and wellness among them. Quite a bit of fuss for a hundred acres of backcountry: moving earth, mowing trees, molding vistas. Quite a trick to try to remain solvent throughout the encounter. Quite an elaborate commitment to the interconnectedness of things: for the whole shebang had to pay for itself, lest our philosophy, our ecological theories, our credit, and our credibility all collapse entirely. In retrospect, it seems amazing that it worked out. Which it did. The new well, which is forty feet from the pond, is also deeper than the pond: perhaps in dry seasons the pond may do for the new well what the eaves did for the old one. Our systems are still interconnected.

The first principle of ecology, some say, is this: you cannot do just one thing. I agree, just one thing we could not do. And not just two, either. We tasted bad water and eventually triggered entire chain reactions, whole systems of interdependence of which we had not dreamed. We did more than one thing just to quench our thirst.

One last time now I pry up the cover of the old basement well, and peer down toward my own bleary reflection near the bottom. I still love the well, and I no longer care what other life is reflected there: the lowly basement critters, nightcrawlers and daycrawlers and all their little ecological cellar cohorts now have the well to themselves. After two hundred years, I hereby transfer title. It's theirs. They can wallow and slobber in the butternut juice all they please for all we care. From the sparkling waters of the new well we gladly toast their health. Cheers!

Part 2

Field and Forest

Within a decade or two of his coming to Washington, Ebenezer Wood had cleared his nearest fields and built the stone walls that still mark the bounds of his farm. He had driven the wilderness back to the western slopes of Lovell Mountain, where he could admire or deplore it at a decent distance. From his back door the fields and pastures he had created spread out between him and the wooded misty mountaintop. It must have been a satisfying sight.

But it would not last. Eventually the hungry wilderness would creep back down from the mountainside and gobble up the fields again. Not in his lifetime, perhaps, but it would begin in the generation of his grandchildren and go on from there. These fields and that mountain have played "give and take" for a long time, and now they play it with me.

The farmhouse that Ebenezer Wood built still stands each summer morning late in the long shadow of Lovell Mountain, and in the winter the rising full moon sometimes comes up like a ball of fire directly out of the mountaintop. House and mountain seem naturally linked. Though a home doesn't have much need for a name, sometimes one just settles upon it and sticks. The name *Lovellwood* has settled comfortably upon our home.

7

Riot in the North Meadow

One of the self-imposed yokes we are casting off is the false idea that farm life is dull. . . . [There is] drama in the red barn, the stark silo, the team heaving over the hill, the country store, black against the sunset. All I am saying is that there is also drama in every bush, if you can see it. When enough men know this, we need fear no indifference to the welfare of bushes, or birds, or soil, or trees. We shall then have no need of the word conservation, for we shall have the thing itself.

—ALDO LEOPOLD

"All I am saying is that there is drama in every bush, if you can see it." All I am saying is that I saw it. It was a riot.

The more or less open space northward from our house is a lapsed meadow, extravagantly untidy, scenic, and beloved. It has been the stage of pitched battles for more than a decade. Except on the garden side it is encircled by woods. From generations of farmers—the Woods who created it and the Powerses who sustained it—it has inherited a simple and explicit mandate: keep up appearances and keep the forest at bay. For years the field stood its ground while we cheered it on by calling it a meadow, sometimes The North Meadow. But always we vaguely realized that time was running out, for the woodscape in that direction showed a vacuum, abhorrent to nature.

Years ago, on the day the last farmer of these acres sent his last cow to market, the forest nodded and took an option on the meadow: it would be only a matter of time. Inevitably, the issue was joined.

As I reconstruct the early skirmishes in the campaign, partly from memory and partly from field research and close inspection of the carnage, it appears that the forest assaulted first directly through the barway, sending two reconnaissance lines of young maple seedlings up the ruts of the wagon trail toward the old apple trees. These first efforts were casually beaten back, inadvertently, by my traffic to the woodlot; indeed, at that time I was unaware that a coup d'etat was in the works, or that I had interfered.

It is quite clear now—though it wasn't then—what happened next. The forest crept in under the stone wall along the left flank—a shrewd place to infiltrate because the line there has been irresolute for decades. The wall itself is somewhat fallen and disheveled, and the disarray created by strewn boulders and fieldstones of yesteryear produced the kind of vagueness that made the line vulnerable to aggression.

Farther afield, a series of subtle rivalries was underway in those early years, quiet dramas, all inconspicuous to inattentive eyes. Alien goldenrod quietly eased its way in as the varied pasture clovers hunkered down or simply slunk away. Who was to notice, really, that where husky red clover had stood, slighter alsike and white clovers were now digging in? And what did it matter? The goldenrod invasion was well camouflaged in green and in grass, and it was hard for us to remember, August to August when the bloom was on, just how much of the meadow was supposed to be golden, and how much was to be clovered or covered with the pale beige of ripening grass. And was it broom grass or timothy? It became difficult to recall. Yet, in one August of indefinite memory, the goldenrod bloomed, lo, everywhere. Or rather, not quite everywhere, for there were other contenders for the field.

That same summer a cluster of milkweeds appeared beside the wild blueberries in the very midst of the growing chaos. They spilled their fragrance but did not stay to argue. Was it that they were bound ultimately for faraway fields and had put in here only to produce, in two seasons, offspring enough to survive the next leg of the journey? Anyway, convoys of seeds set sail one dry September day, just at noontime; they hovered briefly near the battlefield, circled once or twice and then faded into the blue. Another summer, upfield from the milkweed patch, a battalion of wildflowers gained ascendancy and raised their flags in a pageant of wondrous color: brown-eyed Susans, hawkweeds in three shades, daisies, and evening primroses led the way, sneezeweed, steeplebush, and asters followed suit. The next year the goldenrod simply closed down the gaudy show, and that was that.

For us, preoccupied with retrieving an old house, encouraging a garden, and reassuring passing strangers, there was forever something new and nearer to divert us from the deeper contention in the old meadow, and from its growing scope and depth. I suspect now that there are no battlefield innocents, charm and spontaneity of wildflowers notwithstanding; but it seemed at the time that there were. And there may be no such thing as the loyal opposition either: a forest on the march is a totalitarian movement.

Everything worships the sun. But within the meadow's stone walls there will ever be only four acres of it. How would it be parceled out? The scuffle among the clover and wildflowers, the sedate give and take of competition had evidently shaded into conflict. In fact, it was suddenly evident that meadowsweet had slipped in and put down firm roots, without ostentation and also without mercy, merging with the natives, but inexorably enlarging every bit of turf it held. Here and there armed junipers showed up, even within beds of wild strawberries which had just positioned themselves among the weakened clover. Under the protection of the knee-high juniper and goldenrod, insurgents of many a texture and hue sprouted and spread—shadbush, pin cherry, alder, even gray birch—each lying low for some years, sinking strong roots, digging in. One August an early autumn tinge of blood-red showed that scattered chokecherry bunkers were emplanted along the fringes of the field. Apparently, everything under the sun was at stake—light, food, water, Lebensraum—and full-scale subversion was afoot. Conflict became combat.

Meanwhile, dead center in the meadow, eye of the storm, a long-suffering apple tree, now an elevated thicket of gnarled and crusty limbs, past bearing but still too robust to die and too demoralized by abandonment to persevere, had capitulated. Having been for a century or more the emblem and ornament of the meadow, it now aligned itself to wilderness; it did so by fostering a welter of wild sprouts in all directions, far as it could reach, far as its fruit had ever rolled. Here was treason to the meadow. There was no chance that the gesture would ever pay off. The apple tree would be assimilated by the advancing forest: first, all its offspring would be systematically choked, but only after sending final slim and futile branches gasping toward the sun; then the old tree itself would be slowly starved to death in shades erected around it. Promise of this fate was spelled out vividly in grotesque shapes, bleached and bare, of dozens of former apple trees still upright in the surrounding woods: broken skeletons every one.

Forest trees leaned in from all sides of the meadow, patient and predatory as vultures. At their feet gentle beds of ferns shifted among the shadows and probed the thinning strands of goldenrod: sensitive fern moved in spots and jumps; hayscented fern in clusters; bracken, quarrelsome and resilient as ever, seemed to move at random; woodfern patrolled the DMZ. Smothering any tree seedlings that failed to overtop them, smothering the last stands of meadow grass and clover, the ferns advanced implacably upon the larger battle raging in mid-field. Whose side are they really on? Ultimately it will not matter; they are canon fodder now and eventually refugees on the border of no man's land. There was no hospitality in the meadow for mere ferns when the grasses and the clovers owned it, and if the forest finally prevails, they will retreat again to the margins.

In the heart of the meadow the rabble was fully roused, and some regions seemed completely out of control: alder ran riot, gray birch thickened, young pines and ash were astir, raspberry was waylaid by chokecherry at the border; maple seedlings, long crouched at weed height and bent by winter snows, now stood upright to charge. At the near wall the forest forces feinted with quick stands of yellow birches, then made a surprise attack near the far wall and took firm possession of an entire corner—a squad of young poplars did it in one blitz. Lance-leafed goldenrod, suddenly on the defensive in the territory of its own recent pillage, still held flags aloft—but who now cared for these wispy yellow plumes beneath the sleek and successful poplars? On the right, wild rose and blackberry, so recently triumphant, huddled in barracks of briar, knives drawn, awaiting the onrush of chaos. Young hawthorn toughs with fixed bayonets joined the rabble. Drama? This meadow is in an uproar.

A few summers ago a disciplined platoon of slender maple saplings two rods abreast rose from cover and marched almost to center field to take up a stand which appeared invulnerable. Forest reserves massed at the edges were ready for a direct thrust through meadow center, past the old apple tree to the blitz of poplars, cutting the field in two. If this were achieved, only consolidating would remain, and the mopping up: I should be bidding farewell to a favorite meadow. Bidding farewell, too, to the wondrous drama of a stage whereon all the familiar polarities—life/death, bondage/liberation, growth/decay, conflict/harmony—do not so much collide and cancel as excite and reinforce each other.

What is the aim of all this commotion? A mature forest, perhaps, serene and composed, at peace with itself? But how pallid a speciman of life is that compared with the tumult and the gore of the meadow in its throes!

Last year, in a move calculated and unsentimental, I entered the fray on behalf of the underdog meadow—to divert it from its destiny. But there was, I decided, no point in rolling back history and wiping the meadow clean like a slate. Better to make a selection: what in all this raucous confusion was to be spared and encouraged? Trampling through the tripwires of cinquefoil and dewberry, waist-deep in the largesse of Creation still going full throttle, it was not for me then to muse on the aesthetics of nature's violence. I had an existential choice to make: maple sugar orchard in two generations? pine forest in one generation?

I chose a blueberry patch—for this generation—reasoning thus: Let us try to beat down the uprising for a few harsh years, working as an ally of every wild blueberry bush. Let us change and direct the course of history in The North Meadow.

On D-Day in early spring, following a brush mower and savoring my omnipotence, I moved in on the wildness like a tank attack, starting from the garden edge. Meadowsweet, last year's goldenrod, seedling, sapling, sedges, hardhack and juniper, et cetera, et cetera, rank upon rank, I mowed them down and chopped them up. Well into the field I encountered a defensive Maginot Line: wild apple saplings not reckoned on, spikes and barbs in full array, inconspicuous at first, camouflaged by birch and blueberry and nearly face-high, espaliered on each other and barbed on top with a snarl of wiry hawthorns—these made a wonderfully supple and surprising deterrent to my mighty advance, and a completely successful one. As a result, my beachhead in the meadow, though temporarily secure, is shaped far differently from the one I had mapped in my mind, and somewhat smaller, too, humbled everywhere by embattled bulges where my progress was stayed. There are also patches of liberated space where, at the last moment, I deferred to noncombatant natives of the meadow. And blueberry bushes abound.

One culture overruns another, roughshod, and builds upon its ruins. There are warm words in some books about the balance of nature, an idea which easily summons images of gentleness and grace—as if the flowers of the field would adorn only peaceable kingdoms. Don't let them beguile you with sentiment, or with partial views. Out there in the real world it's a battle to the death, bedraggled and splendid beyond the singing of it. There is an elegant ferocity there, riots to revel in, without any sense of restraint or uneasiness. Oh, it's a question, maybe, whether I committed an act of conservation, or of mercy, or of hubris, to intervene and impose a settlement in the meadow, one which I may not in any case be able to sustain, such is the vigor of the wildness there. I'm obviously tampering with a potency so extravagant that I can see new faces of carnage and glory every time I look.

8

The Woods

One of my neighbors here in New Hampshire has a set speech about the woods which he delivers often and well. This discourse is always the same, and it serves to explain and justify much of his behavior. It's not a long speech, and I'll quote it shortly, but I should introduce him first.

Ralph, who was born here in our town, is fond of hunting and of cutting wood, and he does these things as recreation and sport and also to supply his fireplace and kitchen cookstove. I believe he takes to hunting and working up firewood with about equal devotion and both serve for him a further, finer purpose, that of being in the woods. He tells me that after dropping a tree and sawing out a few blocks, he usually finds that it is time to sit down, fill his pipe or pop a top, and just look things over. My sense is that he looks things over pretty carefully and often, for I think he cuts firewood mainly to be where the trees are, not the other way round. I've heard him say—I can't tell if it's concession or boast—that he seldom spends more than half the time there actually working.

Anyway, this speech isn't just casual chitchat for Ralph: he is bearing witness to the important points on his moral landscape. Having worked up to his subject with some standard preliminaries, he throws me a glance and says warmly: "I just like the woods." That's his entire stump speech, so to speak. I believe every word of it.

My neighbor shares this sentiment with several others I know, and they are about equally articulate about it. Usually I don't try to probe their testimony. If I do I get only the answers I deserve: they like to watch the squirrels, they relish the peace and quiet, enjoy the chickadees, or whatever. That much is certainly good and true, and the rest is left to me to figure out. I work on that sometimes when I walk our own woods, for though I share the sentiment of my neighbors, I can't explain and justify it as succinctly as they.

There is nothing surprising about these attitudes. My neighbors' attachments to these woodscapes have accumulated over generations, and go deeper than mere words convey. It's as if some natural harmony overtook them unawares. Ralph has lived all his life in the presence of woods, and I think he does not really know, and could not love, a landscape spare with trees. New Hampshire is eighty-six percent covered with them, and in our town it's well over ninety percent. When I first moved here I reported those figures to my father in rural Michigan who found them hard to believe, and who said: "Well, you'd better like the woods."

Well, we do. And I expect never to finish trying to understand and communicate that.

What is wide landscape in Michigan is knolled and knobby woodscape here, and that's part of the story. To the north the White Mountain National Forest sets a lavish standard, but even outside that, and certainly in my town and the surrounding ones, most of the terrain is extravagantly untidy: furrowed with brooks, strewn with boulders, carved with cliffs. There are scattered one-hundred-year-old giant maple veterans of last century's pastures, ancient hillside ponds slowly dying into bogs, sudden fern beds in unexplained clearings, and sprout lands and rocky juniper tangles that are impenetrable except on snowshoes in February. How disheartening to a lumberman! That's just a rough description of the rough slope between our house and the top of Lovell Mountain, less than two miles away, but it holds for millions of acres around here. Such exuberance at our very doorstep salutes our instinct for wildness.

And it's an instinct worth cultivating. One place where I do that is right at my desk, thinking about forests. Another and better place is the woods itself, walking or working in it. Behind my desk—but not in the woods—I recognize that many of us are unconscious heirs of a long and lusty tradition of nineteenth-century nature romanticism, whereby the forests of America, New England especially, took on a load of symbolic meanings. Here in the still-New World was virgin forest (or was it pagan wilderness?), places for physical challenge (was it spiritual regeneration?), spellbinding scenery, copious natural resource; and here the Muses sang in the trees and the poets declared the groves as God's first temples; and here the fate of forests became a perennial political theme. Many of us have something of that drama in our blood, or in our head, including my neighbors, whether we know it or not. It's part of how we think and feel.

Here I am walking in my own woods, remembering my neighbor's simple set speech, which I repeat aloud to no one in particular. I scramble over a great gray stone wall that was erected by Ebenezer Wood with oxen and block-and-tackle two hundred years ago but hasn't been used for a hundred, and will never be used by me, except as balm to the eyes. The wall curves through a pine thicket, takes in a sharp hillside, and exits into a green sea of hayscented ferns which part for the wall to pass through, ferns which hide so many rocks that it is troublesome even to walk here. Ten rods later I spot a cellar hole under the trees, granite boulders laid up in walls seven feet high and without mortar and still in place. Rough and wild they are, but these woods harbor an explicit human past. I sit down on a mulch of fragrant pine needles to think this over, but not before I marvel yet again at the hardihood of yesteryear's yeomanry. Did *they* like the woods? Like it? They fought the woods to a bitter standstill. Thereafter the land and forest stood still for generations. Then their failed farms faded, their cellar holes and their abandoned stone walls were permanently etched into the landscape, and the woods crept back over the fields. Is it proper for us to like the woods that stole their hard-won meadows? To like it even more just because we know about the theft?

Farming was easier where I came from. That was a sector of Michigan's lower peninsula where all the roads are straight, as is the horizon, and where perhaps eighty percent of the land was under cultivation. Each farm had a woodlot, but there were few places where the trees stretched for a mile in any direction. On the face of it Michigan's terrain has little to compare with the unabashed confusion of New England's.

It's hard to imagine my New England neighbor responding to a Midwestern woods as he does to his own. To "just like the woods" in my native town would have seemed a precious sentiment, and quite superfluous to the farmer who used the woods regularly as the storehouse for the farm supply system. As I remember it, the forest just lacked presence. It required no particular response. It was patches in the background, scenic sometimes, a shelter for wildlife, a commodity always, but not environment; it was something to *go to* as hunters and woodchoppers do, rather than *live with*, as New Englanders do. In New Hampshire we speak of a "woodlot," but in Michigan we always called it a "woods." Though of the same size and serving the same purpose, they may not be quite the same thing. A woodlot is a small portion of woodland bounded by more of the same; a woods in Michigan was a small section of a farm usually bounded by fields. The Michigan farmer, his words following the contours of experience, thinks of a woods (singular—a *this* not a *these*) as a resource located in a particular place just beyond the fields, and of a forest as a distant place on the map. What was true of Michigan a generation ago may be somewhat less true today, but here in New England each individual "woods" became part of the communal "forest" a long time ago.

Much of New England is like the spot where I now sit: in every direction the woodscape is unbroken to the horizon, forming a single forest community where a lowly red squirrel can travel in a straight line all day and scarcely touch ground. Our own woodland doesn't just adjoin our neighbor's; it's really all the same woods, something it has achieved over the last century by casually absorbing meadows, orchards, pastures, boulders, walls, boundaries. Its texture, seamless.

Almost. From my perch I can see on yonder hillside a sharp seam in the treetops where pine or spruce are lined up face to face against the lighter-colored hardwoods. Chances are excellent that I could walk to that place and find beneath the seam an ancient mossy wall: once two different fields, two farmsteads, two farmers met there, but now the different histories of the land show up only at leaf level and at a distance. From an airplane I would see the outlines of fields of a hundred years ago. It pleases me to think of that. I like the woods.

When I walk in the woods I sometimes take along for protection two sentences from Thoreau: "If a man walk in the woods for love of them half of each day, he is in danger of being regarded as a loafer; but if he spends his whole day as a speculator, shearing off those woods and making earth bald before her time, he is esteemed an industrious and enterprising citizen. As if a town had no interest in its forests but to cut them down!"

It would be impractical to look at New Hampshire's forest as something simply to cut down. In many places, my own included, it just wouldn't pay: the terrain is too formidable, the timber is too poor. Which is our good fortune. Viewing the woodscape, we are obliged to set our sights beyond economic opportunity, even beyond simple utility. For generations, everybody around here has more or less understood that. How, then, shall we value it?

The woods' lack of utility has a special poignance for those of my Midwestern rural generation. We remember that the small woodlot of the typical family farm was first of all an economic entity. Whereas our own New England woods is a hundred acres and not very useful, my father's Michigan woods was about six acres and extremely useful. He could not have farmed without it. For more than half a century, from the 1920s to the 1980s, he and his sons culled that plot, taking for fuel the weed trees, the weak, the crooked, the superfluous, and the fallen. One year in the mid-1940s my father cut down a dozen large hemlock trees; with horses and wagon he lugged the logs to a mill, hauled the lumber back, and built a garage and workshop. Later we made and sold hundreds of potato crates in that workshop with elm logs from the woods. Firewood, lumber, and potato crates led the way, but that was only the beginning: year after year, decade after decade, dozens of farm essentials came from that storehouse. We probably grew more farm repairs than we bought: fenceposts and gates, stakes and ladders, building materials of uncounted kinds, even wagon tongues and dump-rake shafts and tool handles, to say nothing of the rabbits for the larder that sprouted from the forest brushpiles every winter, the spontaneous wild strawberries and raspberries every summer, and the buckets of spring flowers. Here was an indispensable harvest of raw materials.

Perhaps it was a harvest of wisdom too. Today there still stand in that same woods stalwart beech and maple and cherry trees that my father eyed with quiet satisfaction for sixty years: always too good for firewood and never really demanded for lumber. They might have gone either way but slipped by on a narrow judgment call, saved perhaps by the fact that they were both good and good-looking. Survivors, they serve now to accent the discipline and grace that integrated the routines of that life. Though the woods never brought in much cash, its function was broadly economic, and beyond that also moral and aesthetic—a locus of value that transcended utility, for my father saw more than trees there. He was close enough to it so that it would have been superfluous to say that he liked the woods. Better to say he cared for it.

The woods was an organic part of the system that was the farm, like the orchard and the pasture and the pond. My father dealt with it judiciously because there was, in the culture and the agriculture of his times, a judicious use for it; and when he died he left it more vigorous, more productive, more handsome than it came to him. There is a biblical idea at work there; its name is stewardship, and its rhythms are still echoed in his Michigan woods. And not in his only.

I am aware that I cannot bring to our New Hampshire acres that sort of discipline and grace. For all its robustness, our woods does not make that kind of integrated economic sense. Like all the woods around here, mine too has lost its proudest species, the chestnut and the elm—a loss too sad to contemplate. I can still find the outlines of chestnut stumps: they send up sprouts that rise quickly in a few years to twenty feet, then the blight claims them, they die down, and other sprouts replace them. It's a very long and slow dying for the American chestnut, lasting generations. As for the American elm, just a single young elm tree now grows on our property; and I hope it outlasts us and believe it may. But a lot of sugar maple is left, and ash and several kinds of birch and some cherry, also pine and oak and spruce, much balsam, patches of ironwood and hemlock, and an inordinate amount of red maple. Well, we have fenceposts by the thousands and cordwood for a whole town, but so does everybody else. And who would make a ladder or a wagon tongue from the woods? I don't know anyone who needs hen roosts or dump-rake shafts. Our available timber is modest and not very accessible: although we harvested some to pay for a pond and well, cutting much more would simply make chaos. At least, my trees absorb more carbon dioxide than I and my family exhale, so the world gains, and that's good to know.

Yet my feeling for these woods is pretty strong, like that of most of my neighbors. With simple economy pushed to the background, we find room in the foreground to cultivate other responses, enjoy other aspects of our woodscapes. Respect. Serenity. Rugged beauty. Historic dramas of conquest and abandonment. Experience of just leaving something alone. Call of the wild. America's immemorial romance with her forests. Within our memory and experience there is an entire repertoire of answering echoes; and fortunately, we can't turn many of them to commodity or cash.

My personal stewardship of these woods? It lies not in the harvest of trees but of impressions. My woodscape is a resource of another kind, part of an economy of understanding, and perhaps for me a source of useful woods words. Some of the best ones I've come across lately derived from a neighbor who said: "I just like the woods."

9

Farewell to Hunting

Woods and hunting seem to go together naturally. In the farm country where I grew up after the Second World War, the mystique of hunting was keen in the October air and in the fertile fancies of us farm boys too: the beckoning forest, the lore of firearms, the chase and its trophy, camaraderie afield, game for the larder, machismo, all of it set to the music of baying hounds on a hot trail and the sweet damp smell of woods.

Farmers, we lived close to the soil, eating only our own vegetables and meat, harvesting most of our food, whether wild or tame: chickens and potatoes, blackberries and rabbits. Occasionally, deer. For us and for most farmers of that time and place, game hunting was a cheerfully overblown celebration of the rock-bottom fact that we lived off the land. That is all the rationale it had, all it needed. The rest was imagination and ceremony.

Memory of such experience runs deep, and I have wondered if any of its elements can be transplanted to other environments. To our New England rural setting, where I do not really live off the land? A few decades ago when we bought this place in the countryside, with its stonewall-bounded "hundred acres more or less" of rocky woodscape, I had it clearly in mind that we were buying a piece of good hunting territory. Actually, we were; but since then others have hunted here far more than I.

Hunting happens on a peculiarly intense sector of the boundary between man and nature, a boundary that is a favorite haunt of mine, however, and one to which I often resort. On a recent excursion there I went as both deer hunter and reporter, well-armed with pen and rifle, and for six days I both hunted deer and took testimony from the woods. I did not have a plan. I accepted duty as inspector of the boundary, and relied upon impulses from an autumn wood to teach me more of what I had to know. Such fugitive game as I gathered this way I aged and simmered for a time, and then prepared from it this report.

DAY ONE: BOULDER THOUGHTS

I am sitting in the woods, about a third of a mile from our house. The temperature is in the upper fifties, much warmer where I sit in the sun, warm enough to write. I have note pad in hand, pen cocked to pick off any passing thoughts; otherwise I'm unarmed. Tomorrow I'll have my rifle, but today's adventure is a dry run, the day before the first day of deer hunting season. I seem to be alone in the woods, and I'm here just to scout the territory and pick the most likely spot to rendezvous with a white-tailed deer, Odocoileus viginianus borealis. My perch is a huge granite boulder, large as an automobile, here since the Ice Age, and graced on top with a two-inch cushion of rich, dry humus. The cushion took about half a century to make, I'll bet, catching a layer of leaves and needles each fall, and it's ready just in time, pressed and dried, for my arrival today.

I take my bearings from this cushioned rock and from two enormous maple trees to the south, five feet in diameter, hugely knobbed and scarred from lost limbs. Among living things they are the real old-timers of this realm, well over a hundred, I'm sure, beautiful in their misshapen ugliness, awesome trees, heavy with slow death. What account can they give of this place? Wide-armed, those trees obviously had an airy and spacious youth, unhemmed by any forest. I mentally push them back into their maturity, then back into their prime a hundred years ago. I wave my pen like a wand and transform the woodscape, pushing it backward in time: those maple trees stand proud and alone on a side-hill pasture, and wide vistas of the rolling townscape are everywhere, for we are back in the nineteenth century on Anson Powers's farm. Instantly the stone wall sheds its lichen and snaps erect to divide *this* pasture from *that* meadow.

The meadow where I sit, long since wooded again, was first laid bare by Ebenezer Wood in the 1780s, and by 1800 he and his four sons would have cleared this hillside and built these walls. Surely they hunted deer here, for they were abundant in those days. I dot the slope with sheep, and put corn and potatoes beyond the stone wall. The years roll by in the wide open places for half a century and crops rotate: the sheep are in the meadow, the cows in the corn. Timothy Wood, the boy who looks after the sheep, took over his father's farm in the 1830s, and before the Civil War somebody let these very maple saplings sprout in the pasture. The Powers family came here to live and farm, and Anson let in some pine seedlings too, say about 1875. Alas, no longer did deer graze here then.

In 1950 those pines were mature and cut for timber, and today I can see some residual stumps, three feet in diameter, forty years from the saw and now soft as ashes. These ancient pre–Civil War maples, the survivors, once shaded those seedling pines, lived among and even beneath the highest pine plumes, and now they remain to lean toward the wall and over the decaying pine stumps. Not in this century has the wall really divided the field from the forest. Here in the vicinity of my rock the rhythm of two hundred years has come full circle: forest to farmland to forest again.

That is how I read my November terrain from my carrel on this boulder. In the fall when leaves drop, contours of the land appear, the woods reveals its archives: now the landscape is an open book, eloquently inscribed in gothic strokes of twisted maple trees and rotting stumps and mossy marbled walls.

But not for all that did I pick this boulder. I chose it for deer hunting over another candidate, sixty yards to the east, though initially there seemed nothing to choose between them. Both command a fair view of the surrounding brushy woodscape for a radius of about a hundred and fifty yards, and both are well within range of a deer path crossing the stone wall near yonder barway. Testing each boulder for half an hour, I found the choice easy. Near the other one is a beech tree, which disqualified that spot for deer hunting, for a beech keeps half its leaves until midwinter or later. They drop reluctantly and one by one, in ice storms, heavy snow, high winds. Throughout the winter the slightest breeze will stir the old bones left on a beech tree into a noisy rattle: the tambourines of nature. That sound is not like the sigh and murmur of a pine tree filtering the wind through its fingers, nor the busy rustle of green leaves in summer. It's a death rattle. I don't want such improvising of beeches to interfere tomorrow with my listening for the light step of a deer walking toward me on tiptoes, so I chose this boulder, which commands the quieter space. Here in perfect repose I can watch the woods and watch for deer, and also watch myself watch the woods for deer.

Today, all the fallen foliage is crinkly dry from ten days of sunny weather, and with every step a pile of brittle leaves explodes and sends a clatter echoing through the trees. No stalking of deer for me tomorrow, for any deer could hear a hunter half a mile off. I shall simply return to this boulder and be patient, quietly rubbing one thought against another to keep warm, and let other hunters stir the game.

DAY TWO: WOOD NOTES

Always, as I have known it, deer hunting requires that on the first day of the season you take the stand well before daylight—an early statement of commitment. Following that rule, I left the house at 5:15 A.M. under brilliant stars, a bright moon high overhead, and east of the moon shone Jupiter, this month's Morning Star. Hanging low in the west I saw the constellation Orion pursuing the Pleiades, which had already hidden in the treetops. All I know about the Greek myth of Orion is that he was killed by his sister Artemis, a huntress herself, for boasting that he would hunt down all the animals and kill them.

Only rarely—and never gladly—do I rise in the morning before the sun puts out the stars. My theory is that there are dawn people and dusk people, an ultimate division, like male and female, north and south. I cast my lot with the dusk people and with the night owls, always have and cannot change it. But on this sterling morning, finding my way to my chosen rock among the sharp shadows cast by the morning moon, then watching those shadows fade away to indistinctness, it is easy to empathize with the dawn people. They have a sense of the promise of each new day. I recall how the Old Testament psalmist exulted "when all the morning stars sang together." They sang today.

As I now write, the morning moon has burned down to gray ash. I have put myself in tune with my landscape. A hundred trees of yesterday emerged in the dawn's early light with a reassuring familiarity, each one still etched into my visual memory, limbs and branches exactly where I left them. To the north the brook is mumbling under its froth, and now I try to think about venison steak and wait for deer. I am a hunter.

An hour after sunrise, I hear faraway twigs snap. An imprecise rustling resolves itself at last into the sound of heavy distant footsteps. Bear? Moose? Man? Not deer—too heavy. Several hundred yards to the east I see an orange flash, and eventually a hunter tramps down the wood road near me. We spot each other from far off and exchange a small fraternal hand wave. As he draws closer I see that he is perhaps slightly overequipped: one rifle, two ammunition belts, one handgun, two hunting knives, a small hatchet. Under this armor is a large middle-aged man, and I wonder if perhaps inside the man is a small boy.

My mind is roving, but my eyes and ears are beamed on this little circle of landscape. Am I watched too by eyes I do not see? Sounds of distant gunfire drift into my clearing. A small voice inside me wonders: Suppose it had been nearer, and were now followed by the sound of rhythmic hoofbeats, a deer in full gallop toward me. What then? Then something would send a message from certain wild cells in my brain that would command adrenalin to flood my bloodstream, speed up my heart to a hundred and twenty, tense my muscles, cup my thumb on this rifle hammer, curl my finger on the trigger, and transform my entire body into eyes and ears. Maybe then a hundred and fifty pounds of handsome venison would canter into my view and I would try to stop it. If it does and I do, I shall dress it in a hurry, my heart still beating a hundred and twenty, and in half an hour the whole assault will be history—just venison all the way, if I work fast enough. Easy as snatching fruit from over the wall.

And the small voice wonders: But what if, instead, a tender young doe in the full flush of innocence steps slowly down the beaten path, and pauses to look you in the face? What is the plan for such a gift outright? Hunters have told me that it has happened to them and they have only sat and watched, spellbound and impotent. It is true that I sit here with a loaded .30-.30 rifle on my lap waiting for such an event; it is true, too, that I simply do not know for certain what I should then do. Some hunters say they would not shoot a standing target. I have a fantasy that I might only watch without stirring, and when the deer left the clearing without a sound I might leave the woods without regrets. Other fantasies I have also. One of them finds the first fantasy repellent, and another regards the whole perplexity as ridiculous: I have the impulses of a trained hunter, after all. If at times our minds are more permissive than our feelings, how do we decide which counsel to take? Do we decide beforehand, or await the moment of truth? One reason for being in the woods, perhaps slightly overequipped with rifle and pen, is to sort that out.

If hunting generally arouses ambivalent feelings, *deer* hunting does so far more. Every deer is at once an extraordinary fact of nature and a powerful symbol to boot. There is, first of all, the sheer beauty and grace of the animal, its seeming innocence, its instinct for survival in adversity, and its astonishing fecundity on the very edges of human habitat, now and for ages past. Second, and no doubt connected with this, is its varied symbolism: more than any other animal in history, I suspect, the deer (as hart, roebuck, hind, stag, doe, fawn, buck, roe) has been represented and idealized in story and song and art. In some traditions (medieval art and Old Testament poetry) deer are very much eroticized: the deer as object of desire, and the deer hunt as parable for erotic love. The Romans painted deer, though didn't much celebrate hunting them in the wild, while the Greeks gloried in deer hunting, very much a masculine sport of conquest. It is a tradition that reaches all the way to Cooper's making an American wilderness hero out of the deerslayer. The Jewish Bible is more gentle: in the Psalms the hart is an image of tenderness, and the Song of Songs is most explicit: "My beloved is like a roe or a young hart . . . He feedeth among the lilies." "Thy two breasts are like two young roes that are twins." For thousands of years deer imagery has been a richly varied resource for the aesthetic imagination, and the stag hunt was often an important ceremony within it. Greek mythology puts Artemis, a masculinized virgin goddess, in charge of the hunt.

Goddess? I came out here to sit on a rock and watch the woods hunker down for winter. Deer hunters do not consciously go forth to wander in regions where a virgin goddess hovers. I wonder if they sometimes do so unawares.

DAY THREE: SHARED GARDEN

It is eight o'clock and I am again on my rock and cloaked once more in my vigil, a familiar garment. Yesterday, I was often cold while sitting still. Is that too what the sages mean when they recommend "getting back to nature"? While some hunters justify hunting as a return to elementary things—food, life, death, nature—they don't put getting cold among these natural virtues. Rather, these hunters want "to become reacquainted with man's place in the natural order." That will also do as a rationale for gardening and raising chickens, but I think it's not meant to. It's meant as deep stuff, and probably is, but if I try to plumb it today I'll never get acquainted with the little piece of richly endowed natural order where I sit right now.

For some time since daylight I have been eyeing a bobcat

sitting on a log seventy yards away. It has not moved at all. From time to time, if I move a little, it turns into a fox. When I move a bit farther it turns into a bunch of leaves. There are Rorschach leaf-blots all around me, corralling native animals of the woods. I can read a forest bestiary out of the surrounding shrubs and boughs. Every hunter knows how bear and deer can turn to stumps and juniper bushes before his very eyes. It's part of the sport.

On the way to the woods this morning I checked to see if there were fresh deer tracks in the garden, and there were. My father used to say simply that he deserved to harvest a deer in the fall because he had fed them all summer from the corn and clover of the farm. The deer feed on our New Hampshire land too, and sometimes on our garden. We don't often see them because they easily spot us first, and every opening around here is only two and half bounds from a thicket. If I saw the deer more often, would I find it harder to think of them as game?

The deer don't hurt our garden much, for they seem to have figured out a way to apportion things. In the early spring they eat the strawberry plants, the budding border hostas (a passionate favorite of theirs), and the tops of parsnips—which is about all there is. Then they withdraw, visiting the unfenced garden sometimes on a summer night as if to check on progress, make notes for future autumn visits, and sample a few special items. It is easy to plant extra for that purpose.

Why aren't the deer more of a garden problem for us? Here is my homegrown hypothesis: Deer much prefer summer apples to garden greens. Surrounding our garden are a dozen apple trees, originally wild sprouts on which I grafted scions of many better varieties, mostly summer apples. Often they bear very heavily—tangy, juicy apples, unsprayed and half of them wormy, but tasty to rabbits, dogs, small children, woodchucks, maggots, and white-tailed deer. I carefully select the few we need and donate the rest to wildlife. The deer bed down daily in nearby thickets and gorge all summer on apples and apple sauce, and leave the nearby garden entirely to us. In October, and especially if the apples are gone, the deer eagerly finish off all carrots and brussels sprouts, but they usually wait until we have taken what we want. There is competition for our late October broccoli and lettuce, but I fool them by covering the best plants, pretending it's for the frost. On the whole, it's a very satisfactory setup, and I'm glad to be a partner in it.

Nevertheless, right now I am deer hunting. I recall the time I brought down a deer when I was young, and I shall not forget how satisfying that was. No sentimental regrets for me then, nor now. Rural people of that day who made their entire living from the land, who fed their families from what they planted and what they found, and who ceremonially hunted game every fall, were perhaps as much gatherers as hunters. The venison roasts we enjoyed on the farm cemented our partnership with the land and its bounties. Going to the woods with our fathers, brothers, and friends we took home food and experience and memories, a harvest of goodness, as it seemed to us, and a celebration of life. For us, the mythic meaning of hunting bore a direct relation to its role in our rural economy.

DAY FOUR: SOUNDS OF SILENCE

Again I am seated on my humus-cushioned rock as the day dawns, and the music of this moment, sunrise in a cloudless sky, is a perfection of silence, the special silence of forests, of trees without leaves. Hush of autumn before the dead of winter. In recent days I think my eyes and ears have grown noticeably keener. Today, absence of sound is palpable everywhere, near at hand and far away to the edge of earshot. I feel that I could hear anything whatever within miles and miles. But nothing is happening that I have heard of. It is acoustically absolute zero.

Why is this early morning stillness so terribly explicit? Is it that, with countless objects about me, there is so much undischarged potential, so much sheer possibility? I have never stood alone on an empty prairie on a silent morning, but I believe that no flat land, empty of objects, could possibly know the richness and purity of this kind of wooded silence. Nor is any summer soundlessness ever so thick as this, for then there is always a whisper of leaves, a hum of insects. Here and now every tree contributes its note to the general repose. I just felt one leaf drop; it was a dozen rods away, but I heard it tinkle lightly like a piece of tinfoil. Surely a gunshot here would create an earthquake. I am watching, watching for deer, for any movement at all, absorbing peace at every pore. It feels to me that my watching is the only thing happening in the entire world. Nature is immobile. Silent. Watching. . . . Time passes. Silence.

I am aware that the stillness of the woods can wrap itself around you like a mantle, become itself a presence palpable enough to elicit from within you a solemn reverence. Deep calleth unto deep. You watch for deer, yes, at attention but at ease, and tranquility itself seeps in past your gaze and settles down upon your will. First you *do* not tamper with the spell, as if you *ought* not; then you do not *wish* to; then it is as if you *could* not. Something has laid a firm and gentle hand upon your will, bade you to slough off your pale otherness and align yourself on nature's side. Acquiesce in that for one serene moment, then another, another. You are becalmed, then absorbed. Maybe you are lured across the line, your will tranquilized. Your eyes are roving and your thoughts are calm and glazed. Your body, conspiring with nature and your will, yields, and melts into the rock. Did they mean this, the poets, when they spoke of oneness with nature?

. . . Now the morning silence, so intense and tangible, has abated to a lesser quietness, flecked with small and distant sounds: nervous chickadees, nuthatches, here and there a worried mouse. And now too the air stirs slightly, just enough to carry to me rumors from the reticent brook. And now that distant beech tree whose company I had first renounced, flexes its bleached bones and seems to curtsy to a passing thermal. Or maybe the beech's gesture was for the hawk which caught that thermal on the wing and now sweeps in graceful spirals against the blue. Not much is happening, but the woods still seems astir. My ears are being fine-tuned, but all day long they picked up no sound of deer prancing toward my clearing.

In recent years in New Hampshire about one hunter in ten gets a deer, and each hunter hunts about ten days. Call that a hundred hunting-days per deer. Suppose a dressed deer weighs a hundred pounds. Then on the average every hunter harvests a pound of flesh every day.

DAY FIVE: FEWMETS FOR THE QUEEN

I sit atop a different rock today, one kept in reserve in case I required a new oracle. This one has an extra luxury item: the little brook from Lovell Mountain offers a soft monotone of music against the background hush of autumn. I had just settled in to listen to the faint rustle and gossip of old leaves behind me when a handsome red fox trotted by, pausing now and then to cock his ears for mice, but taking no heed of me. Easily distracted, my thoughts casually drift to English fox hunting, which Oscar Wilde called "the unspeakable in pursuit of the uneatable." Behind that dandified aristocratic pastime lies the long European tradition of the even more ritualized stag hunt, a favorite sport of idle royalty, courtiers, and gentry. It is hard now to credit the elaborate rituals built up around the stag hunt: hunting dress, deportment, carving technique, distribution of the body parts, and the proper use of elaborate lingo for every aspect of the ceremony. Once upon a time books were written on the etiquette of stag hunting. One such book is hard to forget: *The Noble Arte of Venerie or Hunting*, 1576, a rare copy in the Bodleian Library. It contains a fine woodcut of a huntsman dressed fit to kill and presenting, on a pillow of leaves, fewmets of the hunted stag to Queen Elizabeth. The Oxford English Dictionary defines "fewmets" as "excrement of a deer." If these be hunting trophies, then ritualized hunting is a beast exeeding strange.

Within two generations of this time, that is, in the early seventeenth century, other Englishmen were pioneering colonies in New England. Here they found an abundance of white-tailed deer for food and clothing, and right from the start deer from the forest were a critical element in the survival of the colonies. From the beginning, hunting was as American as apple pie (more so, since the apples were imports). But turkey, deer, and fish were native staples of the colonial survival kit. The pioneer experience has given Americans a lasting and powerful image of hunting as a natural activity and an economic necessity, an image hunters often strive to keep alive. For this American version of the stag hunt there were, at first, no books of etiquette, no rituals, and no rules—only necessity and expediency.

Is is any surprise that within a century most of the deer had been exterminated from eastern Massachusetts? In another century the same was true of much of New Hampshire. Restrictions on deer hunting during spring and summer months were first imposed in New Hampshire in 1740, but the laws were not enforced and were eventually abandoned. Not until the last quarter of the nineteenth century were there serious efforts to control deer hunting in New Hampshire. A total ban was declared in 1878, which lasted two years, and then the slaughter resumed. Hunting for market was the big deal; the preferred technique was using dogs in snow or a mesmerizing jacklight at night. It worked, of course. The deer were being wiped out of New Hampshire, and by the 1890s there were few deer left south of the White Mountains.

Knowing this, I may assume that Anson Powers, who farmed this farm from the 1850s until he died in 1899, probably never harvested a deer from his farm. I may also assume that his predecessor, Ebenezer Wood, probably depended heavily on hunting to feed his eleven children. Today the deer are back. The reason is that in the twentieth century, in place of the old colonial liberties, we have had a state game management program.

The low point of deer population in New Hampshire came just a hundred years ago, and today the population is about what it was three hundred and fifty years ago when the English settlers and hunters first arrived. Wolves checked the population then; hunters do it now. How many deer today in New Hampshire? A consensus puts the number somewhere around thirty-five thousand, which would be about four per square mile. Let me suppose that my region here on Lovellwood is about average. I mentally attach a mile-long spoke to this boulder as hub and run a circle around me, from the slopes of Lovell Mountain on the east to Ames hill on the west. Now I square the radius, multiply by pi, and come up with about a dozen deer inside my wheel, within a mile of me. I can believe that. Last night three of them braved a moonlight visit to our garden.

Suppose all the New Hampshire licensed firearms hunters were out today, seventy-five thousand of them, and some of the twenty thousand bow-hunters too, and that they were all evenly scattered in the state's hunting areas. Then there would be over two dozen of them within my mile radius. You'd think those dozen deer would be in deep trouble. But they are exceedingly swift and wily, and they won't have to evade jacklights and dogs. Ten of them will escape unharmed, perhaps to come back to share my garden. But it is no surprise that I see more hunters than deer, for there are twice as many of them, and they run more slowly.

DAY SIX: BACK TO SENSES

Yesterday, the red fox led my thoughts astray. Where were my eyes and ears? Was I watching for deer as sharply as I had the first four days? I saw a big deer that startled me so much I jumped, as if I had no longer expected it. Without so much as a hello it was suddenly there, a distant beautifully bounding deer, out of range and too fast for me, but with white flag unfurled waving a hurried goodbye. A lovely moment. Today I'm paying close attention to the forest.

I've seen no deer hunters but I've shared the woods with other gleaners: one robin who missed his southern flight, one small mouse, one noisy red squirrel, five jumpy chickadees, six pine grosbeaks, all hunting like me, but more overtly. The mouse, busy at my feet for the last hour, appears to be packing down leaves around his home under a rock. To avoid heat loss this winter? The rock is his automatic solar energy collector, a big contraption to have in one's attic, but it's free, it works, and will never wear out. The red squirrel stopped his nervous labors—they have mainly nuts on the brain in this season—just long enough to berate me with a furious passion. It took five minutes for his tirade to simmer down to a few epithets. What's his problem? I'll forgive his rudeness, but I took note of it.

Chickadees treat a stranger differently: they are kids at heart. They came when I called "pissh, pissh, pissh," as they often do, perched and fidgeted nearby, curious and a bit embarrassed, I thought. They chatted and chicked about me a good deal, snickered to themselves and tittered, dee-dee-dee-dee, and then flitted off, heads jittery with gossip. I made their day. I surmised that the pine grosbeaks had come to my call too, and this pleased me since I had never succeeded in calling them before. Then I discovered that they were paying no attention to me at all, but systematically traversing the woods, the ground and shrubs, twenty yards at a hop, hunting and feeding on seeds at every stop. Serious hunters: not for them the cheery mindlessness of chickadees, the neurotic nattering of squirrels, nor the stodginess of just sitting on a rock. It happens that my rock lay athwart the grosbeaks' forage line today, and they skipped right by, three on a side, without deviating and without a nod. There's dignity. They know exactly what they are doing and they do it with Calvinist thoroughness. But can they *enjoy* hunting while being so earnest about it? As for me, I'm enjoying this hunt as much as a chickadee. Surely it was my idleness that bothered the busy squirrel.

Yet, I am aware that hunting does impose a discipline upon an excursion into the woods. How often—if not hunting—do we sit silently on mossy rocks and listen to the lectures of a red squirrel, the twitter of grosbeaks, or mark the falling leaves? So the gun is an outdoor crutch; it may help some of us learn to walk in the woods or to sit still there. In my youth, when I overtly cultivated the intuitions of the farmer-hunter, I assumed (probably correctly) that hunters then were generally more in tune with the natural world than other citizens. It was then mainly hunters who spoke up for the environment. Unquestionably, hunting has done valuable things for some people that nothing else would do. With luck it can even briefly bring us back to our senses: especially do our eyes and ears welcome us back. With more luck we may perhaps even learn to walk the woods one day and leave the crutch behind.

The sun now slants in from the west. Food for the table has been scarce these six days; for thought, abundant. Deer have been elusive, but hunting *itself* is also an elusive quarry. Yet how exhilarating the pursuit of it! How lush and scenic the conflicted ideological territory down through the centuries. You can stalk hunting in a holy autumn woodsy silence. You can try to stare it down from some exalted rock of principle. You can surprise it in the dark or foolish places of the heart. Pursuing the idea of hunting, you encounter dandies and savages, as well as hungry peasants and pioneers, and armies of descendant sportsmen. In six days I saw two deer, both swiftly out of rifle range. As quarry, hunting itself, too, often seems just out of pen range: a strange animal, wily and inexhaustible, old as the hills, touched by romance and gore, and not to be cornered by one argument or by ten. Not to be captured in six days either. Hunting as metaphor for love? It almost seems inevitable. On that note I unload my gun and close my notebook.

Postscript. Six days. On the seventh day I rested. That year just one in eleven New Hampshire hunters got a deer, and I was one of the other ten. Some who hunted in their youth have overtly renounced it, but many more have just quietly withdrawn from it. Perhaps the original inspiration and celebration faded. Perhaps sentiments or rationale that flourished in one circumstance could not be transplanted to another. Perhaps they chose to cultivate different outdoor intuitions, different feelings toward the natural world. One day they realized that every deer they had seen in a long while looked better alive than dead.

10

Peaceable Kingdom?

The prophets dreamed of a world where the leopard will lie down with the lamb, and the calf and the young lion will feed together. But that biblical picture of a peaceable kingdom is not yet the world we know. Consider the lowly mouse.

One quiet winter night my wife and I were awakened by a faint rustling on the floor just above us. "What's that strange noise?" Grace whispered. There came more rustling and then some faint squeaks, followed by a pale thin squeal. What indeed? Ghost? Quickly there followed a muffled patter as of small feet scampering very lightly down the stairway and into the livingroom. Came another very faint and eerie squeak and more rustling. "What *is* that strange noise?" my wife whispered insistently.

Armed with a flashlight I pursued the sound to its source behind the sofa. There I witnessed what appeared to be the last stages of a serious battle between two small mice. There was no way I could intervene to restore peace in this kingdom; I could only watch and wait. I presume the trouble had started as a territorial dispute in the attic, but it became a fight to the death on the livingroom floor. Thereafter, it took an even nastier turn, for the victor mouse was a wondrously agile savage and also an accomplished cannibal. Ignoring me entirely, he not only silenced his larger adversary but then proceeded, in broad flashlight, to *eat* him then and there. I stood spellbound by this exquisitely ghoulish spectacle. For several minutes I just watched in awe as the two mice became one, and then I tiptoed quietly away and returned to bed and hoped I was dreaming.

No such luck. In the morning we found little scraps—part of one paw, a piece of skull, tail and hide fragments—lying on the battlefield. And then we found something more: To one side lay a very bloated, very dead mouse—a shrew. We had to conclude that he had succumbed to overeating. This thing seemed really bizarre.

Was it so bizarre? We had just happened to catch a passing glimpse of a world that usually goes unseen. We checked a book to confirm that shrews are carnivores and, well, I guess voles are meat. That's about all there is to that. The two have territorial quarrels, and we had witnessed the standard outcome. Thoreau said: "Nature herself has not provided the most graceful end for her creatures."

I keep thinking about that incident, which I still find pretty repulsive, as I observe the dining habits of other creatures. Fish, for example, are meat too, and although I do not compete with the shrews, I do compete with other wild creatures, such as kingfishers, herons, and otters, for fish. I feel that the fish are mine, however,—though I suppose my contestants feel the same way.

Our pond is a small and homemade affair, about a quarter of an acre, but deep and cool enough for trout to survive there. For six years now I have purchased a hundred fingerling trout each spring and released them into the pond. There is plenty of natural food for them there, and it is a pleasure to watch of a summer's dusk as the trout leap for flies. But I feed them too, and they in turn feed us. Some years we have had as many trout as we wanted, starting in late summer when they have reached edible size and lasting until the pond freezes in November. But trout have more adversaries than I had realized—or, to put it another way, they draw in other wildlife more than I had anticipated. Kingfishers, for example: we never saw them near the house until the pond was built, but now we see them regularly. Although I seldom catch them catching fish, I'm sure they get their share. They are not here just to look.

The blue heron is another lover of fish. Great long-legged, wonderfully regal predators, they came immediately when the pond was new to add their grace and dignity to its shores. How did they even know it was here? At first we were so impressed that these elegant creatures deigned to visit our humble pond that we simply sat and watched them stalk the shoreline. I hoped that they had a well-developed taste for frogs, of which we already had plenty and to spare. But within the first quarter hour I saw the heron suddenly dive with lightning speed, spear a trout, rush out of the water, spend several minutes getting the fish lined up perfectly, and then let it slip down his thoat, still wiggling. I could see it go all the way down, ruffling the feathers of his long neck as it slid down to the bottom of his stomach. All that was interesting and rather quickly done, and a cleaner job of it than the shrew had done. Not a fin or a scale left over for evidence.

I was hoping that the *next* course would be frog. Well, so it was; but it took several minutes after being speared for the frog to join the fish. The leggy frog, it turns out, does not have so convenient a profile for swallowing, and it had to be, well, dismembered before it could join the fish in the dark cavern of the heron's gizzard. Having torn up the frog and swallowed it, the heron flew off. The next day he was back, and it was soon evident that he came more for the fishing than the frogging; after all, both entrees were readily available and he evidently preferred the one that went down without having to have its legs ripped off. My hapless trout, hatchery-raised and used to being fed in the shallow shores, were defenseless: they would be quietly eyeing a water strider when, suddenly, giant double spears would appear from nowhere to pin them to the bottom.

That weekend the great bird with the long spears took his wife fishing too, and in one day we counted five trout going down the long gullets of two great blue herons. A little late, perhaps, we realized that our trout pond and our friendship with blue herons were incompatible: you might as well have a vole and a shrew together in the attic. Not yet would the leopard lie down with the lamb. Reluctantly, we started to chase the herons off; but by this time they had gotten a taste of things, and it was not easy. I would dash from the house, shouting and waving and clapping, and the birds would rise majestically, circle the pond to inspect the fuss and then gently flap their way to the top of a nearby pine tree and watch from there, long necks craned over the topmost branches, peering down at me. When I calmed down and disappeared, they would return to fishing.

We gained a slight edge when we brought our dog Penelope into the contest. Earlier we had successfully taught her that ducks on the pond were to be left entirely alone; now herons could be chased off. Could she tell the difference? Could she! Chasing the great birds quickly became her favorite pastime. But eventually the herons learned that she was all sound and fury; so it's a standoff. The herons aren't exactly comfortable fishing here anymore, but I'm sure they still sneak in to get more than their share.

And then there are otters. They too bring charm but no peace to this little kingdom. We have always loved to look for otter tracks in winter along brooks, to see the places where they slide and skate and play in the snow like happy children. Otters are famously playful and irresistible creatures: shy on land, they are swift and smooth as silk in water and sportive as kittens. And they swim like fish—only faster. Unfortunately, they also dine primarily on fish. In a small open pond with no place to hide, our trout were no match at all for the swift and hungry otters.

Frequently I'd see one or two otters, but one day I saw four in our pond, all playing, diving, chasing each other, snorting, grunting, whistling even, having a delightful time. I simply sat down to watch the show. Presently, they slid out of the water, humped over the bank toward the brook in that strange loping gait of theirs, and were gone. I had not frightened them. Clearly, they had just come for a swim, for a pleasant hour of frolicking, and for a fish snack. I realized that they could come any morning for such an hour, play and swim and have breakfast at our pond and then proceed with other business of the day. Two years ago I once more put a hundred fingerling rainbow trout into the pond in April. During the summer they grew larger and larger, but also fewer and fewer, and by fall there was not one fish left for us to eat. I have not yet solved this problem; haven't even come close.

I did try a drastic experiment. Last year I put no fish in, and the little kingdom of the pond seemed at peace at last. It was also pretty dead. No trout stirring the surface as they reached for flies, no kingfishers gossiping about fish from the nearby trees, and the herons came but twice and left for greener pastures. I saw no otters at all. In a world without voles, shrews are unhappy. Next year I shall put in fish again.

It is ducks that brighten up the pond in early spring. April offers a minor flurry of activity, comings and goings by twos and threes and fours, and sometimes in even larger flocks. Hooded mergansers, common mergansers, ringed-neck ducks, wood ducks, black ducks, and mallards we have counted so far. Mallards like it the best, and usually nest nearby.

Although there is much that I do not understand in the duck world, sometimes I look out upon a spectacle that appears to be gang rape among the ducks. Two, three, or even four mallard drakes tackle a female with a vigor that does not seem tender to me—nor, I think, to her. Sometimes the roughhousing is so severe that I have a strong impulse to try to stop it, but this seems futile and foolish. The duck flees and the drakes pursue her and each other back and forth across the pond, running on to the bank, back into the water, then under the water, as if to drown her or peck her to death. The game seems much rougher when it is two or more on one, than when it is just a pair doing a mating dance. Is this sexual play, a genuine fight, or sport, or what? Or is this how the final pairing is decided? The one thing she does not do—at least until she has been very severely roughed up—is simply to fly away, and it is this which makes the whole situation ambiguous.

Then peace returns: she picks a mate, the mallards are happily paired off, and she settles on a nesting spot, which will be at least a hundred and fifty yards from the pond. We mark the nesting season in their behavior. Both ducks fly off together and very quickly the drake returns alone: he escorts her to the nest where she will lay an egg, and he immediately circles back to the pond. Typically, he will now sit in the middle of the water, immobile as a piece of floating wood, waiting for her return before feeding again. Later his mate's absence grows longer: as she begins setting she returns only for vigorous bathing and feeding and is then off again, and he escorts her irregularly now. Sometimes he is joined in his long solitary vigils on the pond by a female duck and we will wonder whether this is his mate or his mistress or just a visiting friend.

We are all waiting for the big day. One morning we spot a dozen little ducklings, each of them just an extravagantly vigorous little clump of peeping fluff, paddling swiftly in and out and back and forth among the sedges at the water's edge, never more than six feet from their mother's hovering clucking. It is the sight we are waiting for each spring: the moment when we make way for ducklings.

Some springs this moment does not come. Instead, one day the adult ducks have gone and we will see them only intermittently for the rest of the season. What has happened? I do not know, but I have two theories. One theory is that sometimes the nest is across the road in our west pasture, from which I believe the adults take the ducklings to Bog Brook; they can then work their way down to Half Moon Pond, which they may think better for raising a family than our little puddle at Lovellwood. And the second theory is this: one night a raccoon just happened to come across the nest where it was camouflaged in the bushes. Maybe the mother duck had not yet begun setting and was not home, so the raccoon broke the eggs one by one and drained the contents, licking the shells dry. And when the ducks returned home they were so brokenhearted that they removed to another pond to begin all over again.

But the best scenario occurs when the nest is near to our pond. As soon as the newly hatched ducklings can walk that far—perhaps in a day or two, for by then they will be famished—they are led to our pond, and then we have their company for at least another month. Mallards are extremely easy to tame and train, and ours have learned well before the ducklings came that we feed the fish. We do not have scientific proof that fish food is good for mallards, but hope it is, for they gobble it down as fast as they can swat it up. Initially, the young are too small to swallow the pellets, but within less than two weeks, during which time they have learned to find natural food, they have grown enough to handle the pellets, and when one of us appears they will race across the water to beat the trout to dinner. When very young they literally run over the water at astonishing speed, but as they learn to swim faster, they tend to run less.

At night all the ducklings gather under the soft belly down and open wings of the mother duck. Such a pleasant sight to observe this nightly security ritual! Mother duck settles near the water's edge and the little chirping ducklings gather around and gradually work their way in and under. One year we had a flock of thirteen and it was quite a trick for all of them to assemble under one duck roof. (Here might have been a role for the drake, but he was nowhere in sight.) A fluff of a duckling oozes out one side, runs around and squeezes in at another edge; probably that forces another out, who chirps loudly and runs around to find a tiny loophole where she can shove her way in. This activity—being squeezed out and squeezing in—takes a half hour or more, as they are being packed in tighter and tighter under there. We watch with field glasses, and by the time it is too dark to see they are all settled down for a long nap.

What happens when a red fox or raccoon comes loping along? We haven't seen it happen, but it surely does; and then I presume they all instantly tumble into the water, just three feet away, and have to climb out to do it all over again. Within ten days a couple of the braver ducklings have to stay outside, since there is no longer room in the downy inn for the whole family. Within another ten days or so all of them are squatting beside each other on the shore at night.

One year the ducklings stayed with us longer than usual, and they became a flock of prospering birds, big as pigeons. So there was genuine competition between the trout and the ducks at feeding time, for a dozen ducks made a commotion vigorous enough to completely intimidate the shy fish. To feed the fish I had to outsmart the ducks. By judiciously scattering pellets I lured the ducks to follow me out of the water on to the land and toward the garage. The first day they left me at the garage door, but the second day mother and eleven ducklings followed me right into the garage; my son then quickly closed the door behind them, I slid out a side door, and we had the ducks all neatly locked away. Then I quickly fed the fish, and in less than ten minutes led the ducks out and back to the pond. It worked perfectly—the ducks never knew they had been had—and so it became the daily routine.

But only for about a week. One morning all the ducks were gone, leaving not a feather behind. It happens every year that way: sudden, unannounced, complete. We do not know for certain what happens. Maybe four otters came and gently pulled the ducklings under, one by one, and then swallowed them like fish. Maybe a pair of foxes swooped down like the wolf on the fold. We have no illusions that we preside over a peaceable kingdom in our yard. Still, another scenario is really far more likely. The outlet of our pond joins a little brook, and mother duck knows that that brook, if followed far enough, must eventually lead to bigger waters. How does she know that? Experience? Instinct? Probably both. Anyway, one morning she simply says: "Children, there are larger puddles to splash in; follow me and I will show you greater ponds than you have ever dreamed of." Straightaway the young ducklings set out to see these new worlds, leaving our little backwater pond to the fish—and to the kingfishers, the herons, the frogs, the otters, and us.

When we first moved to Lovellwood we made friends with a very shrewd young raccoon. We named her Ranger and we fed her nightly at our door. As we got to know her ways and wiles we thought that this was no ordinary raccoon, but we suspect now that very few raccoons are. Every night when she came to our door Ranger rang the bell and waited for us to answer.

Actually, ringing the bell was no problem. Once we got her to come for food it was a simple matter to put the food into a coffee can, put a lid on it, fasten the can to a string and the string to a little bell inside the house. Ranger would come for her nightly visit, pry off the cover, ring the bell in the process, and then we'd come to the door. Seeing us, she would immediately rear on her hind legs and ask for more—which she invariably got. Then we changed the rules and put no food in the can. But Ranger had us trained and she knew it: she would just shake the empty can until the bell rang and we came to feed her.

Recently, people worry about rabies in connection with wild animals, but at that time rabid raccoons were unknown in this region, and we wanted to see the whole wild world as a peaceable kingdom. We read Sterling North's wonderful book *Rascal* and thought we ought to let Ranger join the family. Sometimes we would invite her into the wing of the house, but she was very nervous about it. We were only summer residents then, and by the time she was ready to come in and be comfortable, it was time for us to go back to the city and start making plans for next year. Yet for eight summers Ranger came back to ring the bell—her manners were so precise and individual that we never doubted her identity—and once she even brought along several little kits, showing off her family. We never asked her if she ate duck eggs on the side.

In springtime, just after waking up, raccoons around here engage in their strangest behavior. After Ranger, we had a raccoon that did enjoy living inside, hunting by night and sleeping by day on the woodpile in the wing. Our cat warmly despised that raccoon—we could see it by the way he cocked his head and hissed when he went past the woodpile—and with reason. We discovered the raccoon was using another corner of the wing for a bathroom, a foul practice disapproved by cats. And by us. We thought it best to put a little more distance between us and the creatures of the night. We have listened to raccoons fighting at night, at which times they emit terrible screams, second only to the scream of warring porcupines. We have also had raccoons push a window open, get into the basement, and open a jar of jam. And raccoons sometimes climb on the roof of our house, apparently intrigued by the skylights, and look in at us through those windows.

We realized as time went by that living on acceptable terms with wildlife meant we had to make choices we preferred to avoid. How charming at first to see woodchucks browsing on our lawn, but woodchucks and gardening are incompatible. Something similar holds for rabbits. Feeding birds is a natural country pleasure—which soon becomes the challenge of outwitting squirrels. And how do you keep the jays from scaring off the smaller birds? Otters love fish; 'coon, duck eggs. Such is everywhere the story: we intervene in the uncertain balances of unpeaceable kingdoms, adjusting the balance ever so slightly to please us; but in the night shrews eat voles, coyotes eat deer, and the great movements go on unseen.

But not everything fits that pattern: there are all kinds of pleasant marginalia. This past spring we had a pair of raccoons sign on as chimney cleaners. Our dog Penelope alerted us that something was up by periodically barking at the fireplace. Eventually we too could hear a strange rustling around up there in the smoke shelf. A bluejay perhaps?—for once I had taken a live bluejay from the stove. I opened the damper, but no bird came out; so I lit a small fire, and the noise ceased. The next day it was back. Same sequence, same result. Next time the noise showed up I lit both the fireplace and stove and then went outside to look. Aha! A raccoon hopped out of the chimney, jumped down to the roof, shuffled across the ridge pole, hopped up the other chimney and popped in. More experiments led me to the truth, namely, that two raccoons now resided in our three chimneys, choosing whichever one was the right temperature. They had it all figured out: When the fireplace was not on they went into that flue and all the way down to the smoke shelf; when I lit the fireplace the oil furnace was sometimes off for several hours so they went to that flue; when they retired in the library flue they could go down past the intake pipe and get below the smoke. Somehow or other they could always find one of the chimneys that was right, moving to another when life got too warm or smoky.

I then sought to drive them off by stoking up all systems full blast—stove, fireplace, furnace. As the house warmed up I went outside to cool off and to see what I had produced. Two raccoons soon popped out of the chimney—the same chimney. Had I disturbed them in their trysting place? They shook their heads and looked around to see what all the smoke and heat was about; they peered down at me and then shuffled over to try a second flue, which they didn't like, so tried a third and liked it even less. They stared at me again. They had been born in a hollow stump, after all, and these things sure looked like deluxe hollow stumps to them—though they did seem more smoky than they had remembered home to be. They shook their heads and decided they would wait it out. Each one picked a narrow ridge of a chimney-stump and stretched out, prepared to outlast the situation. When the stumps cooled down they slipped back in.

How were we to get them out?

That's when wisdom dawned, reminding us that it's possible to feel more embattled in the country than you are. You don't have to assert your prerogatives everywhere, don't have to do something about everything. These raccoons were doing no harm at all, and their coming and going was undoubtedly cleaning the chimneys, so they may have been doing us some good. The solution to this ticklish problem was to do nothing at all. Of course, we couldn't exactly forget them. I'd often glance up when I was outdoors, and frequently I'd see a raccoon up there and I'd wave, imagining he was waving back at me from his warm and privileged sanctuary in his favorite hollow stump. We got on very well in this manner, and before summer came they went peaceably on to other business.

Coping with Pups

The heroine of this chapter is the daughter of Mountain Crest Backpacker CD and Lady Cricket of Littleton, namely, Miss Penelope of Lovellwood. Her ancesters were bred for sheep work on the Shetland Islands, and she's a purebred, not only in blood but in carriage and in gait. A sensitive dog who loves us unreasonably, she normally appears to have the conscience and comportment of a demure Puritan virgin.

And one night she got pregnant at a private New Year's Eve party which she had arranged herself.

How arranged? Circumstantial evidence is that over the local airwaves she had sent out an irresistible invitation, exquisitely intelligible to other dogs but soundless and superolfactory to mere humans. Thereupon a macho mutt from down the road arrived and dug his way into her yard; and she, breaking precedent, did not set up a general alarm (which suggests her welcome was avid), and did not even come in to hint coyly to us that she had a caller. Clandestine, is what I call the affair, and appalled is what we were when we glanced out at midnight on New Year's Eve and saw her happily entertaining a lascivious mongrel inside her own private yard. Too lightly we had supposed that Miss Penelope was not the sort for holiday debauchery, that she had more breeding, or class, than that. She worshipped *us*, for goodness sake, so how could her taste in dogs be so deplorable?

Yes, we know: it happens all the time. Moreover, the consequences are thoroughly predictable. Soon comes the end of February, fifty-eight days later, and there is no surprise about what happens next. The only questions were: how many would there be? Could we all cope? And the answers are: there are six pups; and, yes, we can cope. This is a report on the coping.

But first, while the results of this scandal are wriggling around in their box, blindly hunting for an outlet, anything to latch on to, somewhere in this enormous hairy mound of maternal warmth which they seem so inexorably drawn to, and from which to be separated makes them squeak and squirm and tremble, let me introduce the *dramatis personae*.

First, Miss Penelope of Lovellwood is known locally as Penny, and she's the family pet—exceptionally good looking, fond of romping, catching snowballs, barking at things that move, handling the kitchen crumb patrol, especially fond of chasing herons from the pond and, of late, fond of New Year's Eve parties. As unindicted co-conspirator she is now, at age just less than two years, lying there filling the implausible role of mother-of-six. Next, peering into her box is our son Colin, twelve, who is definitely offended by this newest of Penny's tricks, by its diversion of her affections. Why did she go and do that? he wants to know. Don't we all?

Back on New Year's Day, when we told Colin what had happened and what might ensue, he didn't forgive Penny.

And he didn't forgive her either when the signs of the unwanted and unwonted pregnancy appeared, that is, when Penny began to substitute a sedate waddle for her normal prance. I had supposed that Colin would offer a full pardon as the puppies started appearing on the morning of the whelping, but he was trying to program a borrowed computer and wasn't sure he could be bothered for long by the miracle going on between the bookcases in Penny's brand-new whelping box. Initially, he counted the pups as they came and even started to name them, but got only as far as Argus and Orpheus. After these first two individually spotted ones, the pups were all pretty much dusky—"generics," he called them—and hard to distinguish. What's the point of giving them names if you can't really tell Hector the pup from Agamemnon? Colin went back to the computer.

Penny's own calmness relaxed us. Together Grace and I began to assess the data—attending now to the beeps from the computer and now to the squeaks from the whelping box. It dawned on us that the computer with all its fabulous programs was stupid and gross as a rock compared with the computer that Penny had between her ears. Here she was attending her own first birth and doing a calmly magnificent job of it. She knew exactly how to lick each pup gently to life as it came, knew when and where and how to bite off the umbilical cord, and knew how to clean up the box after each pup. Recycling the placenta stimulates her milk supply, the books say; but Penny does not read books. She just cleaned house as the pups came. Her brain is considerably smaller than the computer, and the task at hand considerably more delicate than anything asked of it. The machine has a few years of scientific ingenuity built into it, but she has a million years, more or less, of programming experience built into her, and she knew exactly what keys to press, and in what order. I know, I know: it happens all the time, of course. But you have to see it now and then if you want to be dumbfounded by it.

The six pups—the "sexpuplets," someone called them—totalled exactly three pounds of puppy flesh at birth. Not bad, considering that they started from zero two months ago. If she is pure Sheltie and he is pure mutt, what are they? *Smelties* seemed the right answer, and Smelties they became. In the next two months they are programmed to arrive at five pounds apiece, and about twenty pounds of that puppy growth will have to be extracted from Penny's rather modest milk factory. The prospect suggests a bit of care and keeping and coping for us all, to say nothing of the challenge of finding at weaning time six puppyable homes. Two pups would have been quite sufficient, thank you, but had there been only two I might not have kept systematic notes on their progress. Herewith the notes:

Five days. So far Penny seems to think it's all fun. For nearly a week life in the whelping lane has been remarkably calm and well ordered. And Penny now eats like a starved wolf. When the hamburger, eggs, milk, and broccoli are gone, she'll even try dog food—which she has spurned ever since her taste buds developed as if it were a concoction of sawdust, vitamins, and bad flavoring. My own job is easy: I simply spread fresh sheets of newspaper on top of the old ones in the whelping box. Now I begin to appreciate what an extraordinary piece of software is a good bitch's housekeeping program. Every pup gets many a tongue bath per day, top to bottom, especially bottom. Let a pup merely wiggle into range, and a tender bath will automatically ensue. If there are any spots on the papers that I don't cover up immediately, Penny simply mops them up as casually as a chambermaid. Happiness is six warm puppies.

Ten days. The pups can now squat, blink, squeak on pitch, stagger for three steps, and collapse in a spread-eagle belly-flop. They nurse with an aggressiveness that makes one wince. Do we sense that Penny begins to find life a bit too predictable? The same old grind day and night? She steps into the box to do a bit of tidying up and instantly triggers a riot: six scavengers attack her soft underbelly, as Winston Churchill might have put it. These days she can hardly walk or mop or turn around without stepping on some squirming reminder of New Year's Eve.

Fifteen days. Today a young pup sits on his haunches, swaying like a drunk, waiting for Penny to walk near. High above him, half a dozen outlets from the great celestial milk storehouse bounce invitingly just out of his reach. He waits until one bloated teat swings over him, then, with perfect timing, he uncoils and strikes out desperately: a short leap, an iron grip, enough suction to unplug a sink, and he is affixed. Excelsior! Now Penny moves on and he is dragged, dangling in ecstasy, as mom calmly scrubs the underside of his kid brother, and then with a casual flick of her left hind foot she wipes him off so that he lands bottom up where, quick as a wink, he begins to get his bath. Wow! What if there were a way for people to get kids from dinner table to bathtub with such efficiency? Within three minutes there have been four snacks stolen and five baths administered. Penny is good at this, whether she likes it or not.

Twenty days. Penny's demeanor tells me she remembers fondly the happy, carefree days of her lost youth. How did life collapse into thralldom to this endless routine of washing and meals and cleaning up? she wants to know. Resignedly settling into her corner, she is instantly acreep and acrawl with puplets. Today her eye is on me, not them. Would I please go out with her and just let her chase a stick, like the studs down the road? Liberation, meaningful work outside the household—that's what she wants. For several weeks she has watched me go alone for a walk—if she was settled in at mealtime—without a sign of reproach. Not today. I reach for my hat, and before it reaches my head she is on all fours, six pups hanging on for what must have seemed briefly to be the ride of their lives. She steps to the edge of the box, takes a quick jump, and six Smelties lose their grip on life simultaneously and *thonk* to the floor as six sets of stretched tissues snap back into place like so many rubber balloons. The cough and whimper of six little darlings falls on very deaf ears as Penny and I trot forth to encounter the real world.

Twenty-five days. Feeding time, and Penny watches the domestic commotion from a safe post where she cannot be attacked. She'd love to go in and serve dinner, but will they please wait a minute, for heaven's sake, until it is ready, until it's *there*—before they begin to mangle her? I can see that mealtime is what she adores and what she dreads.

If I carry a puppy away to examine it or to dip its nose into a dish of warm milk, she pays me a lot of nervous attention, but I can see too the ambivalence in her face. Half of her thinks: "Good riddance. I could do with one less. Want to drown the little nuisance?" But maybe she appreciates it that I'm working now to get them on their own as much as possible in order to spare her. The little sucker whimpers when I spill milk on its bib, and Penny moves in with long gentle strokes of her tongue.

Thirty days. At two and a half pounds apiece, the Smelties can stagger and gallop, come to my call, wag tails, sit up and yip in high-pitched voices, harass their mother, lap from a dish, wrestle like kittens, and pee like sailors. Penny is cheerfully resigned to it all: resigned to the eternal mop-up, resigned to mother abuse, to being clawed and mangled and scratched and chewed every time she comes home. Yet she hops into the box at irregular intervals to do the chores and get the treatment. We're all charmed by the family routines, and we realize it's easier than we thought to supervise this production.

Yesterday I saw Penny move in to administer discipline, after a new kind of cry had emerged from the sibling roughhousing in the box. She trotted smartly over and was promptly met with the usual litigation: "He bit my nose first," and the like. She gave the young brawlers each a firm tongue lashing, by stroking each face until it turned the other cheek, until the whimpers turned to sighs, and then, about to be waylaid by the rest of the troop, she returned blithely to the serious work of daydreaming by the fire.

What an extraordinary implement, a dog's tongue! Such virtuosity! Wondrous things I have seen her do with that tongue these four weeks—things hygienic, tender, repulsive, healing, reassuring, cleansing, soothing, disciplining. The versatile tongue arranges everything; the master key, it opens every door. It's like "Return" on the computer keyboard: nothing of any importance happens in Penny's family without her tongue flicking things into order for the next step. Penny's instant response to every breach of family decorum is a quick lick. Return to peace.

Thirty-five days. The sexpuplets are now five weeks old, playful rascals every one, with teeth and claws and cool wet noses and individual philosophies of life. Their names ore Orpheus, Argus, Runt, and the Three Little Generics. That wasn't the naming we had planned, but that's what happened. For that matter, the Smelties themselves aren't what we had planned, either. The pups just happened, and it's soon time for us to share the happening with about half a dozen other homes. Penny won't mind. Although the whole family loves a romp in the warm April snow, mealtime is no longer a joy as in days of yore. Lately she has been skipping out on it frequently to go off and lick her wounds in private. Sometimes the pups snatch a swig on the run, when Penny comes near. But frequently she stands on the box out of range of puppy teeth, reaching long kisses down to her offspring; and I suppose she wonders how a few short weeks can have transformed six little blobs of life into this twenty-pound gang of cheerful sadists.

Meanwhile our problem is: How shall we find six worthy homes that want relief from puppylessness?

Reasoning that everybody deserves an equal opportunity to get in on the ground floor with this new canine line, we ran a successful statewide advertisement, as follows:

> Smeltie puppies. Mother (Miss Penelope of Lovellwood) pure Sheltie. Father (Hunk of Neighborhood) pure Mutt. Implausibly charming pups, born February 27, soon to be famous—their life story in a national publication. Free in exchange for believable promise of good home and required shots. Hurry, only six. Call Jager, Washington, NH 495-3618.

That worked. Supposing rightly that we couldn't ask for payment for Smelties, we thought we should seek fame and immortality for them instead. So although we did not apply to get them into the American Kennel Club, I am applying to get them into American literature. The best treatment I know for one kind of unwanted pregnancy is this: give the pups away, but publish their story.

12

What the Old Plow Says

Some years ago I found in our woods, on the southwest slope, an old dump-rake whose reddish brown rust no one had disturbed in many a decade. I left it there for auld lang syne. Some time later I found an old plow: the long steel beam and the well-worn plowshare were intact, though the wooden handles crumbled to my touch. It lay in the pines across the brook. Both tools are still where I found them years ago—found them only because the wild young growth that first smothered them there had grown up to trees and lifted the curtain on the rusting iron. I judge that those farm implements could easily outlast the trees, if left in place, as I recommend. What I believe is that nobody dragged them out into the woods to die; they expired in the fields they worked, when their work was done, and something dragged the woods out to cover them.

Were I a poet I might try to process those old farm implements into poems, but I'm not, and Robert Frost has done it well enough. I suppose a lot of rustic wisdom and experience is wrapped up in such tools, maybe a whole book's worth—if we could only coax it out. I shall leave them where they are. In another century another poet may come by.

Since I am the resident archaeologist of these fields I go out to the woods and kick the old iron now and then to see if it has anything to tell me. There's plenty of life and resilience left in those old farm tools—enough, I hope, so that like Shakespeare's Glendower they "can call spirits from the vasty deep."

Auren Powers was the last to farm these acres, letting them go sometime in the 1930s, and I know he had a yoke of oxen, for I have seen a picture of them. Sometimes he also had a horse or two; I have a newspaper clipping to confirm that. That dump-rake in the woods was probably once pulled by his horse: raking hay is a light and easy job and a horse's pace is right for it. The plow? Maybe it was drawn by oxen, but I can't be sure. It's clear, though, that during the last two hundred years, more oxen than horses worked this land. I think farm tractors left no tracks in our fields at all.

❦

As a small boy on a Michigan farm on the eve of World War II, I knew just one farmer who plowed with an ox. Now and then if we chanced in his neighborhood we would see him moving sedately, ever so slowly, across his far fields with his ox—an unimaginably ancient relic on the horizon, as it seemed to me, from a bygone age. He wore a long beard unkempt and my brother said he was gruff, which I believed, so we kept our distance. Almost all the other farmers, ourselves included, farmed with horses, although one very ambitious farmer had a big leaky steam engine (that's what we called it, not steam tractor), and several had recently acquired new gasoline tractors.

Certain simple images I harbored at the time, if transcribed into adult idiom, would amount to this: here in my community are the four stages of farming history, succeeding each other in their fixed natural order, namely, ox, horse, steam, tractor. To witness so much history so compressed did not surprise me at all. (My mind had no room for complicating information about donkeys, mules, camels, or water buffaloes.) The world was not very old then, perspective is not the strength of youth, and I could not suspect how inexact this compact chronology really was. It was coherent. I knew my grandfather drove oxen, we ourselves used horses and might graduate soon to steam, and when I became a man I would own a tractor.

Such neat patterns are likely to fade away or unravel. Within a few years I noticed that some of the neighbors simply skipped the steam engine stage and went straight from horses to tractors—which streamlined my view of agricultural history. By that time my farmboy friends and I were engaged in hot debates about the merits of horses and tractors anyway. (Our grandfathers had debated the merits of horses and oxen.) The ox man on the river bank still survived, an ever more obscure and picturesque holdout, not often seen, as I recall, but a vivid emblem still of the reality of all our pasts, and always a conversational landmark—the old ox farmer near Clam River. I'd like to think he follows his plow there still, though I very much doubt it. But I believe he may have outlasted the great ravenously wood-hungry steam engine that once prowled our neighborhood.

When I went off to college I forgot about the old ox farmer until seeing a working ox a decade later called him up from memory. We were in Italy looking at the precarious slopes and terraces of the Apennines, terrain on which no large machine would venture and no draft horse be sure of foot. We saw and took a picture of a farmer plowing that unforgiving land with his huge Chianina ox. The man smiles proudly toward us, glad to be photographed. This peasant plowman is ageless—his years stretch far beyond those of Old Man Powers in New Hampshire or the old ox farmer near the Clam

River. In effect, he has resolutely farmed here—this tough clay, this hilly ground—with that great white ox for more than two thousand years, and in that time he has not changed much. On this land a horse would rip and tear, jerk and break the harness. Not the patient ox. The rugged landscape about him declares eloquently that from the Roman Republic onward, without that ox there would have been little agriculture there, and hence very little high culture, either. I am reminded that the economy of Rome was based not on commerce but on husbandry, and husbandry was ever inseparably yoked to oxen. Virgil himself said so, nearly two thousand years ago. At the foundation of Roman civilization stands this peasant, his ox, his plow.

It is oxen, bulls and calves, and not horses that figure most prominently in primitive religion, in icons and graven images. Historically, we associate the horse with majesty and warfare and aristocracy, the ox with religion and sacrifice and the pieties of the field. In cult and cultivation, the horse had a late start.

The story is distilled into our language. "Furlong," for example, is a good old English word, now no longer associated with the ox who gave us the concept. "Furrow long" is what it once meant—more than a thousand years ago—the distance oxen were expected to pull a plow between rests. In more modern usage a furlong is forty rods, or 660 feet, and a square furlong ten acres. It turned out that eight furlongs just about equaled the Roman mile, so a furlong came into the modern world as an eighth of a mile. But today, the furlong has become a unit for measuring racetracks. Of horses.

From Roman times, Anglo-Saxon farms were essentially without draft horses, and only after the coming of the Normans in 1066 did horses begin serious work in British fields.

In the margins of the Bayeux Tapestry, which commemorates the Norman invasion and Norman culture, I can find both mules and horses at work in the field. I have read that Wales had a long-ago law that forbade hitching horses to plows—though it didn't say why. Recently, I found something that may help explain it. Jochen Welsch of Old Sturbridge Village was quoted as saying: "You can work a horse to death, but you can't work an ox to death. It'll stop and say to hell with you. So which is the smarter animal?"

It appears that it was only very slowly, over the course of many centuries, that the horse became competitive with oxen on the farm—this, despite the fact that for centuries too the farmer-writers who compared them typically favored oxen over horses. Oxen, they said, produce better manure, are cheaper to keep, need no harness and no shoes, are more versatile, and are often healthier than horses. In late medieval days, horses were ridden and used on manor farms to pull wagons, carriages, and so on; but the serious part of tillage, as ever, was plowing. Where there was a score to be settled between the ox and the horse, this was the field that mattered. So what pulled the plow?

As far as I know the first treatment of plowing in the English language was in Sir Anthony Fitzherbert's 1523 farm manual, his *Boke of Husbandrye*. Fitzherbert, a lawyer, knight, and wealthy farmer, approaches plowing with a lawyer's caution: "in some places an oxe-ploughe is better than a horse-plough, and in somme places a horse-ploughe is better." But he ultimately concludes that "All thynges consydered, the ploughe of oxen is moche more profytable than the ploughe of horses." Between premise and conclusion he weighs the fact, well-known to Romans and Italians, that "oxen wyl plowe in tough cley, and vpon hylly grounde, where-as horses wyll stande stll." He also observes that horses "wyl goo faster than oxen on euen grounde or lyght grounde, & be quicker for cariage: but they be ferre more costly to kepe in winter, for they must haue both hey and corne to eate."

And there is a final comparison. When the ox is old, lame, or blind

> he maye be fedde, and thanne he is mannes meate, and as good or better than euer he was. And the horse, whan he dyethe, is but caryen.

For a very long time oxen had a very good farm press. I'm sure that Auren Powers in the twentieth century would have recognized and endorsed Fitzherbert's four-hundred-year-old line of thought. The oxen Fitzherbert knew had been bred for work for hundreds of years; the farm horses of the time were a small and not very sturdy breed. The English Great Horse, immortalized in legend and art, was not a draft animal but originally a war horse—large, fast, high-strung, strong for armor bearing. It's a rule as old as civilization: the best resources go to the military, the scrubs go to the farm.

The Bible enjoins men to renounce war and beat their swords into plowshares. That would imply also turning war horses into plow animals, breaking up the military-industrial complex. Now, there are war horses in the Bible, but I do not find there any that drew a plow. Yet by the time of the American Revolution the military-industrial complex was in fact being dismantled on the stud farms of England, as the romance associated with the horse's resume was actually being brought back to the farm. Through careful breeding, draft horses were of much improved stock, became stronger and healthier, and eventually more than competitive with oxen.

Horses gained the ascendancy as draft animals in England more rapidly than in many parts of America. Mules became common in the American South, less so in the North, and as late as 1850 most New England states still had more oxen than horses on their farms. But by that time—in most of Europe and America, at least—horses had won the symbolic contest: they had come to represent the future, the ox the past. During the last half of the nineteenth century, horses pulled ahead of oxen even in New England. By 1900 the ratio of horses to oxen in Washington, New Hampshire, was about two to one. Auren Powers on this farm would have been one of those ones.

Indeed, by the time steam power began to fill the fancy of progressive farmers—last part of the nineteenth century—draft horses had been superseding oxen, with regional exceptions, for nearly a hundred years. When the steam engine ambled on to the farm almost a century ago (only to vanish later like a dinosaur) it was just in time to be widely called, whether in affection or scorn, a *steam horse*, but never a steam ox.

Ox, horse, steam, tractor. Perhaps there was something right after all about my youthful version of agricultural history. I did not know enough to know how little I saw when I saw only the old ox farmer, our own horses, one giant steam engine, and all our neighbors' tractors. There was nothing to stop me then from seeing time condensed, seeing a landscape of centuries framed for my few years and my narrow horizons.

It's been almost ten years now since the last yoke of oxen, Star and Stripe, left our New Hampshire town. They had been residents of the Crane Farm and had a circle of fans well beyond the borders of Washington. Donny Crane was born and reared on a farm here, and in his early youth his father worked with horses. But by the time Donny and his brother Robert took over the family farm the heavy work was being done with a tractor. So Donny decided to raise a pair of oxen. That was of course a deliberately contrary statement of value, such as adds spice to life in the New Hampshire countryside.

Perhaps Donny Crane's oxen were not all that necessary for the work of the farm, but they did enough to make a colorful pretense of usefulness. They dragged Christmas trees out of the woods sometimes, visited local fairs, took their place in parades, gave much appreciated sled-rides to crowds of visiting schoolchildren, and put in a patient public appearance whenever they could. Almost everybody in town made their acquaintance eventually, and Star and Stripe affected to be populists, but they were really aristocrats—here in Washington the last of a line of historic draft animals. Their most conspicuous work was dragging sled-loads of maple sap to the Crane sugarhouse each March, and it was easy to believe they were absolutely necessary for that. Anyway, the photographs were terrific.

Everybody knew that Donny and his yoke made good copy. The oxen were photogenic and their drover was drily witty in an authentic New Hampshire accent: just the stuff for journalists in search of color. Perhaps a whole generation of Washington folk acquired a sanguine, maybe unrealistic, view of what farming with oxen was like, mediated by the press and their own imagination. For these oxen did not know the plow, and they had never heard of a furlong. People might have got a very different idea from Auren Powers a couple of generations back—Auren who had no public at all, and probably didn't want one or deserve it either.

When Donny Crane died, still young, his yoke of oxen went to a new owner in another place, and there were none left here to keep warm the tradition. Although oxen worked the fields of our town for two centuries, the evidence of it is nearly gone now. Prompted by what is left of a rusty plow that's gathering pine needles in my woods, I call Donny Crane to mind, and I call up all the Auren Powerses of Washington's more than two hundred years, and the old ox man of faded memory near the Clam River, and all the Fitzherberts of England, and the patient peasant and his plow on a thousand Italian hillsides. Spirits from the vasty deep.

13

Adventures with a Cub

The Farmall Cub is a pert little machine with classic tractor lines, a boy-sized, boy-dream of a tractor, keen and seductive as a young filly. Too bad they broke the mold.

When I was a farm boy I admired them extravagantly. Though they were low on horsepower, they were high on style to my eyes, and if I'd been asked, when it was designed and christened, I would have suggested they call it a colt, not a cub. But Cub is its name, and it has the lean and honest contours of its grownup relative tractors, the famed Farmall *B* and the *H* and the mighty *M*, those International Harvester McCormick-Deering tractors that helped to feed the world in the 1940s and 1950s. They don't make any of them anymore.

While farmers wore out the big tractors and bought bigger (there was a "Super H" and "Super M" in the fifties), turning agriculture into agribusiness, many of the little Cubs, which were made to be loved and to last and seldom did much hard work anyway, are still calmly prowling the countryside. You can see them in New England mowing roadsides, and you spot them sometimes idling at country auctions, newly painted. Occasionally, they are to be found loitering in dusty barns under leaky roofs—aged Cubs hibernating, secure in the knowledge that they won't die there but will run again and might run forever.

Cubs reached the rural market in Michigan in the late 1940s, just at the time I reached my early teens and began dreaming dreams of future farming—bigger, better, faster than that of my father. Although he farmed his eighty acres with horses, he had the advantage of relentless advice from me on the need to switch over: we should get modern, get with it, get tractorized. We could even start small. A Farmall Cub, I reasoned, despite its modest size and horsepower, could ease us gently into the scientific farming that I saw, or fancied, stretching beyond our narrow furrows toward every beckoning horizon.

True, a Cub could not immediately replace our horses, for a small tractor lacks not just brute horsepower but versatility, and is at a loss in mud or on steep hillsides. But wouldn't a Cub be unbeatable for light hauling, for harrowing, raking, cultivating, for plowing snow from our long, straight driveway, and, well, if it came to that, for just fooling around? My logic was not only airtight but secure on high moral ground: for me there was no very clear distinction between becoming a good man and operating a good tractor.

I knew my father had never driven a tractor and I darkly suspected that he didn't even wish to. Amazing! And I knew that he simply *liked* horses; he understood them and liked their pace and, what was worse, positively loved the mechanical simplicity of horse-drawn farm equipment. The plow, the harrow, the cultivater had ageless advantages. Not only did they not have motors, they didn't even have drive wheels, gears, sprockets—nothing but simple arrangements of shovels, the same for a thousand years. A Cub, he thought, might bring complications he would not understand and did not want. He eyed a tractor as one would eye an intruder.

So my father calmly stayed with horses as long as he stayed with farming, and he left farming only when his sons, instead of buying farms and tractors, bought books and went into college. Then he himself went into carpentry. He never felt the lure of tractorized agribusiness. Although his mind readily acknowledged the charm and elegance of the Farmall Cub, his farmer's soul remained unmoved.

That was another time, another state, another economy. More than forty seasons of mowing and harvest have come and passed away since then. My father too has passed away. Over the years—mostly academic years for me, and years of writing from the countryside, but none of farming—I've not forgotten tractors. Perhaps the Farmall Cub was fathered, or at least nurtured, by something deep in the American spirit: Fondly we imagine ourselves a rural people at heart, close to elemental things, and a Cub may let you believe that you are keeping real technology at arm's length. "Every man has an exceptional respect for tillage," Emerson wrote, "and a feeling that this is the original calling of the race." But can't you love a little Cub and still endorse the truth of Emerson?

A few years ago I had a totally unexpected chance to acquire, dirt cheap, a small tractor from a friend who was moving out of town. I was not in the market for a small tractor; I needed a small word processor. Still, did I want to drop by and look it over? Why not?

Thus the wheel of fortune turns, and stops. I found myself looking into the aged and handsome face of a Farmall Cub! Knowing that there will ever be only a certain finite number of them made that face even more handsome.

Alas! Oh joy! Between spasms of elation and despair, I felt my common sense give way. The Cub was cheap; it was available; I had land for the little bear to roam, possibly even work for it to do. We would call it farm work. In 1948, I had had several dozen reasons, maybe a hundred, why my father should acquire a Cub; it was hard to pick out even one of them that was vaguely relevant to whether *I* should acquire one in 1988. Evidently I would have to proceed without rhyme or reason, which would require courage. Although I was under pressure from obscure sources, I was yet able to summon the grace to do the right thing. I snatched it. Perhaps we are what we are mainly because of what we were. Perhaps, if my father had not been so successfully resistant to my sweet reasonableness of decades ago I might have now been spared the poignance of this moment. As it was, did I really have any alternative?

But now that I was at last on intimate terms with a Cub I craved to know more. I called around the country and eventually made the acquaintance of Louis Vinoverski of Carlisle Equipment Company in Elysia, Ohio, who is on a first-name basis with dozens of Cubs and knows more about them than I had thought there was to know. All Cubs, I learned, were made in Louisville, Kentucky, between 1947 and 1979, and the last four manufactured were in fact sold right there in Elysia. The early Cubs had 11 horsepower engines, and later they were revved up to 15. The small postwar farmer (my father?

me?) and the truck farmer were the initial marketing target, and cultivating small row crops was expected to be the Cub's main task. For a time there was even a Cub Low-Boy for special cultivating and fertilizing. Cubs are still widely praised cultivators, especially among tobacco farmers, says Mr. Vinoverski. But mowing with a specially designed underslung rotary mower is probably now their favorite job in Ohio and the Midwest.

With matters thus in perspective, I could go to work. The terrain on my New Hampshire hundred acres, for all its rugged appeal, is not at all like the sandy eighty acres of Michigan, flat and stone-free, on which I grew up. My vintage Cub came with plows, hand operated, but my garden here, suitable for a rototiller, is a small terraced slope with big rocks alongside and other rocks lurking just under the topsoil. I should admit it: I am not a farmer, and I really have nothing to plow. The Cub came with a cultivator, but my garden has little space for turning a tractor, and it would take me longer to attach and remove the tool than to cultivate the garden. My Cub has a scraper, but I have now learned from experience that even when it growls deeply it is not husky enough to move my soil or rocks; and as for snow, the blower on my Gravely already handles it nicely. My Cub has no hydraulic lift system, so while it cheerfully drags the rocks to the new wall I'm building, I have to grunt and tip them up myself. I have developed some reservations about 1940s engineering.

Ambivalent but unbowed, I salvaged an old trailer from a neighbor, attached it to the Cub and hauled up the winter's wood. That was such a thumping success that I did it the next year too, and the next, celebrating with bigger fires. Of course I couldn't cross the rocky brook with the Cub, as I would have with a horse, and there were lots of places in the woods I wanted to go where the terrain forbade me. But sometimes when my Cub was at work or play the gentle hum and sputter of its engine was sheer delight—the cheerful patter of nostalgia. All's well in a world that sounds like that.

Of course I should get more attachments, a sicklebar mower for instance, to clear the meadows and drive back the predatory woods. Yet in two years I didn't locate a second-hand mower that I liked and could afford. A more complicated underslung rotary mower was very expensive if available—and was it flexible enough to manage the rocks and depressions in my meadows? It occurred to me that a horse could graze the meadows clear. Meanwhile, I often had trouble rousing my Cub; it was fussy when wet; there weren't devoted mechanics nearby who spoke Cub; I was spending too much time coddling it. Once I hauled it to a repair shop and when it came back it took up precious den space in the garage that other gear had long been standing in line for.

On second thought, did I want these complications? Slowly there dawned the possibility that the Cub was a sentimental visitor from another era, born for other kinds of duties on other sorts of terrain, maybe just disturbing my pace. How could that be? Tractor as intruder? Wasn't that the old heresy I had refuted more than forty years ago? One damp day, trying to start the Cub, I imagined I heard my father's whisper at my ear, something to the effect that I had served my time. And the next day I saw a sign advertising a consignment auction. This would take courage. But was there really an alternative?

Farewell, Farmall Cub—pert little machine with classic tractor lines, tractor of my dreams, keen and seductive as a young filly. We have had our fling together; it's been good to know you.

Memo to my son: Beware! the unappreciated wisdom of your youth may return to vex your middle years. Memo to myself: A horse would look awfully handsome in The North Meadow.

14

Confessions of an Axe Addict

When I came to New Hampshire I bought an axe before I bought a chainsaw. It was a double-bitted axe.

In my youth I learned to swing an axe, as most farm boys did, because farm homes were then heated with wood. Learning to use an axe stood midway on the scale of achievements between handling a gun, which was a genuine rite of passage, conferring adulthood, and handling a pitchfork, which was easy and tedious, conferring blisters. Using an axe required strength and skill and a learning process to boot, it was also slightly dangerous, and it looked and felt like a man's work. So it was attractive to a boy. Splitting wood for the kitchen range served for beginnings, but soon one graduated to swing an axe in the woods.

I was in high school when I acquired my first axe, double-bitted, an axe like my father's, though lighter. You could split wood with a single-bitted axe, but for the woods only a double-bitted axe would do. Chainsaws as ordinary farm tools were a decade away, and that meant that ours was perhaps the last generation of rural Americans to grow up using an axe as a regular tool.

Since then, I have met many men in New Hampshire whose experience echoes mine: they too grew up knowing that a double-bitted axe was the tool for them, they still own one and like it and they have always seen the alternative, a single-bitted poll axe, as a pale substitute, useful perhaps, but not really right for felling trees. They own a chainsaw now, as I do, but they have not mentally relinquished their axes.

A double-bitted axe is perfectly symmetrical and shaped something like a giant bow tie, one edge the mirror image of the other. In New Hampshire I bought one early as a matter of course, finding it cheaper than a chainsaw and more familiar to my hand. Very soon I was very fond of it and used it whenever I had a plausible excuse, sometimes cutting and limbing trees with it as I had long ago, even though a chainsaw would have made the job easier. It seemed such a perfect tool for its purpose, balanced and handsome and smooth to the swing. To those who respect their senses in the woods, the crisp ring of a chopping axe is music compared to the smelly rattle of chainsaws.

It was almost automatic that I lapsed into print on the merits of this tool. That effort was called "A Sermon in Praise of the Double-Bitted Axe," and that's pretty much what it was. The editor even arranged for the sermon to be graced with a Winslow Homer watercolor, "The Pioneer," portraying a woodsman reviewing a hillside of stumps. On his shoulder rested a double-bitted axe. And I was glad to be linked with Homer and, through him, with the larger mythos of the

American landscape, ambiguous though it be, for Homer was undoubtedly celebrating the axe as an emblem of civilization, a weapon against the wilderness.

What had prompted my sermonizing were some claims I'd read in a country magazine: the double-bitted axe is only suitable for professionals, too dangerous, too big, too much axe for the weekend chopper. Nonsense, I thought; that can't be a testimony of serious experience. It's not congruent with what I learned as a youth in Michigan and as a man in New Hampshire; it sounds like suburban overreaction to half-remembered Paul Bunyan legends. Preparing myself to put down those modern heresies, I did a bit of casual research on the axe's local reputation. I talked to several people, starting with Hubie Williams, a friend and veteran of the woods from a generation older than mine.

"Why do you like a double-bitted axe?" I asked.

"Smooth swing. Best balanced axe there is. Besides, you get two axes in one," he said, quick as that.

It was easy to find others who said similar things. On the matter of two-axes-for-one, I did run into a misunderstanding. People who haven't done much axe swinging but admire the double-bitted axe sometimes fasten on the notion that the advantage of two edges lies in the less frequent need for sharpening. But no: sharpening is not a problem if the edge is not nicked. The chopper keeps one edge razor-sharp and leaves the other dull and nicked. The latter he uses for splitting, which requires a dull axe, and for chopping near the ground or on a hard dead knot, or any place that might damage the good edge. One edge of my own axe I have never sharpened and don't expect to, though it has now seen decades of use.

Continuing my research, I went to a friend who doesn't cut much wood but runs a good hardware store.

"John, do you sell many of these?" I asked, fondling a double-bitted axe with a Collins label.

"Oh yes," he said, "but fewer than I used to, and personally I don't like it."

He saw my arched eyebrows.

"Too dangerous," he said, quick as that.

"Meaning . . . ?" said I, practicing my repartee.

He grabbed an axe handle to demonstrate. Spreading wide his legs, he joined hands and threw both arms high over his head and behind his back, puffed out his cheeks and extruded his belly, and sober-sidedly simulated one of the most ungainly and comical chopping postures I had ever imagined. But yes, by golly, it is possible: someone with a double-bitted axe and double-jointed back and no common sense could contrive, with determination and practice, to thonk his bottom side on the backswing of the upswing preparatory to clobbering a slab of maple on the downswing. I have never tried that. I imagined that one could achieve the same sad result without calisthenics by simply sitting down directly on the upright edge. I have never tried that either. But, yes, as with a gun or a car or a chainsaw or any other major implement, there are unsafe things to do with it. I suppose that if someone thinks it unsafe, he should not use it.

But I doubt that questions of safety had any influence on the history of the double-bitted axe. And it does have a most remarkable history.

Over the years my interest in the double-bitted axe, casually formed in youth and casually reaffirmed in New Hampshire, has taken a serious turn. Perhaps initially this was because I learned that there were very few historical facts about double-bitted axes that you could reliably just look up in books. This attracted me—like virgin territory. For a time, I kept my interest at the benign level of hobby and flirtation, but in recent years it has become a full and far-flung romance.

It is not easy to explain an affair such as this to normal people. If I prowled junk shops and collected axe specimens, puzzled friends would understand; but I prowl archives, libraries, museums, and sometimes travel to far places, collecting only notes. Like a man who drinks furtively and alone, not willing to own up to what he is doing, I have sometimes let folks be misled about my addiction, hiding my notes like empties. So this is the first installment on my confession. The full story would require a book and I expect that eventually it will.

When Europeans tackled the New World wilderness they came equipped—so an old slogan said—with three essentials: the axe, the Bible, and the plow. That pretty much goes also for the next generation of settlers, such as the Massachusetts migrants who came to Washington, New Hampshire, in the 1770s and 1780s, including Ebenezer Wood, who came to this very spot. It is amazing that these settlers did so well against the forest, for I think they worked even harder than our historians have realized. They had a good Bible, a fair plow, and a bad axe.

The single-bitted axe they brought from Europe, no matter what country, was a sad tool, not something fitted to slay a wilderness. Of course, they went to work anyway. But their axe was clumsy, unbalanced, too small and the iron too soft, a generally bad design that would not be used today. A gross defect was that the weight of the head was mostly in the blade, forward of the handle, tiring the arms quickly and making an accurate stroke extremely difficult. This axe had ruled the forests of Europe for over a thousand years, though it is hard to understand why, and it survived in America for two hundred years. A deeply conservative rural psychology appears to have been at work, for this axe was eventually discarded as inferior. It took specific American innovations in axe design to correct the inherited design faults.

The first improvement came about the time of the Revolutionary War. Blacksmiths shortened the blade, lengthened the handle, and added a massy butt opposite the bit to balance the axe head. This new axe, with wedge-shaped head and a hard steel bit, became quickly and widely known and admired as the "American felling axe." Since the butt opposite the cutting bit was often called a "poll," the axe was also called a "poll axe." By the early nineteenth century it was familiar everywhere in America and heavily exported to Europe, while the inherited colonial axe sank into well-deserved oblivion.

It cheers me to suppose that the improved American felling axe may have been available to Ebenezer Wood in 1780 when he built our house, though I cannot prove it. I study axe marks on our posts and beams and speculate about his tools, but I do not know. Broad axe and adze he certainly had, but what axe felled his trees? In fact very few eighteenth-century axes in collections are reliably dated: you cannot go to a museum and confidently point to the axe in use in New Hampshire in 1780. Moreover, although the development of this felling axe was a major breakthrough, the double-bitted axe that followed two generations later was far more revolutionary.

By 1850 Americans had been hacking a civilization out of the wilderness for over two hundred years. But nobody was swinging a double-bitted axe. It appeared just after the Civil War—nobody knows exactly where or when—and before 1900 the design had spread to the entire country. Ebenezer

Wood may have had an American felling axe, but he certainly never laid eyes on a double-bitted axe, nor, for that matter, did George Washington or Abraham Lincoln. But I'm sure Auren Powers did. In one generation the double-bitted axe came from nowhere to become the preferred felling axe in the land. That is an astonishing turnabout—for men had been cutting trees for thousands of years in Europe and for hundreds of years in America. Woodsmen are conservative by nature; why would so many of them suddenly switch tools? There is only one answer: they saw it as a superior axe.

. . . As I review these thoughts in my woods, I am facing an eight-inch ash tree which I plan to transform into firewood, and I have deliberately left my chainsaw in the garage. My weapon is my double-bitted axe. That choice is a gesture to history and tradition, for I know the chainsaw is far more efficient. I am reminded of the deep conservatism of farm people throughout all history, their inclination to do as they have always done, their tendency to disparage the new. "Call that thing an axe?"—that must have been the greeting suffered a million times by the double-bitted axe in its early years. Surely there was a strong prejudice against the very idea of an axe with two edges. Maybe the skill and familiarity the old-timers had achieved with their poll axe kept them from believing any design improvement was possible. Whole nations in Europe resisted the double-bit idea for generations until the chainsaw made the question nearly moot. Perhaps the full story here, unwritten as yet, is as much a footnote in the history of psychology as of technology.

But what of those American woodsmen who, a hundred years ago, went against the traditions of their fathers and bought the new double-bitted axe? What did they discover that helped them overcome their prejudice?

Foremost, no doubt, was the marvelous versatility of having two axes in one, a sharp edge and a dull one. Next, they would have soon realized that matters of balance and aerodynamics go together. A fully balanced axe, equal head weight on each side of the handle, is easier to swing accurately, and therefore safer and more efficient. Moreover, the trailing blade of a double-bitted axe works as a rudder, supporting and steering the stroke, like the tail of a bird or a fish or airplane. The axe cuts the air and slides smoothly through it, unlike a single-bitted axe whose blunt rear end, or poll, actually creates turbulence. Once you are alert to this, you can feel the difference as you swing the axe. And gradually, of course, choppers began to appreciate the looks, the timeless symmetry, of the new axe.

. . . Well, my axe worked splendidly when I chopped down the ash tree, but my own performance gets a lower grade. I am reminded again that it takes practice to hit the mark; swinging an axe hard is very tiring work, and the more tired you become the less accurate your swing. If I miss my target by more than half an inch I give myself demerits. But here is a puzzle: If the double-bitted axe really is so superior to its predecessors, as its quick adoption suggests, why didn't it appear earlier? The idea of a balanced double blade is not an esoteric concept; indeed, the design would seem to be almost inevitable. Yet timber harvesters had to wait centuries for such a simple invention. Why didn't Thomas Jefferson invent it? Or Benjamin Franklin? It didn't take a Leonardo to do it (come to think of it, why didn't *he* invent it?), just an obscure American blacksmith, whose name nobody knows. Was it maybe invented several times over before it found the right conditions to catch on?

An axe is not only a tool; it is a potent symbol too. Some few tools have an especially powerful mythological life—the sword, the pen, the plow, the Grim Reaper's scythe. And the

Roman cross. Consider the hammer and sickle, ordinary tools of making and harvesting, but mighty political symbols for two generations in our own time. The mythological meaning of a tool may far outstrip that tool's original significance. When the double-bitted axe entered modern history by entering the American forest, it greatly enriched our storehouse of myth. Paul Bunyan, the legendary American lumberjack of Russian-American descent, is always portrayed with a double-bitted axe. For many decades, until disbanded in 1970, there was a brigade, called "Pioneers," attached to Canadian Infantry Regiments. The Pioneers' chief task was to repair and build bridges. They were regular infantrymen but for two exceptions, which were their trademarks: like Paul Bunyan, they all wore beards and they all carried double-bitted axes. The double-bitted axe early became, and remains, a symbol of masculinity for the advertising industry: a recent two-page example shows a huge pile of logs, a very conspicuous double-bitted axe, a brawny lumberjack smoking the advertised cigarette, and the claim that "when your taste grows up" (like that of this man with that axe) you will select that cigarette.

Memoirs of earlier generations of lumbermen invariably mention the pride the chopper took in his double-bitted axe. In dozens of photo archives I've looked into, one thing stands out: early twentieth-century lumber photos rarely show posed lumberjacks with a single-bitted axe in hand. If he poses with an axe, it will be a double-bitted one. No wonder: in its elegant symmetry this tool is photogenic almost to the point of exhibitionism, an axe with clout and class, a tool to be celebrated. With the massive American timber industry as backdrop, this axe easily lends itself to multiple symbolic meanings, and this may also help explain its triumph in the woods.

Yet, it remains puzzling that it came so late to the American scene. What makes it especially so is the fact that the Greeks and the Romans had known and loved the double-bitted axe many centuries earlier.

Two thousand years ago the Romans appear to have known things about these axes that we had to relearn a hundred years ago: balance, aerodynamics, versatility, compelling appearance. Nor was the power of axe symbolism lost on the Romans: they sometimes put double-bitted axes into the hands of their gods. A carved relief dating from the second century A.D. in the Boston Museum of Fine Arts shows two examples of a deity with a double-bitted axe. They also put it into the hands of woodsmen: a Roman soldier cutting trees with a double-bitted axe is carved in stone on Trajan's Column, dating from the first century A.D. Other archaeological specimens come from Sicily, Pompeii, and elsewhere.

But the Romans didn't invent this axe: they inherited it and used it for hundreds of years. And then somehow lost it. The double-bitted axe disappeared from European forests, disappeared from art, painting, literature, sculpture, disappeared from Western civilization. Somewhere in the Dark Ages Europeans abandoned the double-bitted axe, for reasons unknown. Time and again Europeans devastated their forests—for construction, for metalworking, for naval supplies, for fuel—but not with a double-bitted axe. I make these sweeping statements not relying upon any axe authority (I know none), but because for years I have ransacked archives and museums for evidence that even one medieval tree fell to the strokes of a double-bitted axe. Haven't found it yet. Medieval paintings, sculptures, engravings, sketches, texts, tapestries, manuscripts, icons, etchings, woodcuts—here one can find axes all right. But not a double-bitted felling axe in the lot. Double-bitted battle axes? Just a few. The very idea seems to have gone into recession. But why? The question may be for addicts only.

The English word "axe" itself has a troubled medieval history. It appears to me that English culture has always been less interested in the design of the axe than in the spelling of the word, and a cheerful dialogue on *that* has been under way for about fifteen hundred years. The earliest efforts were conducted in Old English, and involved "aex" and "echze," and also some experiments with "aces" and "acus." Later, Middle English gave "exe" a shot, and even played around with "ex" and "aex." About five hundred years ago the spelling "aix" cropped up, but soon thereafter things settled down to a stiff two-way contest between "axe" and "ax." "Axe" took the lead in the early seventeenth century, when Shakespeare and the Authorized Version of the Bible took its side. That should have settled the matter, for those were also the days when the axe itself, such as it was, got exported to America and the spelling "axe" was shipped over with it. American blacksmiths redesigned the English axe, of course, but American wordsmiths wisely kept the English spelling "axe" just as they got it. Meanwhile, under reactionary forces, "ax" made a modest comback in England in the eighteenth century, but faded rapidly in the nineteenth and all but disappeared, leaving "axe" in charge. However, in the early twentieth century the *Oxford English Dictionary*, never one to abandon a lost cause, came out flatly for "ax," declaring: "The spelling 'ax' is better on every ground, of etymology, phonology, and analogy, than 'axe,' which has of late become prevalent." "Of late?" Then we remember that that is the OED's quaint way of referring to the previous two hundred and fifty years.

In the face of so many uncertainties the world needs some firm doctrine. The correct spelling is "axe."

Before the Romans had the double-bitted axe and lost it, the Greeks had it and loved it—and passed it on to the Romans.

In the Boston Museum of Fine Arts there is a Greek vase made and painted about 500 B.C., and on it we can see, in effect, two snapshots of classical Greek daily life. One shows a cobbler shop, the merchant fitting his customers with leather shoes; on the other side is a Greek blacksmith shop. Such scenes could fit comfortably into the daily life of Washington, New Hampshire, a hundred and fifty years ago. Various tools are shown hanging on the blacksmith shop wall: a hammer, a saw, and two double-bitted axes. What catches my eye is the fact that those Greek axes look almost exactly like mine, the one I hold in my hand, use in my woods. My axe is separated from them by twenty-five hundred years, fifteen hundred of which didn't know this sort of axe at all. My axe descended from the one reinvented a hundred and thirty years ago by some nameless American blacksmith.

I have an interesting hypothesis, but not a shred of evidence: Maybe the unknown American blacksmith who reinvented the double-bitted axe saw a Greek axe on an ancient vase and leapt across the centuries to copy what he saw. Or maybe he just reached back into the collective unconscious of the human race for some archetypal axe.

But what was the intended *use* of the axes in that Greek shop on the vase? Probably they were made for cutting down trees, the labor of slaves, and thus not a proper subject for the conventions of Greek vase painting. The Greeks frequently put double-bitted axes, suitable for woodcutting but employed as weapons, into the hands of their mythic heroes. When early twentieth-century Americans mythologized the double-bitted axe by putting it into the hands of legendary lumberjack Paul Bunyan, that was not new: thousands of years earlier the Greeks had put one into the hands of their legendary strongman, Heracles. (The American mythmakers may not have known about this.) The evidence is painted on a vase now in the Louvre. The Athenian hero Theseus appears on vases with a double-bitted axe, as does Electra. The famous myth of the birth of the goddess Athena holds that she sprang fully armed from the head of Zeus when Zeus was struck with the axe of Hephaistos. Greek vase paintings and sculptures render this scene with a double-bitted axe.

The Greek gods and heroes wielded double-bitted axes, but archaeology has made it clear that real Greeks had real double-bitted axes too, like the ones on the Boston vase, made of iron or bronze, axes that they used as tools or weapons and passed on to the Romans.

But it's unlikely that even the classical Greeks invented this axe.

The Greeks probably got their double-bitted axe from the Minoans, the Bronze Age people who are an axe addict's delight and frustration, for their commitment to the double-bitted axe is by far the deepest and most mysterious of all.

Around the year 2000 B.C., on the island of Crete, the Minoans developed Europe's first civilization. These remarkable people controlled a vast Mediterranean trading network, constructed elaborate palaces and villas, created intricate artwork in metals and precious stones, frescoes and vase paintings, invented a system of writing—well over a thousand years before the classical Greeks painted axes on vases. Their artwork shows plainly that these people, at the dawn of European civilization, worshipped goddesses and employed double-bitted axes in their cult ceremonies.

Archaeologists have found hundreds of Minoan double-bitted axes, many of them miniatures, not weapons or tools, carefully wrought of bronze and silver and brilliant gold; also large ceremonial double axes, made of bronze sheet metal. Double-bitted axes are also painted on Minoan vases and frescoes where they seem to be cult symbols of some sort. But in addition to ceremonial axes there are many heavy tool-like bronze double-bitted axes, which look to the casual visitor like something you might buy today in a hardware store. What was going on back there?

This wondrous story was opened up first in 1900 when Sir Arthur Evans began his excavations at Knossos on Crete. And the end is not yet. Evans called the civilization he uncovered Minoan, after the mythical King Minos, who built a huge labyrinth to confine the fierce minotaur who fed on human flesh. ("Labyrinth," most authorities believe, is an old Greek word that means "place of the double-axe.") Evans and his followers believed that the Minoan double-bitted axe came straight from the realms of prehistoric myth and religion. Evidently it did, but it seems likely (to me at least) that some of these big bronze axes also came straight from the hands of ancient woodchoppers. If they did, we are in the presence of something very perplexing indeed.

But is it possible that these people with their bronze axes four thousand years ago knew things that were forgotten for fifteen hundred years by medieval lumbermen; knew things about tool-making, tool balance, aerodynamics, versatility, still unknown to the American pioneers who settled Washington, New Hampshire, two hundred years ago? Yes, it is possible. Certain it is, at any rate, that the Minoans, for reasons that remain utterly mysterious, fell so heavily under the spell of the double-bitted axe that they made gold and silver miniature axes and deposited them in their holy places.

Addicts tend to lose perspective. Someone in thrall to a muse as mysterious as this needs the tonic of ordinary reality. When I don't have the support of a skeptical friend I can usually sober up by leaving my notes and taking the twelve steps or so to my garage. I keep a chainsaw there and often use it, recognizing that within my lifetime the chainsaw has pretty well rendered obsolete all the metal axes that got us from the Stone Age to now. Before cranking up the saw, however, I may reach up and take from its hook my favorite double-bitted axe.

I hold the axe at arm's length and simply stare at it long and hard. Soon enough all the enveloping myths dissolve, the mystification fades away. What is this strange thing I hold in my hand? It seems but a dull lump of matter, without history, without meaning or magic. I see but a slab of steel on a stick.

From steel and stick I mentally reconstitute an axe. The handle is straight, oval, made of hickory, thirty-six inches long. The head is ten inches long, five wide, and weighs just five pounds. An axe for chopping. Made in a factory. One of thousands, millions. As a tool it is exquisitely simple, elegant, efficient, dangerous if misused, perfectly symmetrical. The cutting edge is hard steel and exceedingly sharp. I see a perfect marriage of form and function.

And I see a symbol immemorially old, mysterious, and more compelling than I can comprehend. The thing in my hand, my axe, has exactly the same form as something I saw in an 1895 Sears Roebuck catalog—and in dozens of far more ancient settings. The form that I saw on Trajan's Column, on

Greek vases in London, in glass cases in Athens, and on a tiny and exquisitely carved sealstone in Crete. The vases were but twenty-five hundred years old, the Minoan carved stone, thirty-five hundred.

It is as if this form, this symbol, has been with us forever and can never be wholly lost, even when it was not embodied in an axe for a thousand years.

Part 3

People and Community

In most of New England the word "town" signifies a political unit and a geographical area, not a cluster of stores and homes. Geographically, it is like a Midwestern *township*, but politically and emotionally it is a very different thing. A New England town may be entirely rural, or it may contain several villages, or it may be an urbanized suburb of a city. But it is a unity. A town forms a community in a way a township almost never does; it has emotional as well as geographical boundaries. Initially, it was the Congregational Church and town meeting government which brought this about; more recently it is still town meeting government which creates community and holds it. A New England town-community is a collective mind and memory, with a sharp awareness of locale and boundary, of tradition and connection. It is a self-conscious unity.

From the earliest days of New Hampshire the town was the unit to reckon with. The state's historical founding may be dated from the moment—the year was 1640—when its four autonomous seacoast towns voted to band together for mutual protection and join themselves to the Massachusetts Bay Colony. Their manner of local government—vesting authority in an assembly of voters, called by themselves—was not lifted from books, or thought up by philosophers, or imposed from above. It might have been too radical to propose as an idea. It just grew as a practice, and *then* became a theory, and then a matter of law. And now a great tradition.

The town meeting is an old New Hampshire institution.

The presidential primary election is a young one. What they have in common is this: they both grew up haphazardly, without anyone intending or foreseeing the importance they would assume. Neither had a blueprint. I think both are too subtle for that. They could only be built slowly by citizens from raw materials that came to hand. Some of the following chapters are about such raw materials.

15

Perambulating the Bounds

As small boys in Michigan my brothers and I would now and then take it into our heads to walk completely around our father's eighty-acre farm. Following the woven-wire fence row, where the fieldstones grew, we tramped from corner to corner—a half mile, a quarter, a half, a quarter mile, exactly eighty acres—and made sure that we touched each corner post and most line posts as well. We had no clear reason for making this ceremonial circuit: it just seemed a very appropriate thing to do. We found nothing new. The lines were conspicuous even to small boys, and only one area, through the swamp, was much of a challenge. We celebrated these excursions by checking out the gooseberries that thrived among the fencerow fieldstones and by recommending cake and milk for ourselves when we returned and made a full report to our mother. It was a mysteriously satisfying way to spend a morning, and we assumed that it merited some official recognition.

Other farms in the neighborhood were friendly and familiar to us, since we had worked or played on them, but we never had the slightest impulse to walk their bounds, although there would have been more novelty in that. Evidently it was not at all the discovery of new things but the assurance of old things that impelled us. Some ineffable tie between ourselves and our family's piece of land was reaffirmed by our little ritual—which we supposed had been invented right there and by us.

These forgotten childhood treks came abruptly to mind

recently as I was staring at an old stone wall. I had formed the practice, for no reason that I could recognize, of occasionally walking the bounds of my own small piece of New Hampshire, something more than a hundred acres of forestland and overgrown pasture. On a recent excursion I had a sudden sense of déjà vu, a flash of recognition, of having been in precisely this circumstance at some indefinite past time. Eventually I traced this feeling back to my walking the bounds ("lines" they are called in Michigan, being straight) of my father's farm, and so restored to mind the charm of a minor memory I had nearly lost.

However, but for what I had caught in that momentary flash, there is not much similarity between that tame Michigan land and these robust New Hampshire slopes. Most of my bounds are stone walls, lichen gray or mossy green; they lie not by open fields but in spruce thickets, in maple thinnets and pine groves, across brooks and steep hillsides. For a century or two everything visible about them has intimated that they are part of the landscape, natural facts and not boundaries at all.

I understand them better because I know something about who built them. Lt. Ebenezer Wood and his boys, the first farmers of these acres, probably put up most of them; it would have been one of their early orders of business after building a house and clearing some openings for planting. A deed of the 1790s, just a decade after the Wood family came here, refers to a particular stone wall that is still easily identified, and that wall contains rocks that weigh three and four hundred pounds, so evidently oxen and tripods were used to lift them. Putting up the walls did several immediate things for the original settlers: it got stones out of the way and it helped fence the livestock. It also did several long-range things: it permanently marked the boundaries of farms and—the chief marvel to twentieth-century eyes—it left upon the landscape stately, sometimes stunning, lines of order and beauty, prompting admiration and gratitude from residents and passersby alike. I know no scale to measure the value of gifts so fortuitous.

Not all the stone walls on my place mark boundaries or roadways: some just seem to veer off at random through the present woods. Only seem. They are not random but follow a route carefully chosen in terms later made plain by Robert Frost: "Before I built a wall I'd ask to know / What I was walling in or walling out." Study the terrain and you can see what Wood was up to, and you can read his mind by reading his wall. He was walling *in* land that could be plowed or at least mowed with a scythe if some of the rocks were rolled away; he was walling *out* land too rough and rocky to plow or mow, land obviously left to pasture.

But now? Even Robert Frost's neighbor would not engage in mending a wall here. Nothing is or needs to be walled in or walled out. My ritualized walking of these boundary walls serves no practical purpose; I leave everything just as it is. I am not trying for good neighbors through good fences. Owners of half the adjoining land and ledges I have not met, hardly neighbors. And still I regularly walk the bounds, needing no reminding where they are, going all the way to the cornerstones—corners, once, I know, of cornfields, pastures, meadows—now half buried in leaves and humus.

If my musing ramble along these walls accomplishes anything it may be some kind of inward validation of my relation to this particular tract of land. In some unspecifiable sense it is reassuring to know that the bounds are there—not doing but being—practically immovable, participating in the very substance of the land, giving a visible sense of order and definition to the arrangements of my imagination, confirming my obscure affection for handsome inanimate things. At least I believe that's what this liturgy's about. The trees, rocks, stumps on this side of the wall are my responsibility: I have entered into their history, they into my stewardship. Those yonder side of the wall are aliens; to the camera they are all the same, but not to me. At any rate, something there is that dearly loves a wall. Undoubtedly these bounds, like those lines long ago surrounding the family homestead, have far more meaning to me than I can say or know. But I do know that my intimations are not unique.

We live within boundaries. Our boundary lines reach out into politics, history, religion, and mythology.

For over two hundred years it's been a New Hampshire law (similar to laws in other New England states) that the Selectmen of each town are obliged to "perambulate the bounds" and renew the marks "once in every seven years forever" and to "return an account." Their task is literally to walk the perimeter of the entire town, thirty-five or fifty or more miles, reidentify all the boundary marks, note the trees blazed, lines remeasured, monuments erected or restored, and the like. "Perambulate"—the very word suggests that something auspicious is afoot.

The law requires that both the adjoining towns be represented when their shared boundary is perambulated. Since the urge to take this vigorous stroll may not strike two towns simultaneously, the law also provides that the older of the adjoining towns must take the initiative. Many towns have half a dozen or more abutting towns (Washington has seven), and in many of them perambulating is done less according to schedule than according to the Selectmen's impulses. Although the law may be honored more in the breach than in the observance, somehow every town does the job now and then, and feels uneasy, though perhaps not guilty, if a decade goes by without a fairly brisk bout of perambulating: after all, the neighbors might be encroaching somewhere. The law provides for a penalty upon Selectmen who neglect the task, but in this state the penalty is never applied.

One reason the itch to perambulate may not come every seven years as the law prescribes is the sheer physical challenge of the thing. Many New England towns, including my own, were laid out hundreds of years ago in the office of a developer, the lines being then transferred to the contours of a mountainous countryside which the map makers had not seen. The results were usually perplexing. There were overlapping town boundary claims and consequent disputes between towns (some residents taxed in two towns and allowed to vote in neither); and there were leftover pieces of land, unassigned to either abutting town, called gores—land subject to sly appropriation by a wily abutter or town official. In rural New Hampshire we've been sorting this out for the past three centuries. It still requires an act of the legislature and a two-thirds vote of the residents of both affected towns to change a town boundary.

So it is to be expected that the law would instruct Selectmen to perambulate bounds regularly, and that they would do it irregularly. Originating the way they did, the boundaries themselves descended to rural earth without regard to hill or dale: they may go straight down cliffs, across bogs, along the face of bare ledges, over mountaintops, or through ponds. This is not the Midwest, where most townships are marked by straight blacktop roads, with no emotional resonance at all.

Walking or perambulating the bounds of something, whether it is a perfectly rectangular farm in the Midwest or a misshapen piece of bristly and jagged townscape in New England, is body language. It is an intimate gesture of linking oneself to the life of whatever is valued within those bounds. As a political gesture it still has a faintly mystical or religious character. Perhaps that is because it also has definite religious origins.

❦

Perambulating the bounds of a town is rooted in the ecclesiastical practice of "beating the bounds" of a parish.

Like so many other things, peramabulating the bounds was transferred to the politics of New England from the parishes of old England. We are back to the days before maps—even the bad maps of early New England: "when maps were rare it was usual to make a formal perambulation of the parish boundaries on Ascension day or during Rogation week," says my eleventh edition (1911) of the *Encyclopaedia Britannica*. This is how they did it:

> The priest of the parish with the churchwardens and the parochial officials headed a crowd of boys who, armed with green boughs, beat with them the parish border-stones. Sometimes the boys were themselves whipped or even violently bumped on the boundary-stones to make them remember. The object of taking the boys was obviously to ensure that witnesses to the boundaries should survive as long as possible. In England the custom is as old as Anglo Saxon days, as it is mentioned in laws of Alfred and Aethelstan. . . . A parish-ale or feast was always held after the perambulation, which assured its popularity.

Evidently my brothers and I were participating, quite unaware, in a a far more venerable ritual than I could have imagined when we walked the lines of the family farm and touched its corner posts. I thought we had invented our own protocols; in fact we were mysteriously in touch with historic rites. No wonder we asked for cake.

So far as I can determine, the Selectmen of my town have not typically sponsored a parish-ale feast when they have perambulated the bounds. The challenge of the ambulating would seem to justify a celebration even if local tradition did not. Perhaps we should schedule the completion of perambulating the bounds just before Old Home Day, Firemans' Muster, Church Picnic, or whatever blast, ball, fair, or feast is already on the town agenda. We could revive a custom that goes back to English parishes, one too good to last:

> . . . in Henry VIII's reign the occasion had become an excuse for so much revelry that it attracted the condemnation of a preacher who declared "these solemne and accustomable processions and supplications be nowe growen into a right foule and detestable abuse."

There you have it! Offhand, one wouldn't have supposed that ordinary "solemne and accustomable" perambulations could get out of bounds to that extent, but here is eloquent proof that bounds beating is a potent business, tapping deep reservoirs of obscure passions.

Despite the bad press in King Henry's day, four hundred years ago, there is no doubt that the ritual has staying power, transcending politics and religion. Today the mystique and the heroics are still alive in British parishes. In Newbiggen-by-the-Sea (Northumberland) perambulating and beating the bounds has been practiced since 1235 and now takes place annually in May. The Tower parish bounds in London are beaten every third year, the choirboys striking each of the thirty-one boundary marks with willow wands. One of the bounds of St. Clement Danes's parish is in the river Thames and is reached by boat for its beating; another of the parish bounds is in an awkward place in Temple Gardens; a choirboy is lowered by his heels to beat this one. In Richmond (Yorkshire) the perambulating procession used to include a wade in the river Swale—a task now performed by the official parish Water Wader. In Crompton (Lancastershire), to beat the bounds (every seventh year) requires swimming across Besom Hill reservoir and climbing over the King's Arms Hotel. The pageantry goes on.

I've mentioned these representative parables of pluck for their inspirational value, but also to strengthen the faint hearts of perambulating New England Selectmen—they who contemplate the pleasures of following town bounds through the swales of boggy brook, across the ledge and up through the puckerbrush and juniper on the face of Old Baldy Mountain. They do not walk alone. If Yankee resolve and shrewdness fail, they have most of Western Christendom at their side.

And the tale has not yet reached its terminus.

Medieval parishes got their practice of perambulating and beating the bounds from the the Romans.

My big book tells me that "it may have been derived from the Roman Terminalia, a festival celebrated on the 22nd of February in honour of Terminus, the god of landmarks, to whom cakes and wine were offered, sports and dancing taking place at the boundaries." Cake again! Surely someone will observe that on February 22—Terminalia—we Americans celebrate George Washington's birthday, he who grew up to mark bounds as a surveyor, and later to reset the boundaries of the British Empire! It may be a coincidence and it may not.

Who, then, is this god Terminus? From the *Oxford Classical*

Dictionary we learn that this great god of landmarks was a deity to be reckoned with. Something immensely grave lies behind these cheerful medieval parish revels, these New England town laws. When an important boundary was set in ancient Rome, an animal, together with fruits and wines, was sacrificed and burned on the bounds, after which the boundary stone was anointed, crowned with garlands, and solemnly set in the hot ashes. The penalty for moving such a boundary stone was death. Termination. Old Testament Hebrews heard similar warnings: "Thou shalt not remove thy neighbor's landmark, which they of old time have set" (Deuteronomy 19:14). Undoubtedly, such landmarks too were set with ceremony and sacrifice. The ancients were solemn folk; not like the medieval rabble at the cake-and-ale parish parties!

I imagine that the only sacrifice involved in setting the corner posts of my father's eighty acres was the labor involved, and I am glad now that as a boy I added some simple ceremony to them. I thought we were walking, but we were really perambulating. The landmark posts we touched were wood and won't last much longer, but I'll never forget where they were. The stones by which the original settler, Ebenezer Wood, marked the bounds of my own land in New Hampshire were set with permanence more in mind, and with a larger investment of toil and ceremony. It wasn't easy: they were anointed with plenty of perspiration, and now the years have given them a garland of lichen and moss, the land's own emblems of endurance. My hat's off.

I daresay that old god Terminus hovers over a long list of human habits and traditions, not just the casual perambulating of my youth and more contemplative inspections of my own New Hampshire boundaries. He broods over my state's perambulating law and the bound-beating in today's England too, over the parish-ales of the medieval church, over ancient Roman festivals and Old Testament laws. Having come to understand this, I find it a wonderfully satisfying set of perfectly implausible connections, proving beyond doubt that the continuity of human experience goes deeper, and through remoter channels, than I had suspected. It's fine with me if checking out the rocks on my boundaries ties me to the Roman Empire! May there be henceforth a new spring in my step as I "walk" and "beat" with the Anglo-Saxons and "perambulate" with the Romans from one "terminus" of my property to the other.

16

Reflections on a Church Fair

Washington Congregational Church was organized in 1780 and that year the Reverend George Leslie, declining a professorship at Dartmouth College, came here to serve as first pastor.
—WASHINGTON CHURCH BULLETIN

In the early days the minister was chosen at the town meeting, and the church was supported by taxes: nobody had heard of separation of church and state.

The Congregational Church has been here a long time, having originated even before its Meetinghouse, which dates from 1787. That Meetinghouse, still the pride and glory of the community, served both town and church for over fifty years. The present church building was erected in 1840 and has helped since then to sustain a Congregational presence in the center of town. (There is a Baptist Church in East Washington.) Three structures, Town Hall (1787), Congregational Church (1840), and School (1884), are carefully arranged on Washington's town common, a bouquet of classic buildings. The much-photographed scene restates an idealized image of the rural New Engand town—now a cliché, certainly, but a beloved one for all of that.

The church on our town common has had some dry times. For a period of about sixty years—from 1918 to 1977—there were only summer pastorates, seldom worship services in the winter. My wife and I clearly recall the first Sunday we attended the Congregational Church—it was the late 1960s—and how we were greeted with enthusiasm: "Looks like a crowd today," said a cheerful voice. Altogether, there were nine of us that day. That would not be a crowd today; so something has changed.

The bulletin explains: "Since 1977 the regular pastor has been the Reverend H. Gardner Andersen, and worship services have been held throughout the year each Sunday morning. During this time membership and attendance have grown considerably and Washington Congregational Church is now affiliated with the United Church of Christ." In addition to holding its regular Sunday worship services, the church is a community presence in various ways. While some of these involve doing good deeds quietly, others, like church suppers, are very conspicuous fund-raisers.

The semiannual fair is, among other things, a fund-raiser. Now I know that I was born with a flat-out lack of affection for the whole church fair idea—the clutter and hustle, the sheer bother, all that tired merchandise. To say nothing of the insidious cheerfulness. Wouldn't it be far more fun, say, to explore a swamp? Didn't our forefathers "sell" pews and then simply tax them? Do we really need to do this? Oh, we need to, all right, say the wiser voices. And, indeed, we might do it even if it weren't necessary, for fund-raisers of one kind or another, for one good cause or another, are a serious cottage industry up here. The town of Washington never saw a good cause—make that Good Cause—it didn't like. Every voluntary organization in our town—eight or ten of them, depending on how you count—has fund-raisers regularly, or feels ashamed if it doesn't. Anyway, some years have passed, and I have capitulated—having come to understand the church fair as a transcendental transaction, and therefore part of the church's liturgical calendar, like Christmas and Easter.

For some time we had all known that there were foundation problems under the church. The good people who built it long ago left undone a few things which they ought to have done, and they also did a few things that they ought not to have done. So the church needed support. The bulletin tells us: "During the years 1984 to 1986 the members of the Church undertook a major restoration and renewal project. The hundred-and-forty-year-old building was raised, a foundation and full basement installed underneath, then lowered again to its previous elevation. This added space for kitchen, restrooms, library and Fellowship Room . . . and provided opportunity for expanded church programs." Paying for all that is one impressive reason for having a fair.

So after years of trying to keep my hands clean, minimally helping on fair day, assisting with the cleanup, trying to be a supportive presence while being absent as much as possible, and above all, avoiding all responsibility, I got roped in. Jean Murdough was in charge and summarily handed me an entire department to organize, set up, manage, be responsible for. I was put in charge of selling rusty tools.

We didn't admit that, of course; plain *Tools* was what the sign would say in my department. "Just do a good job," she said sternly, "and try not to think about it too much." Well, it's a lot harder not to think about these things than you'd think. I decided to fight the temptation by taking careful note of what happened and to present an exact report, hour by hour, of my experience. This is it:

Eight o'clock. Everyone knows that church fairs begin on summer Saturdays at about ten o'clock. They are wrong. It is *selling* that begins at ten o'clock; the fair day begins at dawn. I was told to report for work at 7:30 A.M.; so I arrived a decent and fashionable half hour late and found the entire town common in upheaval. Tables were coming out of the church, the school, and town hall, tarps were getting propped up, people were driving stakes, bustle and energy were everywhere. All over the place Good Cause sentiment hung in the air, thick enough, I reckoned, to recharge the batteries of the entire New England Good Cause Movement. People were smiling. In short, it was an assault on a person's normal demeanor.

Inside the church itself the pews were chock-a-block with all sorts and conditions of hardware and dry goods. We were instructed to empty the church out on the common, everything to a place near a sign that might fit it. For the next half hour a gang of deacons and similar servants of the church lugged stuff out and onto the lawn. I didn't ask how it got in there. Well before ten o'clock some of the elderly faithful already looked exhausted. So much for the notion that fairs just appeared about midmorning by spontaneous combustion.

Nine o'clock. The hour finds me puttering around at my tool area, mainly a picnic table, arranging things into what I hope makes the least sad display—saws, hammers, screwdrivers, rasps, wrenches, rakes, hoes, forks, pails of rusty nails. I will cheer myself by taking a stroll to get the general lay of fairland The morning mist is lifting, something like order is settling on the common, and people seem to know what they are doing. Fortunately, they don't know what *I* am doing, namely, taking notes.

I mentally name the streets. This one on my left must be Tacky Row, though the signs said *White Elephants* and *Clothes*. It runs straight to Castoff Corners, where the places of business are named *Toys* and *Books*, and then heads past a sweet-smelling place named *Food*, which has stacked up enough pastries to stuff a starved elephant. In the old days that would have been the whole fair right there: toys and books, elephants, clothes, and baked goods—your basic five-star garden variety church fair, where a bargain was meant to be either played with or read, reused, worn, or eaten.

No more. Here is Highbrow Alley and three classy departments: *Antiques*, *Crafts*, and *Dolls*. I had heard that the church had a hard-core fair faction in its midst, and that they had held meetings for months. This display is the result: tables of weavings and crewel work, exotic wreathes of grapevine and herbs, dried flower arrangments, handcrafted furniture, and lots of other classy artsy-craftsy stuff. I greet Martha among the crafts, Gwen among the dolls, and Helen and Andy among the antiques—no puns here, just heads of departments. The seductive intent, I can see, is to use quality to entice early Christmas shoppers. Personally, I find it difficult to sustain a properly depressed rummage sale mood in this environment, so I take a short cut back to Rusty Lane, and retreat to my own lair behind *Tools*.

Although I evidently work in a low-class neighborhood, I also have my family nearby: my young son Colin heads up *Toys*, and my wife Grace stands bravely with the rest of the team behind the dreary and elephantine pile of former household goods in *White Elephants*. I bring out from the church some more files and shovels, several wrenches and rakes from far better days, and also the third and fourth rusty saws, and I lay them out as bait, casually assuring curious bystanders that some of these are actually *objets d'art*. I wonder which ones I could possibly have in mind.

Ten o'clock. But I'm right; there is value there after all. At the fair's opening signal people begin reaching over each other to get some of my tools. What do they see in them? Apparently, I am dealing in usable bargains. (Soon I even wanted to buy a couple of the things myself: I found a rasp for a dollar and a huge screwdriver and stuck them under the table, but somebody spotted them while I was distracted, retrieved them, and bought them—from me.) Sales were, as they say, "brisk" for a full twenty minutes. Followed by a forty-minute lull.

Eleven o'clock. Time to take a break and tour the other departments. I stop to see Rod Phipps at *Books* and he tells me he is doing well selling trashy novels. Bob Wright had also come by, he said, and had spotted one of his own college books—his name was in it—and had quickly bought it back. The suspicion was that his wife Jo Ellen had donated it, so I didn't ask if it was a history text or a trashy novel. Rod said that *his* wife had bought him a corduroy jacket to replace one she thought he had lost, not knowing that she had bought the very jacket that he had donated to last year's fair—when it hadn't sold. It's a good thing this is a Good Cause.

Over in *Clothes* I got rumors of the day's leading foul-up. Rev. Andersen had worn his new London Fog raincoat ("The first good coat I have ever had!") to the fair this morning. Discovering he didn't need it, he had folded it carefully and put it down in the front pew of the church. Somebody carried it out with all the other things and put it down under the *Clothes* sign, where it was sold for a few dollars to a stranger before the truth was discovered. It's a very good thing this is a very Good Cause.

I realize now that this is going to be a confusing day, but I cross over to *Toys* to ask my son for his news. He has just sold himself a ticket to a 1946 World Series game at Fenway Park, a six-dollar ticket at the bargain price of two dollars. The other good news, he said, was that toys and games and all kinds of things were selling "wicked awesome," and he couldn't figure out why; and the bad news was that two presumably adult customers had actually quarrelled, loudly, about who had rights to a twenty-five-cent ceramic doll. This spectacle so rattled him that I feared he might develop an early disdain for the church. Without realizing it I lapsed into a fatherly pep talk on the theory and practice of the church fair. Oddly bouyed by my own rhetoric, I headed back to Rusty Lane.

Twelve o'clock. I have to note that as the sun has gotten higher and the day hotter, the prospects appear dimmer for the sale of my two big items, which are, as it happens, both wood-burning stoves. I promoted them early as good Christmas presents, but results have been meager. There is a fifty-dollar price tag on one, and at twelve noon, with the thermometer at 85 in the shade and no shade, a man offers me twenty. By twelve-thirty it is 87 degrees, my brain is getting blanched, Christmas seems far away, and we agree to split the difference: he gets it for twenty-three, my biggest sale of the day.

One o'clock. Time for another break, this time to visit the folks in *White Elephants*, a large and prosperous department. It should be said that in our part of New England, the white elephant is a prolific species, well adapted to its natural habitat in and about the homes of our town, where it thrives like the mosquito, the mouse, and the green garden weed. White

Elephants actually come in many colors and shades (including lamp, eye, and window), also in many sizes, shapes, vintages, varieties, values, and volumes. Here, for example, is one small elephant implausibly disguised as a hairdryer of yesteryear, complete with hoses, pipes, and bags, and two large boxes to stuff it all in. Next to it I find these: a sack of shoelaces, many used, a pile of pot covers, a curious lamp made from a fishing rod and a bowling pin, six ladies' plastic handbags, half a jar of Evening in Paris bath salts, a fireplace waffle iron that stands on its own legs, a smoking stand that doesn't, a great gray wig, thirteen saltshakers, some empty, a chipped milk bottle, a toilet seat cover, four objects that nobody can identify; and least but not last, a rather familiar-looking triangular "one-side" toaster.

I arrived at the elephant kingdom just in time to relieve a young woman's puzzlement about the toaster. I gave her a quick and knowing demonstration: "You snap open the door, like so—it's hinged on the bottom, see—and the toast slides down on the open door and gets flipped top-to-bottom and back-to-front as you let the door spring shut. It's state of the art, circa 1939," I said, "and unlike modern toasters this thing will never burn both sides of the bread at once."

Further details I might have withheld, but her encouraging smile elicits a spasm of candor not usually associated with salesmanship, and I plunge ahead: "Yes, it really works. However, about one time in four you may burn the toast (on just one side); about one time in four you may burn your fingers (both sides); and about one time in four the toast may not slide down at all. But, about one time in four it may work like a charm."

"How do you know all this?" say her eyebrows.

No stopping me now. "Years and years ago we had a toaster of this kind, which we got secondhand at a church fair. We liked it for a while, but there came another longer while when we didn't: it got so that we'd begin to flinch or twitch when we approached it. We had to send it back. To the fair. You know, it used to show up now and then, making the rounds in town, I suppose, looking for a permanent home. It was just like this one, only . . . Oh, no!"

And indeed it *is* this one. Our renegade toaster has got religion again and is once more riding the church fair circuit. But we may be grateful for small things: every time the old burner passes through the fair, the current Good Cause collects a few dollars.

Two o'clock. The fair will wind down in an hour, and already the common is becalmed. Soon I shall have time to think about this fair—despite instructions to the contrary. Why has it been a good day? Although the items left, some not yet positively identified, are under stern judgment, unlovely and unloved, everyone is cheered by everything that has been redeemed, including even some attitudes.

Back on Rusty Lane I have just a few tools left to peddle. During the final hour, with lowered prices now, I sell a wooden rake, another bucksaw, old but shapely, and an older two-handed crosscut saw, the latter seemingly completely worn out. What is going on? Someone cleans out the back of his father's garage, his neighbor's attic, and someone else is elated with the yield? Yesterday a discard, today an *objet d'art*. Those old rakes and saws: today they are utterly converted from their old way of life and made new again. ("The stone which the builders rejected has become the chief cornerstone.") Here on the town common, flat on the grass in front of the church, these old rakes are born again—as interior decorations. Their new owners told me so. Many of the tools of the day, I now realize, are leaving the countryside and moving to the city to adorn the walls of a den or a living room. Only the first phase of their life is over; everything in their derelict past is forgiven as they are born again. There are sermons in junk.

At three o'clock we dismantle the tarps and gather up the fair's scattered fragments and figments.

So what is a church fair, after all? Well, in my town it is at least twenty or thirty things. A great gathering of castoffs; an advance guard for a Good Cause; a place for the summer folks to furnish their cottages; an automatic community attic cleaner; an all-American institution; a charming way to restore the church's foundation; a stylized means for the neighbors to swap their crockery without the vague burdens of giving and accepting; a vast social machine for transforming junk to treasure; a covert theology of forgiveness and renewal; an addictive local habit; a clatter of irony and clichés; a thick slice of rural life; a money-maker; bargain center; corny sideshow; summer picnic; craft exhibit; summer theater; church liturgy; revival meeting; whatever you choose to make of it. If I were a preacher and had to make something of it, I'd go straight for an old saw: A church fair is a parable of the Christian doctrine of conversion, of rebirth—which may be why we continue to reenact this ritual right in front of our church on the town common.

17

Can't Hurry a Rock

Most of us in rural New England have a hearty respect for the rocks and stones scattered throughout our fields and forests. We feel ambivalence about them too: recalling the pioneers who farmed here, or tried to, who worked around those great gray rocks; admiring the implausible but still handsome stone walls they slowly, patiently built in years gone by. Something there is that dearly loves a wall.

We need to be serious about rocks and stones, of course, but we don't always have to be solemn. The whole weighty subject can be lightened now and then with a sense of play. I acquired my perspective largely thanks to Wendell Ashley, Curt Rowe, and Charlie Kulbacki, all of them scions of the tribe "Yankee Handyman," a legendary race. My views on rocks may be still a little unsettled but this is a partial account of their genesis.

Very early in our time here I was directed to Wendell as a possible assistant, and I spoke to him about helping me deal with some of my local challenges—fallen stone walls, listing buildings, forest attacking every meadow. Wendell assured me he would tackle any odd job I had, anything at all, without fear or favor. Then he added firmly that he would not do—would not even consider doing—anything whatever that involved work with rocks. Seeing my surprise (What doesn't involve rocks?) and my evident disapproval, he proceeded immediately to denounce with passion all the rocks of New

Hampshire. He cursed the rocks of the land, even the small ones, with a fury and eloquence that, had he been a holy man instead of a handyman would have shriveled stones to dust and ashes. I listened open-mouthed. Eventually he simmered down enough to justify his feelings, which he did by declaring that he had always hated rocks and always would.

Well! The bald strength of this opinion, and its unabashed eccentricity, made it memorable for its own sake but also for the way it started to rattle my own ideas into shape. I was new to this field, and promptly set out to explore my feelings about rocks. At the interior of my own sentiments, however, I found nothing much: bland regard for stone walls and a deep pool of indifference toward individual rocks. Evidently I was exploring what was—compared with Wendell's—an entirely undeveloped sensibility: he was earnestly wallowing hip deep in regions of passion I hardly knew existed. Take a modest example: while building a stone wall, if I accidentally drop a stone on my foot I can manage to despise that stupid rock fervently for perhaps a minute, maybe two—while the pain is at its fiercest—but no more. Where is the amateur who can point a beam of convinced hate at a dumb rock longer than that without the mind wandering to higher things? Try it; it is not easy. Wendell can do it effortlessly; he is a pro. He has held his favorite hates rigid as a ramrod for a full lifetime without faltering. Marvelous.

For me the point was that, at one stroke, I was cured forever of my complacent lack of partiality in this matter. Neutrality would not do. To this day the inspiring picture of Wendell doing his devotions over the rocks of New Hampshire remains an indelible inspiration. It turns out, however, that I may be countersuggestible: for I suspect it was the purity and passion of his animosity that first aroused in me the glimmerings of what has since then become a genuine affection for rocks and stones. Indeed, I was quickly reminded that Shakespeare, after all, had commended sermons in stones—sermons I would gladly seek out and attend before making up my mind.

❦

I recalled that Wendell in his passion had seen only *rocks*, whereas I in my innocence had seen only *stones*. There is a difference.

A philosopher by training, I began to ponder this difference, but concluded that you cannot comprehend it by studying stone and rocks. A more abstract inquiry is needed, for the difference may not show up out of doors, but only inside, within the concepts. While it may be hard to tell a stone from a rock, it is possible to tell a "stone" from a "rock." It is not just a matter of size and appearance, but of reputation, style, and character. To fully understand this you have to survey the field through eyes other than your own, and look in the places where the sensibility and eloquence of our forebears have left their traces in our language.

First off, there appears to be something more ominous about rocks. We know of New England's "stern and rock-bound coast," and suspect certainly that it would have been less stern if made of stone. And while we would never describe a ship or a marriage, or even a martini, as "on the stones," these fragile entities are betimes on the rocks, and the longer they are there the worse they are for it—which tells you something. Moreover, stones are famed for a resourcefulness not found among rocks: it's a rolling stone that gathers no moss, and a lone stone that kills two birds. And not one of them that a thorough effort leaves unturned. Stones but not rocks run to epigram and poetry; rocks seem to have a kind of social and moral obtuseness about them.

But once you start down this road you realize that there is far more to it than that. There are cultural attractions of stone: Stone Age, Stonehenge, the Rosetta Stone, Stone Mountain, the Philosophers' Stone, the Stone of Scone. None of these is remotely matched by, say, Plymouth Rock, or the Rock of Gibraltar, or rocks of that type. And what *is* the Rock of Ages? Nobody knows. Although there are lots of hybrid rocks at large—rock candy, rock salt, bedrock, rock-bottom, rock band, and rock maple, for example—it is fully understandable that there has never been a certified Rock Age.

Stones are more tractable than rocks as metaphors for coldness and insensitivity. More color and finesse are involved, for example, in a good stiff case of stonyheartedness, or a brisk bout of political stonewalling, than in being rock-ribbed, selling out at rock-bottom prices, or having rocks in your head. And there is one spectacular stone, unlike any rock ever reported, which is justly famous for not existing: it is the Philosophers' Stone, with reputed powers to transmute base metals into gold. No rock in history has achieved similar fame by failing to exist. Most hybrid stones are far less exotic and remote than hybrid rocks, and have, indeed, an almost pliable, domestic character: hearthstone, cobblestone, cornerstone, touchstone, hailstone, millstone, milestone, lodestone, grindstone, whetstone, flagstone, gallstone. And, finally, tombstone.

Now, if by these means we have teased out the facts properly—and added the proper proportions of whimsy and philosophy—we might tentatively conclude that stones are fairly resilient and resourceful; at their best, they may indeed be good for sermons. Rocks, in contrast, tend to be ominous, remote, and a bit opaque—no room for sermons there. Perhaps the sages understood all that just by looking at them in the field, but that would take sharper eyes than mine.

The question may be asked whether there is a still more intimate link between rocks and stones, between "rock" and "stone," a connection not accounted for by literature or geology and not visible to the naked eye. Having thought about this too—again without productive answers, of course—first while sitting upon a rock and then while sitting upon a stone wall, I went once more to a higher authority. The matter becomes exquisitely abstract. If you pick up the unabridged *Oxford English Dictionary*, each volume of which is as heavy as a rock, you will find that it makes the most of apparent similarities between rocks and stones. It tells us that a rock is "a large rugged mass of stone" or just a "large detached mass of stone" (page 2,563). A stone is "a piece of rock or hard mineral substance," or just "hard compact material of which stones and rocks consist" (page 3,068). That's the official dictionary summary, an abstract message undistorted by special pleading from geology or poetry. It is meager intelligence, though, for it comes to this: stones are made of rock, and rocks are made of stone. Philosophical dead end.

Clearly, we need insights more down to earth. For me this was supplied by Curt Rowe, a handyman who owns and operates a bulldozer and an earth excavator, and who has a well-deserved reputation for skill in constructing ponds. We were fortunate to hire him for our pond. While he excavated, moving tons of soil expertly, I watched. Sometimes he unearthed a large rock, and when I spotted one I liked I asked him to shove it aside for later use. He thought I must be joking, but eventually I convinced him to do it. He could not fathom my motives, even when I tried to explain that, at the end of the work, I wanted them placed at strategic points on the landscape around the pond. He did not approve. Still, he cheerfully humored me—at least while I watched—thinking me quite wacky but probably harmless. When my back was turned he buried all rocks as quickly as they appeared.

One day after the pond was completed I went to see him at his homestead in Hillsboro. As you drive up the hill to his farm something strange, almost eerie, about the landscape registers with you, but you may not be sure at first just what it is. Then it hits you: here suddenly there are no stone walls. None. From Curt Rowe's dooryard on the hilltop you catch a wide view, but you cannot see one stone wall, and not a rock is visible on the landscape. Around his nearby pond, same thing: no rock in sight. Curt Rowe has a big bulldozer and an earth excavator, and he happens to hate rocks and to regard stone walls as an impertinent nuisance. He has the equipment to do it, so on his farm he killed and buried every one.

Like Wendell, Curt may have excuses. I think I catch in their warm loathing for rocks a thin atavistic echo of the impulse that more than a century ago lured the real farmers of New England off these stony hillsides and onto the fallow plains of the Midwest. Perhaps here at the bottom of their New England souls, beyond the reach of reason or will and unsoftened by time, is the ancestral memory of toil and struggle with a rocky and unyielding earth, a memory and a pain alive still, its message festering through the generations until now: rocks are not to be loved.

Whenever I become too solemn about my own mossy-marbled stone walls I drive over to Curt Rowe's place and gaze around. That is one man's idea of a good landscape, one he has proudly created himself.

It was Charlie Kulbacki who contributed the next bit of wisdom to my education in these recondite matters. His viewpoint was philosophical and moral, like Wendell's, though more refined; and it took in the entire landscape, like Curt's, though not so ambitiously.

Charlie and another friend and I were rebuilding a warped and wobbly retaining wall, and one rock had been especially resistant. For more than a hour we concentrated upon it in stony silence, prying with levers, shoveling, twisting with poles and fulcrums, and it was not yet in place. Our friend was still in there, relentlessly scraping, prying, shoving, eager as a hound dog digging out a woodchuck. Still no real progress. Charlie stepped back, thoughtfully surveyed the situation, looked it over yet again, mentally checked the options, then summoned the relevant wisdom and broke the silence with one smooth stroke of his verdict. "You can't hurry a rock," said Charlie.

Perfect. I am not a philosopher for nothing: I can recognize a genuine synthesis of poetry, morality, and geology when I see it. And this may be the compressed and studied wisdom that has eluded Wendell and Curt. Grateful for such gems, I have tucked this specimen—suitably generalized to other weighty subjects and objects—into my own ideological retaining wall, a part of my permanent defense against the world's wobble and its frivolous erosions, a retardant to its hectic pace. I call it Charlie's Theorem. Already it has saved me untold quantities of energy; and thanks to it I am making my peace with the unhurryable rocks that enrich my dooryard, garden, and landscape. In a better, fairer world Charlie would have been a counselor to Sisyphus, not merely to the neighbors and to me.

Moreover, armed with Charlie's Theorem, I can often

throw a flood of new light on otherwise dark corners of the New England cultural landscape. This is easy to illustrate from well-known texts conveniently at hand, such as the diary for 1712 of the Salem witch-trial judge, old Samuel Sewall. The entry for April 14, which has probably never been understood until now, is especially provocative, showing Sewall to be a spiritual ancester of my New Hampshire neighbors. He writes: "I lay'd a Rock on the North-east corner of the Foundation of the Meetinghouse. It was a stone I got out of the Common."

If we read it aright, it tells us all we need to know. To such a reader it is crystal-clear that the lower-case *stone* he got out of the common had become an upper-case *Rock* by the time he got it into the Meetinghouse foundation. How come? Evidently, he had tried to hurry the stone along, and it turned into a rock. So he had a Rock on the corner, but no cornerstone.

We can mark it down for permanent reference: the sermon in every stone is its potential for rockhood. What we have here is a simple corollary to Charlie's Theorem. I Call it Sewall's Corollary: "A Rock is a stone being hurried."

We call them stone walls, not rock walls. Could we love a rock wall? Warm up to a Rockhenge? Normally, if a lump of our native natural hardware has been deposited in a wall, or even in a henge, it has been handled in a patient and unhurried way: it is still a stone. We know our predecessors built these stone walls slowly, struggling with them over the course of many years, etching everywhere great gray lines into landscapes of the future. Something there is that dearly loves a wall.

18

Chicken Dinner: The Unwritten Recipe

In our part of New Hampshire you can't travel very far on a country road without seeing a homemade sign announcing "Fresh Eggs." That's a rural commodity I heartily approve of, and the recurring signs never fail to elicit a thought: Perhaps this is the year when I will get chickens. For a long time I have had an elusive feeling that I *ought* to get chickens. Maybe it is the eggs. Maybe it is something out of my youth. Maybe I have heard too much of the red meat versus white meat background noise in our culture. A few years ago when the idea of getting chickens came strongly to the fore I took evasive action and bought my wife a big book: *365 Recipes for Chicken*. The first year we got through twenty-seven.

Last year, under attack again, I contented myself with just ducking in at a neighbor's Fresh Eggs sign to admire the birds. I saw nothing unusual, just a flock of hens poised at about the third link from the beginning of the food chain, cheerfully striving to recycle grass and grain into white meat, all the while also working up a batch of fresh eggs from scratch and bugs and grubs. As chickens go they were predictably mindless, carefree, almost jovial, and you could see from their demeanor that they didn't care a cluck about salmonella or cholesterol. It did not seem to be a vivid part of their self-image either that, as chickens, they were not red meat. Still, I would consider getting some. That was last year.

More recently, I found myself standing in the slow line at the supermarket and chose to redeem the shining hour by scanning the least unreadable item available, a magazine article which, as it happened, was dripping with dewy prose about the great days on the family farm of yesteryear. That's where I came from, so I perked up. Here was a soft-core supermarket rhapsody on the old-time religion: independence and self-sufficiency, fresh eggs and thick cream and homemade butter, root cellars stuffed with pesticideless vegetables, sweet water from an ever-flowing well, chicken dinners drawn right from the farmyard. Literary fare of that sort is meant to get your glands going. Probably not unwholesome thought-food, but slightly overseasoned with romance.

I ought to know, come to think about it; for I have been there. What jarred my memory was the quick and easy reference, so blithely unexplained by this cultured city author, to the farm-based chicken dinner! Ah, yes, not white meat, but chicken dinner. How well do I remember the chicken dinner recipe that served the farm family of my youth so well. It's not in the book.

Since the domestic chicken is an ancient fowl, this recipe was hundreds of years old, and used by thousands, probably millions, before our particular family took it up. It needs no recommendation from me. My version may be faintly tinged with personal flavoring, but I've added nothing exotic. In its heyday this recipe was not even written down. All the more reason to do so, for it may nourish both the body and the soul.

Generally, when there was a chicken dinner in the offing, cooperative efforts were necessary to implement this recipe: In our community three persons participated, a farmer, a farmer's wife, and a chicken holder. Also a chicken. The recipe has eight steps.

First: Catch your chicken. The question is: which one among these hundreds? The answer is: no spring chicken has the required character. We want a dowager type, one entering her golden years, and past her prime time for egg-laying. On our farm we put a leg band on every hen so we could tell her age at a glance, for we found that after she had put in three years of unremitting egg-laying, she grew tired of it and was ready for a career change, such as advancing to the city market or entering a local pot. Otherwise, senility might intrude, and she would just drop from the roost some night.

So we select a lady bird of known vintage, a chubby one of course, and preferably one in the henhouse, where cornering her is easier than on the straightaway outside. Simply running down an old hen in the yard is both inelegant sport and pretty hard to do, even if she is too modest or decrepit to fly. That bird can cut capers that will surprise the city slicker in you, and a chase would raise such a rumpus with the rest of the flock that they would produce bloodclots in their fresh eggs for the next three days. So, we resort to the henhouse.

The farmer knows that you can waylay an old hen pretty well with a long stick on whose end is affixed a tight wire crook, something like a large fishhook. You reach out carefully into the cackle of cornered hens, hook the leg of the chosen bird and yank her smartly off her feet. You pounce quickly, and that's it. It's not much like catching fish and it's quite lacking in finesse, but it works. She'll squawk like an old biddy for a while, and you'll be henpecked for sure, but that's farming. The spread of pelvic bones under the soft down of the rump—you can feel this with your fingers—will tell you whether she is laying eggs regularly. Widespread, three fingers: Yes, let her go for now and fish for another. Narrow spread, two fingers: No, she's had it as an egg layer and can now be graduated without regret to a higher place on the food chain.

Second: Slay the fowl. In the tall broom grass near the orchard is a large upright block of wood with two spikes set in it about two inches apart. This is a guillotine. One son, working as the designated chicken holder, holds the bird on its side near the block, one hand grasping both legs, the other hand steadying the body. The hen is no longer a *she*, only an *it*. You can feel its heart beat, and you may suspect that it is probably not amused by this part of the recipe. My father, cool, matter of fact, holds the chicken's head by the comb in his left hand and places the neck carefully on the block between the spikes. This assures that no sudden jerk will make the blow misfire. He learned this method from his father, who learned it from his. Everything is steady and held in place, although the chicken, probably suspicious by now, squawks a meek dissent. One firm stroke with the axe—my father never missed—and hen and head are separated, without pain. The chicken holder immediately tosses the bird gently into the grass a few feet away and then backs off.

The old dame is dead but not down. Every muscle in the bird's body goes into violent spasms, and the chicken starts to flop and bounce about in the grass, gyrating four feet into the air, and throwing a geyser of blood in every direction. We keep our distance while this very remarkable show is under way. Here is a decapitated fowl with more hot-ziggity vigor than it had ever shown in life, dancing about frantically like a . . . well, though I hate to say it, like a chicken with its head cut off. It's quite a way to go, and for overall dignity it undoubtedly beats dropping from the roost at night. A minute later the body is at parade rest, merely twitching, a huddled clump. (You don't know if you like this recipe? Maybe you don't really know if you like the farm, after all.)

Third: Undress the body. Two teakettles of boiling water have been prepared. The water goes into a pail, and the bird, held by the legs, is thrust into the hot water. Out, then in again. And again. That loosens the feathers. My father begins plucking, stripping the feathers quickly in the opposite direction from their natural lay, generally toward the neck. If—or, rather, when—he burns his hands in the hot feathers, he waits; when the feathers won't come off easily, he plunges the thing back into the hot water. This is messier than it sounds: the small wet downy feathers stick to his hands, to his pant legs, shirt, his cap, his nose. He shakes his hands to get rid of the sticky feathers: we are glad we are outdoors. If I am the one conscripted as chicken holder today I hang on to the thing by the feet while he picks feathers from the bird and from himself, finally wiping his hands on his bib overalls. The down feathers go into a separate pile, for they will eventually enter a pillow. When the carcass has been plucked clean, he wipes it off with a damp newspaper (on this farm there is no such thing as a paper towel). Now we see the rolls of rich golden fat under the skin, suggesting that this hen had not been laying eggs for weeks—just getting fat for the ascent up the chain.

Fourth: Transmit the carcass. Although certain pleasantries still remain, on our farm this was the point at which my father, following a pattern followed by most farmers, handed the project over to his wife, in one of those mysterious domestic divisions of labor never discussed, never explained, never deviated from. What comes next is not called butchering (that was for hogs), but "cleaning." It was not just that cleaning a chicken was woman's work; rather it was housework and it happened that farm women did that. My mother cleaned hundreds of chickens, all of them in the house, and my father cleaned hundreds of rabbits, which he had shot in the woods; but he did that job in the barn and delivered only the meat to the house. My father never cleaned a chicken nor my mother a rabbit. Such were the gender roles—fully understood, fully approved.

Fifth: Prepare for radical surgery. Cleaning a chicken requires two more sets of newspaper. First, my mother opens all the lids on the kitchen range, exposing the live coals. She stuffs the opening full of lightly crushed newspaper, which promptly roars into high flames. With bare hands she passes the chicken rapidly back and forth, upside down and backwards through the flames; for when she got the carcass it had dozens of tiny pin feathers, too small to pluck by hand. In the flames they are singed away. She learned this from her mother, who learned it from hers.

At all steps of the process I was alert to the prospect of a little drama: catching the hen might have proved a challenge, or even *finding* it in the crowd, if there were only a few left of the chosen vintage; the chicken might peck your hand and surprise you into dropping it while you were going for the axe; the bouncing of the body after the beheading might reach record-breaking heights (five or six feet were not unheard of); and certainly watching the flames roar out of the stove during the pin feather singeing, sending soot to the ceiling, was a sight worth seeing. For me, being ten years old and big enough to be a chicken holder was not bad, for I understood all this as one of the rites of the family farm.

Sixth: Open the package. Whereas rabbits are cleaned with a jackknife, chickens are cleaned with a paring knife, and it is done over newspapers on the kitchen table, where tomorrow the chicken will appear again. Then it will be the dining table. As to opening the carcass itself, well, it's been said that when you have seen the inside of one chicken you have probably seen them all. (Anyway, I *think* it's been said . . . has now, anyhow.) There is one exception: occasionally we found an egg inside, with a flaky and still-soft shell. "Now, that's a *fresh* egg," my mother says, lifting it gently. She'll honor this egg by saving it for cake. I remember those cakes.

Occasionally, she would find a whole string of egglets, each one smaller than the next, for fresh eggs are not created one at a time but on the assembly-line principle, each egg growing a little each day as it moves down the line. (You *knew* that? Most folks wouldn't have even thought to ask. Some say that if you follow out this string of ever smaller, tinier, receding eggs, you may at last unravel the ancient mystery about the firstness of the chicken or the egg. But I prefer the mystery to the answer, whatever it is.)

During the first times that I watched my mother open a chicken I wondered how anyone could tell meat from guts: it all looked like the same sort of mess. The hands that twice-weekly kneaded our bread dough and nightly tucked us into our quilt covers were now probing with similarly practiced expertise far into the recesses of the carcass, feeling perhaps for the gizzard. But she always got everything sorted out all right. Then she rolled up the residue on the table into the newspaper and handed it to the former chicken holder to take out and bury in the garden, for whatever was not consumed was recycled.

Seventh: Prepare for cooking. Now the chicken is washed, cut into pieces, and put into a kettle for boiling. Being large and fat, the hen might have made a good roaster, but on our family farm we never had roast chicken, we had only fried chicken. On the other hand, being old and fat it might have roasted up as tough as an old crow.

Watching these last steps before cooking, I might catch a glimpse of what is fundamental and profound in these rural rituals: for it was a masculine task to feed and raise the bird, and a masculine endeavor that reduced the hen to a fowl, then to a body, then to a carcass; after which it was a feminine skill to eviscerate that carcass, elevate it to white meat, and finally, and elegantly, transform it into chicken dinner for a family. Therein lies the spirit and the genius of this recipe.

Last: Cook the chicken. The meat is now boiled with a little salt until it is tender, and then fried with butter and pepper until it is crisp and golden.

Although our chicken dinners were always dispatched with universal acclaim and delight, no one on our family farm ever hit upon the modern idea that the steps in the recipe were few, or effortless, or that the good life we lived was easy. I didn't pick that up until a generation later when I started *reading* about the simple life of those golden days.

I know today too, as I didn't then, that there are at least 365 chicken recipes other than this, most of them easier, and all of them starting farther from the henhouse and nearer to the dining room. I have tried dozens of them, and I have nothing against them.

As for my own recipe, although it has brought satisfaction to countless millions for untold generations, it is not guaranteed to do so today, especially for those to whom the real simplicity and directness of the old ways may be shocking or new. Anyway, I didn't lay it out primarily to recommend it. I'm remembering it. Perhaps the recipe, remembered, can help to spare us from shortsightedness, and from the glib and misbegotten idea that a dinner really starts at the supermarket.

19

Six Hundred Road Agents

We in Washington have always had a lovers' quarrel with our roads.

It was our personal fate to join the quarrel before we had even purchased the Old Powers Place. In the mid-sixties Grace and I had our first intimate experience with Half Moon Pond Road. April 30 it was—we remember it well—and we had driven up from Connecticut, ostensibly to check on the daffodils we had planted the previous fall, for we were still testing the place before buying it. We didn't know it, but it was still "mud season," New England's fifth season, which lasts three or four months: by the calendar, much of March and a good chunk of April. It is the season when most of our roads, which are gravel, turn to soup, and just after our blacktop roads have suffered their annual case of frost heaves. At Half Moon Pond we saw the hand-lettered sign: "Mud." A dated sign certainly, we thought, and we blithely hurried past; after all, tomorrow is May Day.

Our innocence lasted just a half mile. Our 1957 VW Microbus deviated ever so slightly from the two road ruts and we were promptly sucked into soup up to our axles. Situation: hopeless. Nothing to do now but to walk back the muddy mile to the last occupied house and put ourselves at the mercy of a stranger—if we could find one. Yet heaven smiled upon us, as that house turned out to be the home of the town road agent, Philip Gaudet. He came with the town tractor and dragged us back to the center of the road, accepted our copious thanks gladly and our payment reluctantly, and we were on our way again. It had been a serious problem directly solved: we could like this town. Had things turned out otherwise, we might have retreated back to Flatland for good and never entered this local lovers' quarrel at all.

And the daffodils were up, another confirming sign. But if our first mistake had been not believing the "Mud" sign, our second mistake was to believe the sign near the house, which said "End of town road." This is the last house, we said, no one drives beyond here, and so parked our VW high and dry astride the grassy strip in the center of the road. But May Day was also the opening day of trout season, so at 5:30 A.M. we were honked awake by an eager fisherman unhappy that we had blocked his way to the headwaters. We reckoned that as soon as we figured out the local code we might feel comfortable in this community.

The code, as we learned, calls for putting our town roads in a special place in our hearts. That is not just my opinion. Howard Mansfield, a writer who lives in the nearby town of Hancock, New Hampshire, drops in sometimes on the Washington town meeting. Frequently, he finds that we are discussing roads—usually with passion, expertise, and detail. His recent book, *In the Memory House*, says:

> The debate on the roads in Washington lasts as long as the entire town meeting in Nelson, a town with a similar year-round population. Washington, it appears, is a town of six hundred road agents. There is an intense, fervent discussion of wing plows, culverts, gravel, farmers mix, sand, salt, frost heaves, drainage, class one to class six roads, scenic roads and "throwing it up" (closing roads). This must have been what the rough-and-tumble sectarian religious infighting was like

> one hundred years ago. Now it's roads. Roads are the military budgets of town meeting: expensive, complicated and you can never do enough. (p. 96)

Six hundred road agents! That's us. If I'd written that I'd be accused of exaggeration. But, fortunately, it's an impartial outsider's view, which makes it believable. Are there reasons why we are all self-appointed road agents? Experts? Maybe it has something to do with the lay of our land, with our townscape. This is a high, hilly, rocky region; we catch the sleet and snow as it passes, and our roads penetrate recesses angels fear to tread. We breathe a thinner air. And all this goes way back.

When in 1780 Ebenezer Wood bought the hundred acres we now occupy as Lovellwood, his deed referred to the road as "the highway that leads from Washington to Bradford." Highway? Sure. At that time, if you cut down a swath of trees you had a highway. It's pretty certain that what they really had was a crooked two-rut cart road weaving through the woods and leading to the next farm, a step farther into puckerbrush. For all of that, this road, now our beloved Half Moon Pond Road, is on a New Hampshire map drawn before the Revolutionary War and published in England in 1783, one of just two roads then marked out in town. Like other roads, its right-of-way was determined by the stone walls which soon grew up along its edges and still give it definition and scenic character. Of course, it has never been paved.

New Hampshire has no county road system, and there has always been a state/town tension about roads. State highway construction was started ages ago, before we were even a state, by Governor John Wentworth, the last colonial governor before the Revolutionary War, but with statehood we entered a long period of private enterprise. Starting about 1800, turnpike corporations with power of eminent domain sprang up like mushrooms all over New Hampshire. Their mission in each case was to build a road straighter and smoother and longer than the cart roads of the towns, and then charge the public for traveling them. It was to be an intertown highway system. (A "turnpike" is a toll barrier, a pole or pike that turned to admit the traveler—the term quickly came to be used for the road itself.) Between 1790 and 1820, about ten major and several dozen minor New Hampshire turnpike corporations were chartered.

A town that was tapped by a turnpike headed toward Boston or the seacoast was lucky. Washington was doubly so. Two major turnpikes joined in our little village center: the Second New Hampshire Turnpike, coming from the Connecticut River at Charleston, and continuing south through Hillsboro toward Boston; and the Croyden Turnpike from Lebanon, which joined the Second New Hampshire here. These important roads put Washington squarely on the thoroughfares from the Connecticut River to Boston—for decades a great economic boon. The town was accessible.

It would seem that the public liked the turnpikes better than investors did. Many turnpike corporations made but slim profits, or none, and within three or four decades most were out of business, leaving their roads to a grateful public as free highways. In Washington no tolls were collected on its turnpikes after 1837. The turnpike experience led New Hampshire—slowly and reluctantly, then as ever—to the painful idea that public roads would have to be built and maintained with public tax money. For a very long time the state legislature, completely in thrall to the more dramatic romance of railroads, chose to leave this mainly to the towns. Washington's population peaked for all time (1,150) just at the end of the turnpike era.

After the Civil War, when New Hampshire was being

laced up with railroad tracks, Washington's terrain was cheerfully bypassed. There was no way a railroad could reasonably scale these altitudes. So the town could then stagnate comfortably on the reserves, moral and economic, that it had accumulated in the more leisurely turnpike days. But it always remained accessible to trains in Hillsboro and Newport by stagecoach on the old turnpikes.

From the beginning and for a hundred years, Washington's town roads were constructed and managed through a simple "Surveyor" system. The town meeting voted a road budget and set an hourly wage, and the Selectmen appointed ten or more Surveyors of Roads who were each assigned a section of road. The local surveyor hired his neighbors to help him work on the road, replace and repair watering troughs, and the like. The main idea was that any citizens who wished could "work off" property taxes in this manner. From earliest days New Hampshire towns were firmly committed to public works programs that offered employment to any taxpayers who wanted it: building roads, pounds, cemeteries, meetinghouses, schools, more roads. No wonder road-building savvy flows in the ancestral blood up here. You inherit expertise, and you pass it around at town meeting.

Although a lion's share of the local property tax went into roads, given the terrain, it was certain that they would often be in bad shape; certain, too, that they would draw endless complaints. Records show that out-of-town travelers especially sought to collect damages for real and imagined injuries from Washington roads. Harlan Pike, for example, swore in 1880 that "by reason of the drifted and unsuitable condition of said highway my said horse became greatly bruised, swollen and badly lamed . . . ; and I claim damage therefore of said town to the extent of two hundred and fifty dollars." Did he expect to collect that at a time when surveyors were paid ten cents an hour? The same year Elwin Nichols swore that "my daughter Minnie . . . was thrown from a carriage and injured from a defective highway and I hereby claim reasonable compensation for damage to herself and carriage." So went the reports of outside experts. Everywhere, "defective highways" in "unsuitable condition."

Late in the nineteenth century, Washington town meetings opened a new debate, lasting several years, about buying a road scraper. Many worried that this would break up the old informal surveyor ways they had inherited. But the town took the plunge in 1894 and bought a Champion Road Scraper for $250, a road machine to be pulled by four or six horses. From that time too the town began to elect one road agent at the annual town meeting and put him solely in charge of operations. He handled the scraper and supervised those who would "work off" their taxes.

Undoubtedly, the scraper got here just in time, for in the 1890s autos were spotted in town and reported upon in the newspaper. True, the turnpikes were out of business, and the railroad wasn't coming, but there was still public transportation. The horse-drawn stagecoach left the center of town every morning and traveled the Second New Hampshire Turnpike to Hillsboro, and from there you could catch the train to Concord, and then to Boston. (There is no public transportation from Washington to Boston today.) However, the town roads of a hundred years ago still discouraged owning an auto. Not until 1911 did one come to stay in this town—ordered from the Sears Roebuck catalog. Sixty-five years later, Caroll Farnsworth, then well into his nineties, wrote down this account of that day in 1911.

> On July 6 Dad, Brother and I got a ride . . . to the freight office [in Hillsboro] to assemble our new Sears auto. The wheels were gotten on, and gas in the tank, and then we cranked it up. I then took the seat at the steering-bar and headed across the railroad and on to the fair-gounds. Then three laps around the race track for my first driving lesson, and then headed for home. Got there safely, took Cranes hills quite easily. It had twin cylinders, air cooled and friction drive, hard rubber tires. . . . I do not know that there was any other car owned in Town at that time.

Carroll Farnsworth died not long ago at age one hundred and four. We who knew him sometimes feel that we know, more or less, the entire history and theory and practice of Washington roads. In full cry at town meeting, we are all experts.

Has anything changed? In the 1890s the town debated for a few years and then courageously decided to buy a new scraper for $250. In the 1990s we debated for a few years and then courageously decided to buy a new grader. A scraper and a grader do the same thing, scrape and grade, although a grader does more of it and does not require horses. The difference, in this case, was only one hundred years and $89,750. The results were identical. The Washington correspondent for the *Hillsboro Messenger* reported in July 1894: "Never in the memory of the oldest inhabitants have the roads . . . been in so good condition as at the present time." One hundred years later, after the purchase of the new grader, all six hundred of us road agents have to agree that our roads have never been in so good condition as at the present time. Call it progress.

It is the 1994 town budget hearing, it is January, and it is snowing. The forecast is for more snow, then sleet, then warm rain, then zero temperatures. So I am taken aback when town road agent David Hunt—who, despite the evidence, is the only *elected* road agent in town—approaches me with the idea that I should spend tomorrow with his road crew.

Now and always, being an elected road agent in this town requires adroit political skills. Road maintenance skills don't hurt, either. The standard of recent memory was set by Robert Crane (see Chapter 21), but currently by David Hunt. Like a good road agent he does not allow me to read exactly what he has in mind. Has he heard rumors that I have the scribbler's disease again? Spend tomorrow with the road crew?

"Why should I do that?" I ask.

"To see exactly what it's like. You need to have that experience," he assures me with utmost sincerity.

I do not know what he means, so I play my ace immediately: "I'm up to speed on roads, you know. Remember, last year I drove the new grader before we had even paid for it."

Phil Barker, a member of the road crew, appeared at David's side to apply more gentle pressure—and to assure me I would not be driving tomorrow. I am to understand that this is a genuine invitation (of the kind hard to decline) to look closely at an operation which, David says, "everybody just takes for granted." I don't tell him that I haven't been able to take it for granted since I passed up the "Mud" sign at the pond years and years ago.

"There is a big storm coming," I say.

"Yes," said David.

It is clear that I cannot avoid this ride with my credibility intact. "We usually start at about four o'clock on storm days. We'll call you then. Okay?"

That man said four o'clock!

It is not okay. So I say "Okay."

On the way home I devise an explanation for Grace: "I thought it might be more interesting than sitting at the lunch counter getting secondhand reports on the roads." By the time I have formulated this I am convinced of it: it is both true and unanswerable. I can sleep peacefully on it, and do.

And indeed the phone does awaken us at 3:50 A.M. It is Phil Barker: we are meeting at the town garage in half an hour. I dress warmly, drive through five inches of new snow, which is all my car can handle on the hills, and arrive at the garage on time. The folks who take care of the town roads may not be fond of this weather, but it brings their skills to the surface, and they don't seem to mind that at all.

By four-thirty we are gathered in a circle, some of us awake, listening to David Hunt's attack-plan: Larry, Kevin, Ed, Phil, and I. Today I am literally a road surveyor but disguised as one of the boys. The plan is pretty basic: we are going to move snow until the weather changes, and then we are going to figure out what to do next. It is snowing an inch or two an hour now and by daylight sleet is promised; after that, it will get interesting. I am to join Phil in the big green Mack and we are to plow, in order, Lempster, Faxon Hill, Valley Road, Bailey, Dole, and Smith.

Washington roads splay out from the center like the arms of an octopus, and soon run into another town, or run dead, or both. By four-forty we are ready: David has the One Ton, Kevin has a Mack, Ed has the army truck, Larry the backhoe, and Phil and I have the other Mack. Our motors are humming, our lights are flashing, our radio scanners squawking. Outside it's dark, very cold, snowing heavily, and there is no other traffic at all. We roar off. We will keep in touch by means of that radio scanner. Four towns are on our frequency (Henniker, Hillsboro, Antrim, Washington), and we can get a sense of how other towns are coping by eavesdropping on them.

We are plowing in second gear at about fifteen miles per hour, and the plow is moving snow with two blades: center and a right-side wing blade, both hydraulically operated. At four-fifty the scanner crackles: Dr. Tate, superintendent of area schools, is asking road agents in several towns about conditions. I know that our road agent thinks this would be a terrible day to send out the school buses, but on the scanner I hear David say, "Our plows are all working, we can handle it this morning, but later in the day it could be a problem." Can Tate translate that into: "Don't send the buses"? At five-fifteen and before we are finished with Lempster Road, we get a scanner report that school is cancelled for the day. That means the teachers' "telephone tree" will immediately swing into action, and at about this moment Grace will be getting a call telling her school is cancelled. She will call another teacher and then, I hope, slide comfortably back into bed.

We hear David talking with the others. Larry says the state plow is on Highway 31 (Croyden Turnpike) salting. "Salting?" asks David. "Salting," says Larry. "There are six inches of snow, and this guy doesn't even have a plow on. Never saw anything like it!" I will learn that state highway personnel often get a surprise when they get to Washington, for we are in the clouds on days like this.

We're moving up hill and down at a steady fifteen miles per hour. Phil says it's going to be a long day, and I don't hear the slightest note of regret in his voice. A short time later we hear "901 to 905," on the radio. That's David calling Phil, who picks up the mouthpiece, flips the switch, and says "905, go ahead." David wants to know where we are, and how his passenger is doing. Phil says his passenger seems thrilled to be doing something useful.

Do I have a job to do? We can pretend my job is to watch out for mailboxes and, by mentally concentrating on it, keep the plow's wing tip from catching them. Hitting a mailbox is an occupational hazard of plowing snow—such an easy thing to do that it has come to be a byword. At the General Store lunch counter I have heard snowplowing described as "nailing mailboxes." But mostly I do my duty by keeping out of Phil's line of sight as he swings as close as possible to the edge. "No point in missing the boxes by three feet," he says, "No skill in that. No fun either." He boldly comes to within an inch and a half of the next one. Long experience operating big machinery has given him genuine skills. Since this is Washington, expertise comes with the territory; skill, however, comes with practice. Fortunately, most people in our part of town pick up mail at the post office, so mailboxes are not a major issue. Phil's favorite story involves the time he heard on the scanner from one of our own crew: "Damn, got my own mailbox."

Now we learn on the radio that Ed "nearly lost it" on Faxon Hill. Did he say he went down sideways? He doesn't tell us more; apparently he's not broadcasting his adventures. Lots of folks in town have a scanner at home and keep it on just to pick up the local news as it happens. A radio scanner does what the old party-line telephone did, namely, deliver the community news raw. Now we pick up fragments from other towns. Somebody in Henniker says it's starting to rain, and although it's snowing here, we have an inkling of sleet to come. Hillsboro trucks are having some bad luck—one with a flat and one off the road. We don't get many details of that, either. Later in the day, back at the garage, I learn that crew members learn to speak in a loose code to their own team. "Slip over and give me a hand," Robert Crane used to say on the scanner, and that meant something like, "I've got one heck of a mess on my hands and need all the help I can get." Ken Fletcher used to say, "Bring me some sand," which was code for something like, "I've ditched a truck."

We're moving down Valley Road, and Phil remarks that you can take pride in plowing well. He points out that by going more slowly you can "avoid big ripples in the road as the blade bounces, and you don't swing out so far when you're avoidin' obstacles if you're movin' slow, and you probably won't bust the wing when it hits a stump or a rock in the snowbank. Like, this mornin', I'd have said: 'Since we have four trucks goin' we can go slower today, do a bettah job.'" As we pass certain homes Phil gives me a synopsis of recent road complaints. They seem to be direct descendants of the "my-lame-horse" and "my-daughter-Millie" crowd of yesteryear.

Except for a few years in the service, Phil has lived in Washington all his life, close to fifty years, one of half a dozen or so in his age group. They all speak with a native's accent, flat and musical and r-less, but theirs seems to be the last generation here with the old New Hampshire accent. He likes to see a road plowed to the edges, he says, so that the entire roadbed freezes. Otherwise, he explains, the edges thaw in the spring when the center is still hard and become a trap for the careless driver. Careless driver? I tell him about my experience on an April 30th, many years ago. "Thawed shoulders," says Phil, "you got innoculated early." The truth is, we all have much higher expectations of our roads than we did just a short generation ago when we ourselves first arrived. At that time—having been innoculated—we just assumed that our Half Moon Pond Road would be impassible during mud season. During our first year here we simply left our car at the pond for more than a month and walked the last mile and a half. Nobody does that anymore.

The sleet has begun, arriving with the daylight as promised, and ahead of us an old jeep is stalled crosswise in the road. It has slid into a snowbank and its battery has pitched off its perch, breaking a connection. We get it started again and round another bend to find a Coors truck with its rump in the ditch. My first thought is: Why would anybody in his right mind try to make a beer delivery today, of all days? My second thought is: It's his job to do it, his pride is in it, and snow and ice are just a challenge. He didn't even consider not going. When he is freed we move on, ever more carefully. We still haven't found anyone who is cursing today's weather. Today is just a little bit unusual, that's all. By now the rain is falling heavily, freezing as it touches, turning everything to crystal, and Phil remarks that even the clouds are freezing onto the trees.

We have been carrying six cubic yards of sand all morning, and it's time to start dropping it. Phil checks this with David on the scanner. We are sent to Valley Road for the second time, now to sand as long as the supply lasts. Through the radio we learn that back at the garage David and Ed are having trouble with the diesel pump. Kevin hasn't been heard from lately. Phil says that our truck carries a special tank of fifty extra gallons of fuel for such emergencies, but how far will that go today? The ice has coated the road so firmly where we plowed a few hours ago that the plow blade slides over it, without cutting through. Phil stops to change the angle of the blade to get a better shot at cutting the ice. He climbs back in and tells me that in a couple of storms like this you can wear out completely the six-inch replaceable steel edge of the blade. I think of all the tons of steel, in snowplow and grader blades, that are worn off on New Hampshire roads each year. Edges with carbide inserts last a lot longer but are more expensive.

I am beginning to realize now that I am learning a lot more today than I thought I needed to know. Did David suppose that my road knowledge hitherto was a little old-fashioned, or historical, or bookish? At any rate, I am now becoming a current expert. It's catching. Want to know about carbide inserts, anyone?

Eventually, we are back at the garage. David and Ed are huddled in the sleet, bare fingered, trying to discover the fault in the diesel fuel pump. Without a working pump this operation could be shut down in a few more hours. Right now, everything is double-coated with ice; it is windy; you can barely walk; somewhere underground a wire is shorted out. It was easier to get around hours ago in the snow. All the roads in town are snarling at us now. And the men are doing a great job of acknowledging the varied charms of the situation. "See what I mean?" David says. (What does he mean?) "Like I said: You need to do this." Whatever he means, I think I detect a note of triumph in his voice, and that helps me to figure out what my job is today: it is to help them savor the nuances of New Hampshire weather.

For me, it has been an unusual way to take a blizzard under advisement, a day rather to be experienced than to be analyzed. The forecast had been for heavy snow, wind, sleet, rain, zero temperatures. Bull's-eye, so far. On the surface, at least, all six of us are having a great time. It's this lovers' quarrel with our roads. We wonder if the other 594 road agents in town will appreciate our labors.

20

Neighbors

Recently a new sign appeared outside the Washington General Store, "Breakfast and Lunch." That was pretty big news in these parts, as it's been many a year since you could sit down at a lunch counter in the center of our town. Bill and Ann Lofgren, who own and run the store, cleared out a few rows of food shelves and had Jim Russell install a lunch counter. That brings to three the number of hot spots in town, the others being the recycling center and the post office.

Once a week or so I stop in during the lunch hour to get a closer view of a cross section of my own community. It's a good place to hook up with the local grapevine. I go armed with notebook and pen, of course, just in case something happens that needs to be captured for posterity. At the store you can also buy a sweatshirt with some town statistics: "Population: 629 Deer: 320 Moose: 29 Natives: Darn Few." That's probably about right.

Bill Lofgren is the amiable proprietor here. He is not a native, but he appears to have been born to the role he has fashioned for himself, namely, holding court at the center of town. "Hey, I figured the town needed a place where folks could sit down, have a cup of coffee and shoot the breeze about local affairs," said Bill. "I bought the store in '89; the economy promptly went down the tube, and I've been subsidizing this place ever since. I thought I could do as well with the lunch counter in this end of the store. Maybe someday I'll break even. Anyway, I figured the town really needed it."

"You mean: since we don't have a newspaper in town, we need a kind of unwritten newspaper, here at the counter?"

"There you go," said Bill.

Two young men in Pepsi uniforms join the four of five of us at the counter. I learn later that they are in the store to work on the Coke machine. One of them says, "Is there, like, a city of Washington?" This brings hoots from us barflies at the counter. He tries to recover, "I mean, like a center, with stores and stuff." We still think this is very funny. Maybe it's his earnestness; maybe it's us.

"You're in it, buddy," says Bill. "This is *it*." He jabs his finger toward the floor for emphasis. Behind his hand he tells us that they are from Massachusetts. I think they hear that, and are meant to, but don't mind at all. Clearly, they are having a hard time believing that they are in the center of Washington, New Hampshire.

Bill is from Wakefield, Massachusetts, and he doesn't use any more "r's" than someone native to this town. That didn't do him any harm when he moved here five years ago. He pours me a second cup of coffee, which is free. This is the kind of easygoing place where it would seem almost a discourtesy not to accept seconds. You get a second bowl of soup too, if you want it.

"So where was I, yeah, I think this place can serve a real purpose in town: people I hardly ever saw now come in here, sit and talk. Yesterday there were thirteen here, which is max. Tell you one thing: you sit here for a while and eventually you will hear the other side of every issue."

On another day we are all sitting around bragging about how cold it was at our places. Evidently this winter is setting some records. Today you can't even play if you have nothing over twenty below to offer. I win by one, with twenty-five below. Wendy Otterson is in on this conversation, and she decides that if she is to rank in these contests she has to move her thermometer out from under the eaves, which may trap a few degrees of heat. "But let me tell you how cold it really was at our house," she said. "This morning I got my car started, finally, and I closed the door and the mirror fell off!"

"Cold!" said Bill.

This reminds Wendy of Joe Smith. "Remember him?" Nobody does. Okay, Wendy is the youngest grandmother in town, but she's virtually a native too. Tell us about Joe Smith.

"Well, on cold days like this," said Wendy, "he'd put newspapers in his trousers; and he would come into town with this paper bag over his head. Really! Little slits cut out for his eyes. Weird!"

I write this down. Posterity will want to know.

"Hey, but you know what?" says Wendy. "It really works great too!—if you can stand the noise."

I don't ask her how she knows. I'm just taking notes.

The day after Christmas we had an unplanned episode here at Lovellwood which gave us a direct insight into the sociology of our town. This little event is known as a chimney fire, and it's the kind of drama that gets your full attention while it lasts. If it lasts very long, you may be in very big trouble. Soot and creosote and miscellaneous other juicy and tar-like chemicals, all combustible and hot-burning, collect in a chimney. One cold day when the fire is hot they ignite and burn with an awesome roar. The fire is often contained within the chimney, burns itself out quickly, and may do no lasting harm. Until very recently, these things happened only in other people's chimneys, people who had made a mistake somewhere.

Then it happened here. For a short while, the last old house on the road was in big touble, probably bigger than we realized at the time. Our fire didn't last long, and the firemen came and went within little more than an hour—leaving us safe, grateful, and humbled. I have carefully retraced the causes of this fire, and I find that there is a long sequence of actions that I can blame—in addition to the fact that I had been burning green wood. The sequence starts way back with the local school budget.

Last fall, the Washington School Board, seeing that its transportation budget was getting out of hand, did the honorable thing and looked about for ways to save money. The Board's bright idea: shorten the bus route; lop off a few stretches of country road that are rough, hilly, or hazardous; play safe, save money, win public approval. It seemed they could even drop the last quarter mile on Half Moon Pond Road, including that wooded curve opposite the Jager house where the big trees are. Five students would thus walk the extra distance to meet the bus.

But this is a a small town and there was a very rough road ahead. Parents of those five students stormed the Board and protested the shortened route, promised litigation, promised state intervention, promised to make life miserable, argued that a road unsuitable to drive is surely unsafe for children to walk. The Board was now caught between budget deficit and citizen wrath.

The Board turned to state officials and also to the Board of Selectmen, the town's executive officers. The Selectmen cleared their throats and scratched their heads for several meetings, and then decided that "addressing safety concerns" sounded like a politically safe course—what with the state peering over their shoulder. So they instructed the road agent to cut some trees on the curve near the Jager residence to improve visibility. It was not at all clear to the road crew just why they were doing this, for they who serviced the road hadn't noticed a particular problem there; or, rather, there are problems everywhere—every road is hazardous. That is why we love them so. But evidently all the people's servants were now pretty far afield from the original question of the bus transportation budget.

A mere private citizen, I had heard nothing of this rich background—for this was before the town lunch counter had assumed the role of town newspaper. One day I did hear chainsaws nearby, went to investigate, and met the road crew hard at work. When I learned of their intent I had to point out that the trees they had been sent to cut were not on the town's land, but on ours. This did not simplify a matter that badly needed simplifying.

The only thing more amazing than the ease with which a rural community can get into such a sticky little quagmire, is the fact that it can sometimes get out of it. Altogether, we probably don't know much of the official academic stuff about "conflict resolution," but we are used to winging it. Here's how we do it. We all gather on the roadside in an ad hoc meeting—Selectmen, School Board, road crew, and I. To each other we are not strangers or bureaucrats: we are neighbors, or nearly so—which doesn't mean we all necessarily like each other. But we each know something of how the others think about town issues, we have chewed the fat together at the same town meetings. Next week we'll be rehashing this one at the store, and if someone wants to bring it up at the town meeting, we'll rehash it there too. But right now we've got a problem to solve and, without knowing just how, we presume we are going to settle it somehow, short of a court order, which we all cynically believe would only exacerbate everything.

We are scratching our toes in the dirt on the roadside, discussing the matter obliquely, needling each other to test temperatures, joking about bus drivers, about the trees under indictment, all suspecting that this meeting is both serious and absurd. And here—though maybe we don't fully realize it at the time—one of the secrets of rural town life is revealed: sometimes it's better to do the ridiculous thing rather than the reasonable thing. Reasonable would be: everybody lighten up, back off, cool down, and reconsider the whole matter next year. Ridiculous would be: cut down some of those big trees, create a dramatic effect if nothing else, and pretend that everybody won a big victory. Gamble half a dozen trees on the peace of the neighborhood. Hey, maybe it's not a bad bargain. I don't know that you could do it better elsewhere.

We agree to cut the trees. Everybody is impressed with the dimensions of our efforts. The road agent tells his men to pile the logs where I can conveniently salvage them for firewood. But it was a wet November day and, alas, while delivering the logs the crew inadvertently rutted and rendered impassible for me the lane that leads to the field where my seasoned wood lay. Am I getting the short end of this deal? Well, no big problem; they can fix the ruts later. Meanwhile, I would just eke out my winter's supply by burning the fresh new green wood for a month.

As everybody knows, green wood leaves an excess of soot and creosote in stove pipes and chimneys, so I watched the pipes carefully and cleaned them weekly. But the chimney itself, which normally needs less attention, slipped to the back of my mind for a month. I had things to do, a book to finish, Christmas to celebrate. Day by day during December the cool chimney collected the creosote that was carried by the smoke that oozed from the green wood that came from the big trees that stood by the curved road that concerned the Selectmen that counseled the citizens that pestered the School Board that managed the budget that started it all. I was out of the loop, of course, just stoking the stove.

Just at dark on December 26, creosote far up in the chimney lit up, and an old-fashioned chimney fire was soon roaring like a huge blowtorch, ten-foot flames leaping from the chimney and slapping across our roof. It was a cold and windy evening and the size of those flames was very impressive.

A volunteer fire department, like a volunteer rescue squad, is one of the remarkable institutions of small-town America. When my son Colin called the Fire/Rescue number at about five o'clock he was setting in motion a complicated chain of events. Indeed, knowing the huge disturbance immediately created by such a call, I had hesitated. The chimney is on the outside of the house, and I believed the fire would burn itself out shortly. But I am also aware of the standard chimney-fire horror story, whose plot is this: the fire dies out or is extinguished, but creosote has previously seeped through a crack and soaked into some hidden part of the wooden structure. Heated by the fire more creosote now runs in, and the fire follows it in, smolders invisibly in the wall for an hour or two, and finally bursts out when the firetrucks have left and everyone's guard is down. This scenario swept through my mind as I watched the flames leap out of the chimney. So we called the fire department. Such calls are answered by a dispatcher in Hillsboro, who covers five towns. At the press of a button he or she simultaneously activates all the radios worn by the forty-plus members of the Washington Fire Department, and repeats the message received. Of course, not all firefighters are in town at any one time.

Meanwhile, as I had expected, the flames in our flue calmed down and finally crawled back into the chimney and died there. I then put in another call, though I believed that once under way the firetruck would not turn back. My second message was: fire no longer visible; so perhaps the truck needn't come, just a fireman or two for inspection and reassurance. Fat chance! We had two trucks and an ambulance on the scene in jig time, and a row of firemen, many of them suited up for action. Since the situation didn't appear dangerous anymore, the banter could begin almost immediately: "Well, you'll get a free chimney cleaning, anyway. Is that what you called us for?"

Ladders and wisecracks come out and soon one man is on the roof poking a flashlight into the chimney. Somebody asks if he is playing Santa Claus, another hands him a chimney brush, and still another tells him to "clean it real good before you jump in." It's pretty cold out here, and that's about the level of humor we can squeeze out of the situation at the moment.

Thirty minutes later we assess the situation. One truck has just been sent back. The fire inside the chimney is certainly out, the chimney has been reamed, the stove is still on. But here are still ten men dressed for firework with plenty of energy and goodwill left over, but apparently not much to do. Has this trip been worthwhile? It is six o'clock, and my wife Grace has been making stacks of ham sandwiches. We all troop inside and upstairs to the library to have a second look at the stove and stovepipe.

It could be that David Hunt, deputy fire chief and commander of operations tonight, was on the lookout for the right occasion for a seminar on stove installations. At any rate, I gave him the perfect excuse by explaining that what they were seeing was a false brick wall, just a single course on the inside, with the wooden wall of the house next, then the chimney on the outside. "Like a ham sandwich," I say. "The bread is brick; the ham is the wooden wall of the house."

This arrangement interests the firemen very much. Wooden wall behind this brick? They all go into alert-mode, like cats ready to pounce. David has already made up his mind, but he moves gently: "Tell you what: we could dowse the stove, remove the stovepipe, pull out that metal sleeve that goes through the wall into the chimney, and check the connection—see if there is any wood close to it, see if anything is smoldering in there." Sixteen firemen's eyes go to the point where the stovepipe enters the brickwork and goes through the house wall and into the chimney. Then they all turn to me, to the pipe, and back to me again. I look at the row of volunteer firemen, my neighbors, though I can't identify some of them under their regalia. Do they want to tackle this nasty little job here and now? Of course they do! Nobody says: "Naah, let's go home." Are they thinking: Well, here at least is something useful to *do*?

"Do you know what's around that sleeve?" I am asked.

"Well, I've always wondered," I admit, "but I could never remove the sleeve to find out."

David nods: "*We* can," he says simply. Here are ten neighbors volunteering to do a job for me I haven't been able to do myself. It is not what I have planned for happy hour tonight. But it may be what small-town America is all about.

David Hunt and Bobby Crane now open an impromptu workshop there in my library. I am permitted to carry the water so Bobby can dowse the stove—very slowly so as not to crack hot iron. David explains to younger firemen what they are doing and why. Two firemen carry the pipe outdoors for cleaning. Two others twist and pull and shove and jerk and heave on the sleeve and eventually it slides out. Then we all crowd around peering by flashlight into the black hole. I get the longest look, since this workshop is also, though by no means exclusively, for my benefit. It is also a kind of minor rally for the troops, a moment to affirm the old values. I have the distinct idea that everyone would have been very disappointed to find the connection in perfect condition—which would have showed that their expertise was not required.

The setup does not disappoint them. The only good news out of the black hole is that no wood is in direct contact with the metal sleeve; the rest of the news spells danger and trouble. David wants all the firefighters to see what he sees: absence of proper sealing around the sleeve, no air space, heat-loosened mortar, places where creosote, probably from the fire, has leaked into the space between house and chimney. "Fire inside that thin sleeve could have gone anywhere," I am told. And it takes him a while to be certain that there isn't any fire in the wall now. He lifts a chunk of mortar to find that less than three inches of mortar separates metal sleeve and wood. "This is how you burn down an old house," he concludes. That's a signal for other members of the seminar to contribute their favorite horror stories about the waywardness of chimney fires. I am duly impressed.

. . . Now the men and trucks have left and David, who had come in his own pickup, and I are wrapping things up. I learn that five trucks had initially headed our way: four firetrucks and an ambulance. As soon as David had determined that they were not needed he had radioed two trucks to return to the station, allowing three to come, including the ambulance, which goes to every fire. "What if I had rolled off your slippery roof in the dark?" 'Nuf said.

I also learned that the basic fire department rule is simple: "Every call is treated as a worse case—until we're on the scene and decide. It gets a total response, all firefighters, all equipment. From there only a fireman on the scene can 'stand down'—such as cancel trucks before they arrive."

"So what about my second call, saying a truck was probably not necessary?" I ask.

"Ignored," he said.

I am not feeling any swells of pride about this whole episode. And I cannot bring myself to tell the deputy fire chief that I had been burning green wood: that would be like driving a car into the ditch and having to admit you had been drinking. And I certainly cannot bear to tell him *why* I have been doing it—the long chain of causes that goes back to the school budget and the trees by the road and the ruts in my lane blocking my seasoned wood supply, and then the easily available green wood. For the deputy fire chief who just conducted the chimney seminar and the road agent who brought me the green wood are one and the same person: David Hunt.

He senses that I am chagrined by the fact that I, who supposedly know something about country living, allowed myself to have a chimney fire. "Hey, the guys love it," he says as the trucks roar off.

"Love it?" This cheers me considerably.

"Well . . . yeah. Hey, it's a volunteer department. They don't have to come if they don't choose to."

I am thinking this over. Don't come if they don't choose to.

"What if they don't come?" I said.

"Never a problem," said David. "Besides, we all learned a little bit." He eyed me sidewise. "And don't forget: we condemned your chimney." He said that in a cheerful, so-all-is-not-lost, tone of voice. "When was it, about two years ago, maybe, when the rescue squad picked you up back in there? Remember, how many showed up here that time?"

I did indeed. I had had an accident deep in the woods, was

immobilized, and the rescue squad had come in with a cast of dozens, trussed me up on a litter, carried me out of the woods, and brought me to the hospital. My complaint turned out to be a broken vertebra and a craving for painkillers, but it eased off in a few weeks. That time too they all talked about what good practice it had been for them. They had never carried a subject (yes, that is what you turn into—a subject on a litter) out of the woods before, and they needed a good case to rehearse their technique. Conditions had been ideal: hills, rocks, snow, woods, ice, approaching dark. They all learned from it.

That time I had landed on my back; this time I had fallen flat on my ego. And my neighbors treated it as practice? They are always practicing, always in training, always getting ready for an emergency. Break your back, come near to burning down your house? Rally the troops for practice. Some day we may be needed. Small-town America does some things uncommonly well.

❦

Two weeks later, early January, and I am back at the lunch counter in the village store. Bill is behind the counter, serving up local news and broccoli soup. He keeps promising venison stew, but I can't seem to hit the days when it is on. He probably makes the stew from deer he has shot himself. Last year he brought back two from his annual trip to a remote Canadian island. I like to hear him talk about deer hunting in remote places where there are lots of deer and the herd needs thinning. I can almost forget that I have withdrawn from the sport.

The deputy fire chief comes in. He is disguised as a road agent today, and he smells of gasoline. It takes a while before we work our way around to the point—after all, we don't want to let on that this is more than a minor incident—but eventually we come to it.

David says: "By the way, get your chimney fixed yet?"

I say, "You know John the Mason?"

Of course he does. Everybody does. He's the one you call at a time like this. "He said he could rebuild the connection for a couple of hundred bucks. Well, last week he came and did it. Did a good job: took out nine courses of bricks on the inside, cut the wood of the house wall way back, left an air space, put in a clay sleeve, and cleaned the chimney. That's when he gave me the real news."

By now I have everyone's attention, which is what I wanted since I am doing field research. "Apparently the fire had been hotter than I had thought. He tells me I've got broken tiles in the flue. He said somebody will have to take out all the top tiles and replace them. David, I thought you had scared me when you pulled that chimney sleeve, but John scared me a lot more when he looked into the chimney and told me what he saw."

I know I'll lose their attention in a moment, for we are going to go into a round of *their* chimney stories, so I hurry to my punch line. "He said that if I used it this way creosote would collect between the tile and the brickwork and eventually the flue would be encased within a pool of hardened creosote. A time bomb. Once that catches fire, he said, it will literally explode, blow the chimney to smithereens. That's what the man said."

Well, I had been suitably awed by this possible scenario, and I repeated it here around the lunch counter so I could run a plausibility-check on it. Nobody batted an eye. They all shrugged or nodded, and started to tell their own stories. Nobody said: "Naah, don't worry about it."

Bill said, "You got problems."

"Same thing happened to me," said David. "Cracked tiles. Tore the whole thing out and rebuilt it from the bottom up." Then he quickly added: "Just the top five tiles? You're lucky."

The cheerfulness of my neighbors is astonishing. On the other hand, perhaps I *am* lucky.

21

Pure Democracy

ACT ONE: THE 1970s

One institution is ambivalently cherished more than any other in Washington, and that is the annual town meeting. Here is the community in a nutshell—democracy still pure and proud and free.

Our town maintains its practice of devoting the entire day and as much of the evening as is necessary to the town meeting. (Roughly speaking: the smaller the town, the longer the town meeting and the larger the percentage of the the town's business done there.) Each annual meeting has its own character, its own combination of contentious issues, filibustering, generosity, high spirits. In the blur of memory all the Washington town meetings of the early 1970s swirl and dissolve and gather into one sustained act, and a representative silhouette stands forth. Let it be 1976, the year of the two hundredth anniversary of Washington:

Townspeople begin to gather and cluster in the Town Hall about nine-thirty. The room is cold and most leave their out-

Portions of Act One are adapted from *Portrait of a Hill Town: A History of Washington, N.H.*, by Ronald and Grace Jager, published in 1977, by Village Press.

door wraps on. Someone says he remembers "when this room was het by a wood stove." But no one now alive ever saw it in its original form, before this ceiling created a second floor above and closed off the galleries. The meeting room is now plainness itself. Only the remnants of the original paneling, the old glass of the windows, the worn floors, the deacons' benches, and a few fine pillars suggest its actual eighteenth-century vintage.

Women are behind the counter at the south end of the hall making coffee, laying out homemade doughnuts, "town meeting cakes," and sandwiches. The three supervisors of the checklist have spread out the large handwritten sheet with the names of the town's registered voters: 184 in 1976. Winonah Babb, town clerk of Washington since 1953, has arrived armed with two ten-pound leather-bound Town Record books. Once in a while the moderator will call upon her to clarify what the town actually decided by asking her to read from The Book. No one ever questions The Book.

More townspeople jostle in as ten o'clock approaches. There will be up to one hundred voters throughout the day; two or three dozen of them will show up only to vote for town officers and to linger a while and leave. Donald Crane, moderator, is checking his watch. The three Selectmen, suitably suited and tied, have joined Winonah Babb in the raised box on the north side of the hall, where the pulpit used to be, and Crane now joins them. The atmosphere is brisk, chatty, informal. Only in the telling of it, or in the selective chambers of memory, is there any solemnity, for everything in this chamber is entirely relaxed, casual, familiar. Washington, a city-state perched in the hills, has assembled to express itself, to enjoy itself.

Yet, imagination needs to strain only a little to see this hall as a stage with a drama about to begin. The actors are checking the props, to see that the pieces are in order. Everyone is part of the cast: living theatre, democracy-in-the-round; and there is no real audience, except the eye of tradition and precedent, and so no one is self-conscious. The neighborly disassembly begins to compose itself now that curtain time approaches.

There may be some expectancy in the air after all, for this enactment reaches back across the town's two hundred years to the first town meeting with more continuity than anything else that happens here. Then as now the agenda for the meeting, called the warrant, was posted by the Selectmen in February, and in March the people left off what they were doing—which was not very much—and came to this place. On this spot they struggled and quarrelled, made friends, made laws, made history; here they debated and shouted, compromised, voted, spent and saved, learned to win and lose with dignity. From these walls, hundreds of times, the independence of the town and the importance of "the-will-of-the-people" was amplified. Here and now, and within twelve hours, the framework for the next twelve months will be constructed with slow and steady strokes. There are several dozen articles on the warrant, and on each one a motion will be discussed until no one wishes to say anything more; only then will there be a vote.

Donald Crane begins absentmindedly to finger the gavel, which is very familiar to his hand, like a pipe to a habitual smoker. He has fingered that gavel, twirling the head in his hand, for several hundred hours since he was first elected town moderator in 1964. Everyone in town simply assumes that he will be moderator for the forseeable future. Now it is ten o'clock and he taps lightly with his gavel on the slab of polished granite at his elbow—the sound is a brittle click, lacking authority—and declares that the annual town meeting is in order. It isn't really in order, but that is because everyone knows what he will do next. He will proceed immediately to read the warrant, every word of it. In 1976 there were twenty-six articles; in 1876, there were thirteen. Almost everyone has picked up a copy of the town *Reports* by this time; many are following the moderator's reading; others are trading quick bits of whispered talk with their neighbors ("Sugarin' yet?" "Thought I'd wait."); others are blowing on a cup of coffee, settling in. At least a dozen people are sitting in exactly the same place they sat last year, and the year before, and the year before that. There is a comfortable buzz: the orchestra tuning up while the conductor runs through the score.

After the reading of the warrant, the next order of business is ceremonial: the moderator takes the large wooden ballot box, opens it, shows the assembled voters that it is empty, locks it, hands it to the police chief, who delivers it to the ballot clerks, who will supervise the voting throughout the day. The voting process for town officers was changed during the early 1970s. Until the recent past townspeople could expect to be met at the Town Hall door by aspiring candidates handing out small slips of paper with their names written on them—a clear signal that the person was running for some office or other, but only the grapevine knew which. Some candidates disdained the brazenness of doorway electioneering and depended on their constituency to write down the proper name at the proper time. One by one the town offices were then filled: the voters passed by the supervisors of the checklist and the police officer to the moderator, who put each ballot in the box as he called out the voter's name to the clerk. A majority of the votes cast was required for election, and this meant that second and third votes were not uncommon. It was a very time-consuming business, but it left room for alliances to form and shift with the winds. When the victor was finally identified, he or she was sought out and sworn in on the spot.

Such, or approximately such, was the practice in Washington for almost two hundred years, a method which dramatized democratic procedure. I think it might now be called "quaint." It certainly was monumentally inefficient: it took an entire morning, and often more, to complete the town elections. For a century and a half, or perhaps almost two centuries, this did not seem a major drawback: there was time enough; elections were important enough. What brought change to Washington had more to do with justice than efficiency: not everyone who wished to vote for town officers could take off time from a job to be on hand through the entire morning. A ballot system, adopted in 1972, which allowed voting for town officers at any time during the day until the polls were closed, at 9 or 10 P.M., permitted every citizen to vote.

Now the meeting is in full gear. Discussions are lengthy, male voices predominate, written ballots are frequent. Time was, years and years ago, when the moderator's uncertainty how to call it on a voice vote was resolved by a show of hands. Not any more; uncertainty is now always resolved by a secret written ballot—just as we used to do with electing town officers. The principle of the secret ballot and the principle of uncurtailed debate are treated in this town with a piety reserved for few other things. Punctuating the long meeting with a frequent "paper ballot," as it is called here, relieves tedium, rearranges the seating, fosters sociability, extends the market for coffee and sandwiches. Other than this, the twelve-hour marathon is broken just once, with a recess of sixty minutes at noon. The meeting presents a neat paradox: the high pitch of political self-consciousness, and the low key of the process itself.

At eleven o'clock we receive a delegation from the village school, the children filing in and sitting for a time at respectful attention. This is a civics class, field trip, and glimpse of the local road show all rolled into one, a you-are-there slice of local history-in-the-making. They have been well coached. But they soon discover that it is not an epiphany: becoming restive, they are led away. Was not Democracy a more solemn and lofty thing than this? Aren't these just the folks down the road talking about that old backhoe? Yet, the subtle mystique, pruned by observation, will grow again, just as it grew again for those who sit here now, and once sat there then. The mystique of the meeting will take on artful and cunning forms, working on the spirit of the populace and making it hard to imagine any other way of executing community affairs, forming a granite sense of local process.

The road agent, Robert Crane, gives an oral report, full of force and forthrightness. He knows "it's a tremendous lotta money I'm askin' you folks to spend," but he reports that "we've had pretty good luck on the equipment this year," the extra help "have been doin' a real good job." Like a road grader he plows full throttle into the uneven qualms and queries of the town, making rough places plain, gearing down to meet the toughest spots: "You people have been awful good to me; and I'm not going to stand here and say we can't get along another year without this new machine; we can." So perhaps we can postpone it? Not at all: "we don't get a chance like this often . . . wise investment for the town . . . if we had to hire this kind of work . . . my thought was, if I see a place where I can save the town a buck I ought to be churning up the sod to get to it." Some say he could sell ice in Lapland.

Steadily, patiently, slow as the early sap, the meeting marches on. ("Please be courteous to the speaker; you may not be interested in what he's sayin', but he is.") Hours pass. By mid and late afternoon, few have any sense of the time, and there is still no sense of hurry. Obligations at home have been arranged for. Mothers go home, nap the children and return; informal rump sessions convene at the post office and the store. Whereas a hundred years ago sixty barns with cows waiting to be milked hurried the democratic process, now there are but two. (Frequently in the 1930s and 1940s the annual school meeting was held in the afternoon on town meeting day after town business was disposed of—years that seem gone forever now, gone without regret.) Time to decide; let the world wait. Talk, tobacco smoke, coffee, and adrenalin substitute for eating. Agreement seems easier; the world more remote; everything that matters is right here. Marathon negotiating and group therapy, those sophisticated urban pastimes, were surely born in the New England town meeting.

Discussion ambles crosswise through the warrant, sniffs and then nibbles gently at the edge of controversial tidbits and is briskly snapped to heel by the moderator. Always there is one formidable issue doggedly pursued, often two or three: the cemetery wall, a new addition to the garage, the town dump, land use regulations, a new road. They are issues that most people deplore—and wouldn't miss for anything. Sometimes we seem to celebrate the length of our meetings just as we celebrate the severity of our weather: we think both derive from natural causes, and both confer virtue.

In 1975 James Hofford took a tape recorder to the town meeting and asked veterans how the meetings of today compared with those of yesterday. Calmer, some said, not so exciting; people don't get so riled up like they did; people used to speak out more, shout even. "Oh, we used to have some warm ones," says Ernest Cram, who has been observing them since the beginning of the century. Others said people are more considerate now, they think more about the town than about themselves. And others that meetings are just the same as always; they were always pretty good; still are. Some remember when men used to spit tobacco juice at the sawdust box beside the stove before they talked; some wish the women would talk more, "but they never have, much—except Elba Chase . . ." Nostalgia for an earlier, heartier race merges with a conviction that things are still fundamentally in place—and entirely unpredictable.

Ghosts of the recent past hover about the chamber: Wally Chamberlain shuffles to the front, removes his weatherbeaten hat (surely an heirloom), grins like a leprechaun, respectfully moves to dismiss the article. Then he replaces his hat. Formality mingles with informality; most stand to speak, and Oliver Chase has kept the "Mr. Moderator" tradition alive for years. An Otterson warns of a dangerous precedent about to be set, a Barker appeals to some civic virtue, a Hofford sums up the views of a dozen others and then joins the consensus he has just postulated, a Crane deplores some new state restriction, a Rolf appeals to decency and detail, a Niven looks to the future, many voices cite the past. About once every twenty years John Tweedy speaks, cutting neatly through the issues with a quiet logic.

Someone asks why the insurance on the Town Hall is so low—would it not cost many times that much to replace it? Is this an oversight, or what? The meeting, suddenly hushed, sucks in its breath, waiting for explanation. And many might respond, but it happens that Ralph Otterson, fireman, puts matters into perspective with succinct eloquence: "The insurance is mainly to cover repairs in case of serious damage; you cannot really insure the building for what it is worth: insurance won't cover that. This building is priceless; it could be repaired, but it cannot be replaced." Silence. The words strike home. The meeting exhales. Today's lesson—"priceless." Then we return to business.

The moderator keeps order and keeps out. ("It's your meeting; I'm not here to sway it, just to run it.") He knows this audience, knows their views; knows whom to recognize first and last, knows from long experience how to elicit the drama and the consensus, and how to keep chaos at bay ("it seems to me there's an awful lotta noise here, not real loud, but an awful lot of it"); knows parliamentary procedure and how to use it; knows how to solicit a motion or frown and puzzle one to death; knows how to inject his fiscal counsel ("that's the policy of havin' it and spendin' it, instead of spendin' it and then tryin' to get it"); knows and employs everything a good moderator needs to know. Knows especially how to sway a meeting, by running it. They say he turns to granite if he is losing, but they don't often see him losing.

The bright image and fame of the New England town meeting—whence do they derive? Not only from its ancient lineage, its storied picturesqueness, its exhaustively democratic format. But also from the solid fact that it is the main self-expression of a very self-conscious community: the town in rural New England is by far the most explicit unit of social and political awareness. It is the town meeting that makes law, raises and appropriates money; there, what the people say matters, and they can see it matter before their eyes. Such self-government is self-conscious to a high degree. Never does a visitor understand what is really happening at a given town meeting unless he understands *that* town—understands its mind and heart by experience and instinct, an understanding hard to acquire by study and not available in books, an understanding that sees how much of every day is symbolized in this one day.

For the annual town meeting is quite inseparable from the political life of the town fifty-two weeks of the year—always was so. The meeting epitomizes the working of the rest of the local government: the sense of equality, casual democracy, local bias, easy access to officers, open meetings, open records. And the same kind of process is at work: time, exhaustive discussion, conversational by-paths, unimaginable patience while consensus gathers. Eventually, decisions are reached—reluctantly, for deciding tends to curtail discussion. The sense of time involved is an organic part of the pace of life, which is itself a feeling that matured in rural New England long ago in an agrarian society. Here the ways of democratic life are slow, not in the way bureaucracies and legalities are slow (full of baffles and maneuvers for advantage) but in the way in which the growing of corn is slow. Things have their season, creating a sense of felt natural rhythm, inviolable, like the stars in their courses.

A free people reared in the town-meeting tradition may have a political outlook slightly different from that of Americans of other traditions. Here people may have a sharper belief that things are and ought to be within their control: have a different understanding of the meaning of the ballot, for our ballot makes law, levies taxes, decides controversies, and does not merely elect others to do these things. Hence too the yearning to believe that all government ought to be like local government—and is creditable to the degree that it is. And from this derives the local wariness, shading into active distrust, of far-off governments and of politicians not present for accounting; and thus the contrast, echoing through the town meeting, between "them and us."

How long will this style of governing endure? It is not fragile, for it is tough as the landscape to which it attaches, but it is a political culture exposed to wear and tear from within and without. Within—these hallowed forms of democracy contain little that has inclined the town, for example, to regional cooperation, or to broad viewpoints, or even to seeking out modern means to preserve the cherished ways of the past. And without—there are many prowling legalities, state and federal, administering life, wearing down the local initiative. Other pressures, just as lethal to inherited ways, derive from the swift pace of life, shortening attention spans and fostering impatience with the familiar manner wherein, by drift of talk, prejudice, and instinct, the latent spirit of the community slowly finds itself. So the margins wherein the local mind can be brought to bear seem to be narrowing and the time available to detect that mind and apply it seems to be shortening. Both facts may breed resignation—and a dark awareness that the same American culture which still idealizes the small town may be quietly subverting it.

But nothing subverts the underlying sense of equality among citizens, which is the strength and the genius of the system. It is a sense of equality that is not so much a theory or an ideal but simply a fact—rooted in long community experience and perhaps even nourished by the natural environment. Here the very frame of life itself is composed, not by the systems and hierarchies of men, but by the earth and its seasons, its beauties and caprices, a system which is no respecter of persons and is a great equalizer: the sun shines and the storm beats on the wise and the foolish alike.

During the 1974 town meeting, the plan to write the history of the town was being discussed, when a blunt voice from the back shouted: "What's the purpose of the history?" The challenge was aggressive, and the implication in the tone was evident: it's likely to cost money, what's it for, what's the point of a book? The inquiry fell into a roomful of glum silence. How respond in few words? Moderator Donny Crane slowly scratched his ear, gazed without expression at the window, twisting the gavel in his hands, and then with an evenness in his words that might have gone for pride, he guessed that the purpose was "just to tell it like it was."

Pride in the town is as strong as ever—perhaps stronger now, because it is deeply attached to the very mode of life which the town represents. It is a pride no longer uneasy with the memory of the pastoral strength and weakness of an earlier age; a pride at peace with a landscape bearing perpetual witness to a very different history: sawdust pits where corn grew, a rusty mower in the woods, the everlasting cellar hole. Certainly today's pride is surer by far than in the days, generations ago, when it was vaguely supposed that progressive people would pack up for the city. The city is not now seen as an image of progress, but as something unnatural, teetering on the edge of social decay. Stability and strength are here, near to elemental things. It is not a faultless outlook, and it is at best but a partial view, but the view was shared by the founders of the town, two hundred years ago. Thomas Jefferson understood this conception of life. So, for that matter, did George Washington.

ACT TWO: THE 1990s

Now it is another town meeting in Washington, nearly twenty years later: March 8, 1994, nine o'clock, and we have assembled for our 218th annual gathering. Today we are nearly a hundred strong, with more drifting in—almost twice the number that gathered twenty years ago. As of old, we will be here for the next ten or twelve hours, and we will love every minute of it, even the parts we came to loathe.

Who are we? We are Swamp Yankees, Natives, Newcomers, and Flatlanders; we are the Knitters and the Needlers in the center, fingers working all day long; we are the Standees in the back, with caps on; we are those of the Folded Arms club, and those of the Flannel Shirt society. We are Everyman: carpenter, farmer, mason, electrician, housewife, teacher, writer, artist, factory worker, secretary, shopkeeper, computerman, radioman, businessman, real estate agent. And we are retired folk: banker and businessman, clerk and bureaucrat, truck driver and factory worker, scientist and civil servant. We are far, far more varied in our professional lives than we have ever been.

How many of us here today were present for the two hundredth town meeting in 1976? A third of us at most. Two dozen, maybe, have an attendance record that goes back farther than that. Yet a few—Cranes and Ottersons, for examples—have been coming to this town meeting all their lives, as did their parents and grandparents. Somebody has to represent continuity.

For today's meeting, as always, many citizens slip into their roles, and some slip into uniforms. At the head of the room is the moderator, Michael Otterson, who continues the town's long tradition, almost unbroken, of having a native son in that position. The moderator always wears a suit and tie on town meeting day, part of his ensemble, part of our tradition. This is a ceremonial occasion, after all, he is king for the day, and he should look the part. Beside him are three Selectmen, executive officers of the town, who are responsible for just about everything. It's sometimes called a thankless job, but when they leave office we always thank them.

The police officer is in full regalia. Uniformed, badged, and probably armed, he adds a touch of color and authority to the air. He keeps a watchful eye on the ballot box until the polls are closed. And usually he presents the police budget for the ensuing year, pointing to the local crime statistics, assuring us that it could have been a lot worse, but for our assistance, et cetera, et cetera—just look at Massachusetts, for example. We think about Boston for a brief minute, gazing out the window at the clean snow, and remember why we live here, and pass the budget with a voice vote. Not every year, of course. Once we drastically cut a proposed budget, and that chief resigned before the meeting was over. This year the chief resigned before the town meeting began, so we cut the proposed budget too. The position may exceed Selectmanship in thanklessness, and we run through police chiefs at a pretty brisk pace in Washington, as do other small towns.

The fire chief is here, also fitted out for the occasion: uniform, badges, buttons, and a name tag that says "Robert Wright, Fire Chief." Not that we didn't know. He will present the budget items for the fire department, and he long ago discovered what the local police also have long known, that when presented by uniformed officers proposals get more support, or at least respectful acquiescence. Anyway, under his chiefdom the fire department has become a well-equipped and highly professionalized organization.

The road agent is here, with a budget big enough "to read without bifocals," somebody said. In fact his budgets have been flat lately and the roads relatively smooth, so he will get what he asks for, which may be less than what he needs, without having to admit, as did his predecessor, Robert Crane, that he is asking for "a tremendous lotta money." Although he is.

The radios are here too, dozens of them, resting like pistols on the hips of firemen and rescue squad members. Wherever these citizens go, they go radio-armed. Like the American cowboys of the mythical Wild West with a holstered six-gun, they can draw their radio and spring into action or form a posse to face an emergency. These are our Minutemen—except that they are not all men and they respond in seconds not minutes. That's one way the community takes care of itself: several dozen patrols always at large, radio-armed, alert for trouble and trained to fix it. Should we wonder that there are but muted votes against their budget proposals? Police, Fire Department, Rescue Squad—you want to vote against apple pie? Not I. I have had their trucks roar in to fight a chimney fire, and I have been carried out of the woods on a litter by these troops. The "ayes" have it.

In 1994 we are no longer meeting in the Town Hall at the center of town. Although we have one of the few surviving specimens of eighteenth century meetinghouse architecture in New Hampshire, it is now vacant on town meeting day after 204 years of unbroken service. On the village green, together with the school and Congregational Church, it forms a justly famous and historic composition. Over the years the interior of the Town Hall has been altered many times, the outside hardly at all; it still houses the town offices, and at various times it has served as school and church and dozens of other things. But the space available for the growing annual town meeting became inadequate, and it is not handicapped accessible.

When erected in the summer of 1787 it was called the Meetinghouse; in the next century, when the Congregational

Church moved out, it came to be called the Town House; the twentieth century knows it as the Town Hall. By whatever name, it housed our annual March town meetings more than two hundred times. No one keeps official track of these things in New Hampshire, but ours is probably the state record for the longest unbroken string of town meetings in the same building.

We wear some traditions very lightly. There just wasn't a lot of sentiment in town about maintaining the record, so in 1992 the meeting was moved from its historic setting into this larger space a mile away at Camp Morgan. Although I had witnessed only the last one-eighth of that record, I felt a personal sense of loss at the move. That's mainly a Flatlander's response, I found; few natives complained. Some suspected, however, that in a new and alien setting, without the brooding witness of the old familiar walls, a chamber alive with memories and echoes of memories, we might make unguided decisions. Moderator Michael Otterson has a different view: he believes we were so crowded in the dimly lit Town Hall, invading each other's private space as it were, that it may have made us edgy and cranky. The brighter light and larger space we now use puts us in a better humor, he feels. Others say our better humor is to be ascribed to the moderator's skills in that office. It's an argument the moderator cannot lose.

I took a casual survey of opinions of town meeting veterans about how our meetings have changed. Among others, I talked to Phil Barker, Robert Crane, Bobby Crane, Julia Dunton, Jim Gaskell, Michael Otterson, Ralph Otterson, Bill Rhoades, Jim Russell, John Tweedy. I asked, What has changed significantly in our town meetings during the last couple of decades? For better? For worse?

Here is a sampling of what they said: "What's changed the most, I feel, is confidence in our leaders. You know, thirty years ago, some people—and usually one or more of them was a Selectman—were simply above reproach. Now it ain't that way. We're suspicious." ❧ "Changed? I think it's the financial complexity of the issues; it makes us mentally withdraw from the process. There are fewer and fewer places to apply plain common sense." ❧ "Oh, I dunno, I think possibly *I've* changed at least as much as town meetings have. I'm not quite so romantic about it. I now sometimes feel: 'do I have to listen to all that?'" ❧ "I think our meetings are more democratic than they used to be. When I came here a few families had almost total influence. There are now more voices, more kinds of voices, heard from today. I think Mike is probably more fair than Donny. Actually, I think the meeting is better than it ever was." ❧ "Like the general quality of life, I think it's probably going down hill. There's bureaucracy and number crunching now, and things are so much more complicated. Less of the Norman Rockwell, I guess—though it is still democratic as hell. I still love it." ❧ "We're more impatient, I think, than we used to be. Twenty years ago we could just worry a bad idea to death, or let it go away; now we think we've got to kill it." ❧ "There are too many people that come up here from the city, with their city agenda. They oughta listen a few years, and find our what's goin on." ❧ "I don't think the meetings *have* changed that much—not that I can see. Wouldn't miss it for anything." ❧ "We've become security nuts: we're forever yakking about liability and safety. Our speech-making is saturated with talk about litigation, insurance, liability, indemnity, state mandates, security. Where is our confidence? Our supposed self-reliance?" ❧ "Well, they're not as interesting as they used to be. We used to have some nice family-type fights. And I really miss Oliver Chase and Wally Chamberlain, guys like that. We used to have some real characters." ❧ "I notice that there are a number of people who don't come anymore, and I wonder about that; and this year the crowd was smaller than last year, even though the checklist is longer. Is that going to be a trend? People are less likely than they used to be to take off from work for town meeting." ❧ As with most subjects, there is more than one viewpoint.

Several remarked on the clearer air in today's meetings. Air? I was reminded of how, less than twenty years ago, we did our business in a haze of thick-enough-to-slice-it tobacco smoke, such as would not be tolerated today. From the first, American democracy was nurtured in tobacco smoke, but those days are gone the way of town meeting spittoons.

Most of my neighbors alluded to the rapid growth of the town, and always with regret. The population census numbers for our town from the Office of State Planning are these: pop. 162 in 1960; 248 in 1970; 411 in 1980; and in 1990, 628. Only a small proportion of the newcomers make a living within the town. Many are retired folk, many are people who can retain their professional connections elsewhere and live here in the countryside, some have day jobs they can commute to from Washington, a few are back-to-the-landers. The town today has almost twice the population of 1976 (628 vs. 320), but three times the number of registered voters (554 vs. 184). (Many registered voters today are summer residents who aim to register cars and take out insurance from a New Hampshire address.) The numbers may be confusing, but the fact is that the town has grown more rapidly recently than at any time since the early years of the nineteenth century—and yet our population is nowhere near the 1140 it had reached in 1840.

Starting about 1850 our town slowly declined in numbers

each year for over a hundred years, beginning to grow again only in 1960, going from 162 to 628 in thirty years, part of a trend echoed in dozens of New Hampshire towns. Reflecting on town meetings of the 1970s, I observed the many threats to the way in which, "by drift of talk, prejudice, and instinct, the latent spirit of the commmunity slowly finds itself," drawing upon "unimaginable patience while consensus gathers." It seems an ever-receding ideal.

Today, as usual, we cover dozens of topics, and we appropriate hundreds of thousands of dollars—a hundred and seventy six in the first five minutes, an astonishing record. We take up highways, cemeteries and trust funds, 911 Emergency systems, and the fire station furnace; we discuss dogs, tax maps, and pagers; we vote on recycling, the library, on complying with American Disabilities Act, on Class VI roads, the town forest plan, the Town Hall boiler, diesel fuel, tax deeds, and the summer program. We consider how to reconstruct Cram's corner, sponsor an Old Home Day, close the landfill, and buy a new computer. Are we knowledgeable about all these things? We will be before we vote—or we just might vote No. We go on to Welfare and recycling and tax deeds and radios. We straighten out the police department, consider Marlow trash removal, and move on to health insurance, retirement benefits, tipping fees, and block grants. We spend nearly two hours on the matter of bringing the Town Hall into compliance with the ADA law, and decide to postpone it. Not much comes up that we can't handle.

All the money appropriated by us today is raised by our property taxes, so there is a direct and extremely well-understood connection between one's vote and one's tax bill. I can easily calculate before I vote that the new grader will add about one hundred and twenty-four dollars to our tax bill. Since no other taxes are so directly related to our decision-making, we tend to take it as a model: indeed, town meeting government panders to the idea that this method of taxation is the only legitimate form. Any wonder New Hampshire has a generally negative view of taxes?

And we like our meat raw. Please don't give us information cooked by committee. In fact, skip the committee step entirely, since any intervention between people and data is deeply suspect. We save our jeers for the idea of appointing a committee to study something. We'll all decide right here, thank you. The basic idea is that a proposal does not gain credibility but actually loses it by having a committee process it! Even departmental budgets that are winnowed by the Selectmen (or a Budget Committee—perish the thought!) interfere with pure democracy. Committees don't clarify proposals, they contaminate them. Give us the bare facts, and then "let the people decide"—that's the battle cry.

Does this make sense? No. But it makes our democracy purer. The visitor new to this process might be appalled at this attitude (some are), feeling that it would make sense only on the assumption that the folks at town meeting have perfect pitch in judging miscellaneous raw data, without advice, study, or investigation. Well, maybe we do; anyway, don't tell us we don't. But the visitor will find it rather touching, too, for its absolute faith that the process on the floor, in all its noise and showmanship, its bluster, confusion, and occasional eloquence, could not possibly be improved upon. And the visitor can eventually see something more subtle: everybody has a chance to put in an opinion or ask a question. The merit of that is completely intangible but very real. Someone might not care to contradict a committee, but she'll tell us what she thinks of the raw idea and go home satisfied. Democracy is a messy business; pure democracy is messier still.

All this works out in practice better than our visitor will think it deserves to. Long-winded discussion often eventually exposes the weak spots in a budget or an idea that needs more thought. This makes it safe to vote against it. Yes, with some committee processing we might have had a matured idea we could be for, instead of a half-baked idea we are against. So there is a built-in conservative drag in the process. Is that regarded as a criticism? Not here.

Last year we had a roaring raw meat debate on the school bell. The bell is old style, heavy cast metal, operated with a rope. We have built a new school, but the old school building still housed the bell in its tower. Should the bell be moved to the new school? Well, there were two schools of thought on this, both eager to pay tribute to local history—or something. One side led off with the assertion that respect for tradition and historical continuity required that the old bell be moved to the new school, to serve a new generation; the other side wanted to leave the bell in its tower in that original historic building, which was on the National Register, after all. During the long and eloquent debate many hands were in the air, as if everybody in town had an opinion on the bell's destiny. Eventually someone managed to squeeze in some simple questions. Would the bell be used at the new school? When had the bell last been rung? Nobody could remember. Somebody thought it may have rung on the Fourth of July in 1976! A teacher said schools, well, don't use those old bells any more. Alas, all the fun seemed to go out of the argument. "Hey, it was a good fight while it lasted," said John Tweedy.

Random advice from recent town meeting discussions: "If you are for it and everyone is speakin' against it, why are you sittin' on your tongue?" On the fine points of the Land Use Ordinance, Hans Eccard, in a rich German accent: "It's insulting and unAmerican." Marty Harrison, perhaps the best Christian in town, being rebuked by the moderator for using a profane phrase: "We'll have no more of that." On the workload of the Selectmen: Donny Crane quoted as having said: "The worst thing that could happen to Washington would be to have Selectmen who had time to do the job." On the town's computer system: "It's a dinosaur, and was when we bought it; but it does a few things slowly and it's bulletproof." On the unpredictability of town meeting: "It's like, you never know what's going to sell at a garage sale." Robert Crane, snapping his suspenders and lecturing a relative newcomer on the rules of Washington: "In this town you do not oppose God, the Shedd Free Library, or the Purling Beck Grange." Moderator Otterson on a question too extended: "If the question is longer than the answer, it's too long." On the noon recess: Whereas we used to break "for dinnuh," the motion in 1993 was to break "for lunch." Probably not a good sign.

Every town develops its own traditions about the shape and character of its annual town meeting. Always there is the tendency to think that there used to be more local color to relieve the beige of business as usual. Some towns still hold all-day meetings as we do. Ours often reaches far into the evening, and three times in the last decade we have recessed after about twelve hours to complete the business another day. Many towns meet only in the evening, sometimes two evenings. Some towns have a Budget Committee, with considerable authority to process spending proposals before they are presented to the full meeting. Every year we read of towns that romp through their work in a couple of brief hours. To our ears, that sounds scandalous, maybe even treasonous. What kind of commitment to democratic decision-making is that? I have never heard anyone in Washington express admiration for a town that does its annual business in a few hours.

We prolong the business by dispensing with certain standard rules. For example, we just don't "move the question" if there is anyone who still wants to speak. The moderator follows the ancient rule that we are ready to vote when nobody has anything more to say. Our tradition of the secret written ballot may be the town's favorite fetish. When the voice vote is too close to call, it is never resolved by a show of hands, but by a written ballot. The law requires a ballot vote if seven voters request it, but we have a standard of privacy seven times that high: we have a written ballot if one person asks for it, usually by just shouting "paper ballot." This quaint practice of a once-small town was elevated into a fixed principle of democracy by Donald Crane, our much-admired town moderator for twenty years, and it still sticks. People believe in it. With a secret ballot my neighbors are shielded from the dangerous knowledge of how I voted on the road grader. Usually it works: the meeting has to take a break now and then, and the "paper ballot" is one way to do it. Someday, sheer numbers and the bother of it all may force common sense out of hiding and we might have to decide things by a show of hands. It will be warmly resisted.

The New England town meeting echoes ancient Greece, but its historical roots go back to the Protestant Reformation. Invented by Massachusetts Bay Puritans, who were looking over their shoulder at Church of England hierarchies, it began with the principle of equality. And to this day a town meeting levels the field and elevates equality. In my state, any group of fifty citizens can call a meeting (though this is rare), all may come and speak, all registered citizens may vote, and the ballot is decisive. The idea of governance by town meeting emerged from experience in Boston and surrounding towns in the 1630s and 1640s. Nobody really planned it; townspeople just did it. The Massachusetts governor and legislature found it convenient merely to acknowledge what was going on. It seemed harmless enough. They recognized that certain local decisions were made by assemblies of local citizens. So? So a mighty tradition was taking shape—although they did not know it.

Equality is still the first principle of our town meeting, and patience is still its salient virtue. Perhaps it takes a special faith to believe that anything so simple and sophisticated, so enduring, as town-meeting government could have derived from a haphazard process, something not thought up or written down. Some may prefer institutions to be invented out of whole cloth—the way the U.S. Constitution was all made up during one long hot summer.

Certainly there are cynics and others who say the town meeting is dated or outdated, that it doesn't work anymore. But those who speak this way are seldom citizens participating in the process. They are those, one native confided to me, who are paid to sneer. But some do quietly fear that the old meetinghouse stylistics are fading: gone or going are the wonderfully leisurely cadences of the day-long, night-long town-meeting decision-making of the the 1960s; gone or going too the "unimaginable patience" that impressed us two decades ago.

Maybe so. But we are not ready for elegies yet. We still

meet for a dozen or more hours every year, and nobody expects or wants less. A larger and much more diverse community, maybe we have now to *create* a consensus where we used to be able simply to *find* it. But we do it. Eventually most foolish ideas are flushed out; most half-baked ideas postponed for a riper day. Yes, it's monumentally inefficient as government; but it's very effective as education. Anyway, nobody around here thinks efficiency is the highest good.

Some of us are now and then concerned that the person who tries to take the measure of the town meeting in Washington again in twenty years' time may be looking out upon a vastly different town. What if there is then only a short evening meeting attended by a tenth of the voters, and no hassle? Then it may be time for elegies. But right now our tradition is still free and proud and strong: three hundred and fifty years old in New England, almost two hundred and twenty in Washington. The institution is still robust and sometimes eloquent, still widely praised and often disparaged, usually surprising and still imperfect, but deeply beloved and believed in, still our purest form of democracy.

22

The Primary State: Parables of Power

Every fourth winter it is presidential primary season in New Hampshire. Then our granite state is acreep and acrawl with politicians and candidates and campfollowers and money raisers and Very Important People, also with media hounds, presscats, and spokespersons, with hopefuls and hasbeens and wannabes, and with lots of homegrown political groupies and junkies. Presidential campaigning, which is chronic here, becomes acute. I know people who complain about it; but, frankly, I don't mind it at all. No one would come to live here because of this spectacle, but many of us cheerfully accept it as a fringe benefit. Some say that the first presidential primary should not be a local but a truly national affair; and some say that in fact it already is. They see here a *national* presidential primary—held every four years in New Hampshire.

In our town of Washington, registered voters numbered nearly 500 on primary day in 1992, and over fifty-five percent of us voted, a modern record for us. Fate sequestered us in the hills far off the worn paths of presidential candidates. You might have to go back to Franklin Pierce, who was born and reared next door in Hillsboro, to find the last future-president to have set foot in our town. In small places like this overt campaigning keeps a proper—that is to say, a low—profile.

However, in the 1992 primary I felt strongly enough about my candidate to do a little local campaigning for him. So I telephoned friends and neighbors, chatted with people at the post office and transfer station, handed out literature, put up a few signs (glancing over my shoulder as I did so), and spent some hours at the polls on primary day. That was more, I think, than anybody else did in this town, and probably about as much as one can do without attracting suspicion.

I was prompted by conviction and curiosity, and together these kept me from being deterred. For there certainly were deterrents: the New England countryside is historically reticent, and overt electioneering outside its formal settings is just not expected. It may even be disapproved. Besides, my candidate had studied abroad, and was a suspected intellectual. Some folks dislike any association with politicians, especially articulate ones, and some are just skittish or shy. For many others, whom you vote for is a matter of exquisitely private morality, absolutely not for chit-chat outside the family. Although some discuss candidates and preferences as calmly as the weather—with similar conviction or despair—and a few campaign and a very few are political groupies, the largest group here are the great Reserved. Most of my neighbors wear no buttons and if asked about their choice prefer to button up.

As a campaigner, I am deeply curious about this rich variety of attitudes. Every four years I have a yen to meet and hear them, study and understand them; for surely no one thing explains all these predispositions, not even in this little town. The first platitude my brief campaigning experience confirmed was this: on primary day different citizens of this town are doing very different things with their vote—which may be why pollsters' predictions are so fallible. For some few, voting is the end result of a complex judgment, and for others it is just a gesture. Some are picking a candidate to run against the opposition and a few are just "sending a message." Some of my friends, I feel certain, picked a candidate most like themselves, or like their own best self-image (though they didn't tell me that). Some vote with their heart, others with their head. Some vote their pocketbook and some vote the public interest. A few vote for the name they recognize or the face they recall. Some are private about their choice and others are private only about their reasons.

Standing outside the polls on primary day for just a few hours I met all the above. For lack of deeper insight I concluded that voting is simple but human nature is complicated. I recalled again that democracy is the weird theory which holds that all these impulses and ideals add up and boil down to the best that can be achieved by the nation. It takes faith.

Politically, our town is serenely lopsided, and my candidate belonged to the minority party, making my modest activism still more conspicuous—gauche, perhaps, though nobody here would have put it that way. Indulgent friends looked the other way for the duration, forgiving me my trespasses. Some of the campaign signs I put up were torn down—perhaps by some passionate defender of free speech. Democracy is a wayward business.

On primary day in February the polls opened at 11:00, and I got there at 11:05 and found the place jammed. Why had they come early? Some because that was all they had on the agenda today; others because they were eager to do their very private thing; but most, I suspect, because they always come early to events in Washington. Having forgotten that this church supper habit extended to the voting booth, I nearly missed the day's biggest crowd. Ten people gave me the same advice in the same words—"vote early, vote often"—and this kept me cheerful for several hours.

In the evening I learned that my candidate, who did well enough in the state at large, did far better in my town. Local campaigning vindicated. I may go national.

The New Hampshire presidential primary has long been a national event in a local setting, and our first encounter with this phenomenon occurred in 1968. When Grace and I went to the town meeting that year, the presidential primary still fell on town meeting day, so we got two events in one. Actually, the bargain proved even better than that. The nation had entered the era when Vietnam war protests reached the higher decibels, when action against the war invaded the American political process and tested the system's strength. That New Hampshire town meeting day, March 12, 1968, was not just doubly memorable for us; it became a political watershed for the nation. Just the previous month the Vietcong Tet Offensive had proved that American forces did not control the ground war in Vietnam; and now the New Hampshire presidential primary, in a peaceful offensive, proved that President Lyndon Johnson could not control the political process either. The preemptive strike came through the antiwar campaign of Senator Eugene McCarthy, which broke upon the national consciousness through that self-same March New Hampshire presidential primary.

For us it was town meeting number one, an experience refreshing as summer rain, but for the town it was number one hundred and ninety two, stuff of tradition. About a hundred people attended that day, off and on, and by late afternoon maybe fifty or sixty remained. I noticed a knot of young people, visitors clearly, leaning against the back wall and soaking up the proceedings with evident satisfaction. They stood out not only for their knowing smiles as they watched a page from their American history textbook leap to life around them, but also for their age and grooming: coats, ties, dresses, no beards. We exchanged pleasantries and I learned that they were a detachment of the "Clean for Gene" troops who were spreading Senator McCarthy's anti-Vietnam War message in New Hampshire. They were not invited to address the meeting, and they did not ask. They were just studying the town meeting process, as was I—something we had both read about but not previously observed—while waiting to take the results of the presidential voting to their headquarters for early reporting. Similar delegations, they said, waited upon every New Hampshire town meeting that day.

The presence of these young citizens, watching and learning and hoping, seemed to me to reinforce all the democratic truisms implicit in this humdrum little town hall drama. It is a remembrance—a first town meeting, a first New Hampshire primary, a group of students engaging the process with their interest and their ardor—that I still draw upon, decades later, if ever I am prone to cynicism about the incessantly wayward tendencies of democracy.

The news which the peace troops ultimately reported to the country that night showed that even in conservative New Hampshire Senator McCarthy could get nearly 42 percent of the vote against an incumbent commander-in-chief. Like President Truman sixteen years earlier when Senator Estes Kefauver received over 50 percent of the New Hampshire primary vote, so now in 1968 President Johnson began to consider the advantages of early retirement.

Meanwhile, the New Hampshire primary achieved even more visibility. And still it goes from strength to strength.

Soothsayers from the media and the political lairs of Washington D.C. sometimes look at New Hampshire's preeminence in the presidential primaries and lapse into Deep Think: Why should this one small state have such massive influence on the selection of presidents? It's not representative, not equitable, not reasonable. We should scrap this goofy system and create from scratch something more representative, more defensible. . . . It's a wonderfully easy observation. To some of us in New Hampshire the familiar critique is about as profound as saying that democracy itself is a flawed idea. Of course it is; and the alternatives are worse.

But it's true that whenever New Hampshire's early primary is challenged on the national scene all our state's officialdom rushes to its defense, getting there just in time to waffle on the question whether this first primary is right for the nation or just good for New Hampshire. We should admit it: it is certainly good for New Hampshire. Rivers of patronage flow our way because of the primary. There are contracts and contacts by the boatload, tons of publicity—all embarrassingly good for our economy and our national visibility. Originally, we just lived with it; then we started to live for it; we should watch out for the temptation to live off it.

From the advantages it brings to New Hampshire one might think we cooked up this first primary in a burst of creative self-interest. Not so. Though technically the offspring of state law, it was really the offspring of the Law of Unintended Consequences. Would anyone, given a blank sheet of paper, have invented this system, just like that? Not very likely. It's a flawed idea. And the alternatives are worse.

Like democracy itself the primary system was not so much thought up as allowed to grow. Which leads one to suspect that sometimes history itself is wiser than our best armchair wisdom.

Fourscore years ago, in 1913, New Hampshire was early but not first among the states to turn a populist idea into state law: let the people, not merely party leaders, elect national convention delegates—delegates more or less committed to a given presidential candidate, but really running on their own reputations. It was a good idea, but not a revolution—only step one of an evolution. A dozen states did the same, and for a generation nothing much was made of it. Evidently the idea went to work underground in the American soul, one place where history secretes its wisdom.

A new state law in 1950 redirected New Hampshire primary voting from convention *delegates* to the presidential *candidates* themselves—called a "direct presidential preference primary." The traditional town meeting day in March was the obvious choice for the voting day. Easily done, and without fanfare. However, there was a little side effect to the new law: it made campaigning among the people by the presidential candidates an inviting option. That idea would have vaguely crossed the minds of a few New Hampshire lawmakers, who remembered that Harold Stassen had campaigned here a bit for his delegates in 1948.

But in 1950 hardly anybody thought the rest of the nation would pay attention to what New Hampshire did at its town meetings (they never had), let alone follow suit with direct primaries of their own. In 1952 General Eisenhower did not come to New Hampshire; Senator Taft came a few times, obviously uncertain as to what exactly he was doing here; and Senator Kefauver, Democrat, came a few more times, since it gave him a safe platform to hammer at President Truman. So something certainly was new here, but you couldn't tell yet if it was important. On town meeting day the strong vote for Eisenhower and Kefauver got national publicity, and the New Hampshire direct primary got its first significance not from design, but from the symbolism discovered in it by those who watched it from afar. One thing they saw was that the presidential vote was dignified and magnified by the New England town meeting setting. But even this wasn't designed, and it wasn't invented; it evolved.

One recent feature *was* designed. For decades, primary voting took place on town-meeting day, always the second Tuesday in March. For small towns, where small things are big, that was good Yankee thrift—two elections for the price of one. Then a problem came up: other states, jealous of New Hampshire's accidental prominence and priority, tried to preempt first place by scheduling an earlier presidential primary. Now the state retaliated swiftly: the legislature took the primary off town meeting day and moved it up ahead of the other states that had tried to cut into the line. Next time, same thing. This kept the predatory states at bay, but the jostling was tiresome. So New Hampshire passed a law decreeing that its presidential primary must be held on "the Tuesday immediately preceding the date on which any other state shall hold a similar election." So there!

And so there it stands today, and has for the last four presidential primaries—a law not likely to be repealed. The Law of Unintended Consequences, sanctioned by history, not legislators, is the one that's least likely of all to be repealed.

In primary season crystalballing is a serious cottage industry: last time our phone rang seven times from out-of-state professional pollsters. There are two ways to win the primary in New Hampshire: one is to do better than opponents, the other is to do better than expectations. In practice that computes to quite a few candidates claiming victory; and surely that is just the way it should be so early in the game. But who would ever have dreamed up such a system, with predictions about the outcome a structural part of the process?

Undoubtedly the drumbeat of the pollsters does induce some voters to fall in line behind the loudest bandwagon. But if polling tells us something of how the electorate is leaning against the blast of propaganda, its greatest value may lie, ironically, in its fallibility, in the possibility that it may flop and let someone win the expectations contest. It's not always easy to figure out just what these Yankees are thinking, and many of them believe that's all right: they'd just as soon mess up the tea leaves. I know people who puckishly misinform pollsters, and others who will tell them nothing.

In 1992, after absorbing months of campaigning, over 61 percent of New Hampshire's three hundred thousand voters went to the polls on primary day. Nobody suggested that these voters did not know the candidates or their views, for this is a setting where policy discussions have a unique opportunity to prevail over images. Two weeks later, after one fortnight of strictly media campaigning before seven million voters in Georgia, Maryland, and Colorado, the newspeople said: these voters do not feel they know these candidates very well. And just 35 percent of them voted in the primary.

It is the style of New Hampshire campaigning that serves the country by serving the candidates so well. Here there is a relatively inexpensive opening for anyone with plausible credentials and a plausible message. It gives the candidates a training ground to refine their style and message. It exhibits their strengths and flaws. Finally, it passes tentative judgment on their qualifications for the rest of the country to consider. It does this within a retail, homegrown, personal politics not possible except in a small state. The effect is to revitalize democracy at its roots with the richest possible nutrients: a vivid sense that the individual's vote, individual commitment, matters; the sense that *I*—as felt by thousands and thousands of *I*'s—contribute to this process and to its outcome. The New Hampshire primary, at once so personal and so conspicuous, dramatizes this political intimacy on the national scale, just as the town meeting does on the community scale. Probably the idea of the primary could only have taken root and flourished in a state with a strong tradition of direct democracy, the town meeting. But nobody figured this all out beforehand. Wisdom sneaked up on us unawares.

If the process serves the candidates well, it also serves the public well. Here the candidates face the people: they cannot hide behind surrogates, ads, and handlers. Senator Bob Kerry, campaigning for the Democratic nomination in February 1992 was having lunch at a senior citizen center in Manchester. A sharp voice from diagonally across the table said, "Bob Kerry, eat your peas." The Senator did.

Two centuries ago when the founding fathers gathered in Philadelphia to draft our Constitution, they were concerned about the small states, and they brooded over those inconvenient and irrational state boundary lines. How build a unified nation of states so manifestly unequal in size and population and wealth? Strong voices even said: scrap the troublesome old state boundaries, born of accident and competition; chop the land up into thirteen more equal pieces. Voices of reason they were, taking the high road, speaking for justice and equality. Fortunately, the voice of reason was promptly throttled at the Constitutional Convention by the voice of common sense: they would do no such thing. State boundary lines, crazy-quilt pattern of inequity though they made, had already been sanctioned by historical experience. So the Philadelphia delegates drew upon a deeper wisdom, and they gave us, for one thing, a Senate with equal representation from each state, and they taught us, for another thing, to live comfortably with state boundary lines that nobody, given a blank sheet of paper, would ever have thought up.

We should rejoice that democracy has such resilience in the face of the unreasonable. Philosopher Plato, who deplored democracy for excellent reasons, didn't appreciate that its very sloppiness fosters unexpected virtues. If the New Hampshire primary serves poorly some abstract notion of national equality or representativeness, its close-to-earth campaigning, it civics-book style of election discourse serves other democratic aspirations magnificently well.

Upon reflection, I'm very glad I put up those campaign

signs for this year's primary. I regret only that I felt furtive about it. This is the preliminary, not the final winnowing, and New Hampshire voters are very experienced at it, sometimes even sophisticated. We do this job about as well as it can be done.

But early winnowing itself may be the least of it; the best of it is the political parable enacted. From New Hampshire we send so very few delegates to national conventions that our strongest contribution is not numerical but symbolic. Listen carefully every four years and you may hear the New Hampshire primary saying something solemn about the political process, voicing an intimation from deep within the national consciousness:

> *Whoever would preside over this vast republic, define its agenda, command its armies, let him humble himself and acknowledge that the starting point of the race for the crown is among the people: in someone's living room, around a neighbor's kitchen table, at the supermarket, high school, or retirement home—among the people.*

A parable of power so valuably subversive, making such a downright assault on political hauteur, is too simple and profound for anyone to have just thought it up. Nobody did. It just bubbled up, unplanned, in the New Hampshire primary, as it happens. And we live with it because we sense that it says something charming and scandalous and deeply wise—something we haven't found another way of saying better.

Epilogue

Just outside our west window the morning sun strikes the great gray stones of the wall where Ebenezer Wood's barns once stood. I have not yet been able to figure out exactly what was barn wall and what was yard wall, what was being walled in or walled out. If Wood built it, and it was just a barnyard wall, why did he use stones so huge, and set it upon a ledge of rock outcropping? If it was a barn wall, why are the top stones laid with a slope to the northeast? Anyway, with stones of that mass, no one has moved them since the oxen and the tripod hoisted them into place.

Whenever I am certain that I understand New Hampshire rural history, building, life, culture, then I look at that silent wall—which has never explained itself to me at all—and I realize that often I cannot answer the most simple question posed by the landscapes of Lovellwood. Our lives are constantly annoyed, and wonderfully graced, with unsolved rural mysteries.

But nowhere is it written that we must solve them. It is merely our pleasant privilege—as stewards, coming on the heels of pioneers like the Woods and of survivors like the Powerses—to try to retrieve some scraps of their times, and link them with our own. Our excursions into this particular rural past are forever brief and incomplete, done for our sake and not theirs, and bring back only fragments of a narrative—which is all we really seek: history in the present tense. Here is a stoned-up well, a granite hearthstone, hand-hewn beams above my head, and wallpaper peeled back to the bare walls of yesterday; and all are as shards of broken pottery, never a vase entire, just fragments of a fable. Wholeness, if anywhere, is in composing our own chronicle with the pieces and inspirations that come to hand.

To our east, Lovell Mountain always appears soft, spruce-padded, but close up it is bony, like the ledge under that west wall. In many places the granite skeleton sticks out, reminding me that one unified rock underlies all. When the sun goes down in our valley its last rays travel far over our heads to strike the high western slopes of the mountain, there to squeeze the day's last color from the hills. Lovellwood itself is always early into the evening shadows, but the mountain, a singular rock towering to nearly nine hundred feet above us, enjoys a longer, sunnier day. Evenings, which are soft and lovely and melancholy, the shadow of the western tree line climbs the mountainside, dimming as it goes all the varied hillside colors, though sometimes the clouds above flare up in vivid violet hues. It is as if night does not fall here; it seeps up from the valley, gathering shadows piecemeal, like fragmentary thoughts, and rolling them upward toward the mountaintop where they unite, to await the tidings of another day.

Acknowledgments

Earlier versions—in most cases very different—of some of these chapters were published in *Harper's, The Atlantic Monthly, The New York Times, Country Journal, Country Life,* and *New England Review*. I'd like to thank them for permission to reprint portions of those essays. I must also thank Annette and Bill Cottrell, who were instrumental in our finding this last house on the road, and whose friendship has been a blessing for many years. In addition, there are so many others who have encouraged the writing of this book, and who await its appearance—they range from national treasures, such as poet Donald Hall, to dear neighbors, such as Marty Harrison, and dozens and dozens of others. I wish to thank them all for their friendship and support.

RJ

The text of this book was typeset in Weiss by Wilsted & Taylor. Display titles were designed and composed by Janet Perr. The text was designed by Sara Eisenman. The book was printed and manufactured by R. R. Donnelley & Sons, Harrisonburg, Virginia.